Strategies for improving race relations

To Mae Shapiro, whose patience, strength and advocacy made it possible for one contributor to withstand the adversities of change agentry.

Strategies for improving race relations

The Anglo–American experience

edited by JOHN W. SHAW
PETER G. NORDLIE
RICHARD M. SHAPIRO

with a preface by BHIKHU PAREKH

MANCHESTER
UNIVERSITY PRESS

Published by MANCHESTER UNIVERSITY PRESS
Oxford Road, Manchester M13 9PL, UK
Wolfeboro, NH 03894–2069, USA

British Library cataloguing in publication data
Shaw, John W.
    Strategies for improving race relations: the Anglo–American experience.
    1. Race relations
    I. Title   II. Nordlie, Peter G.   III. Shapiro, Richard M.
    305.8   HT1521

Library of Congress cataloging in publication data applied for

ISBN 0–7190–1789–0 *hardback*

Photoset in Linotron Ehrhardt by
Northern Phototypesetting Co., Bolton
Printed in Great Britain
· by Bell and Bain Ltd., Glasgow

Contents

Preface

Thanks to such unequal and exploitative historical encounters as the slave trade and colonialism, the relations between blacks and whites in Britain and America today are profoundly unequal and asymmetrical. In both countries blacks are subject to racial prejudice and discrimination, are socially and economically worse off, occupy the bottom rungs of the occupational ladder, wield little economic and political power, bear signs of deep psychological damage done by the perverse dynamics of slavery or colonial domination, and find it difficult to break through the cumulative cycle of deprivation. Racism, or belief in racial superiority, is obviously not the monopoly of whites, and is sometimes shared by blacks as well. However black racism, such as it is, is inherently impotent, defensive, reactive and lacks sting. Blacks have little political power, and are hardly in a position to harass, persecute, inflict indignities upon or oppress whites. They also have little economic power and are in no position to refuse jobs and promotion, or discriminate against, and damage the life-chances of, whites. And since they inhabit a world culturally dominated by whites, they are hardly able to destroy or weaken whites' pride and self-respect, scar them with a shattering sense of inferiority or unhinge their psyche. Racism is therefore basically a white problem in the sense that racism is a relationship of subjugation and whites are the subjugators. If that relationship is to be changed, then, short of violent overthrow of the social structure, whites alone are in a position to make that change.

The so-called 'racial question', which bears remarkable resemblance to the 'social question' that dominated the nineteenth century, is ultimately about ending the historically generated and self-reproducing pattern of inequalities and injustices between whites and blacks. It has not always been formulated in these terms, and as a result, its discussion has tended to become mired in the swamp of foggy generalisations and rather soggy sentiments.

For some the racial question is about how to create love and goodwill between blacks and whites and enable them to live in harmony. Now love has no meaning outside the world of intimate interpersonal relationships, and is a politically irrelevant and unrealisable goal. As for racial harmony, it is a vague and indeterminate concept. Further, when relations between two groups are unequal and conflictual, the language of harmony only subserves the interests of the dominant group. That language calls upon the weaker group to remain content with whatever concessions can be secured from the superior group, and is inherently biased and even offensive to the group without power. For some others, inequalities and injustices between blacks and whites are integrally tied up with the capitalist mode of production, and hence the racial question is ultimately about overthrowing capitalism. Although this view contains important insights, it is seriously flawed. As the Marxists are beginning to realise, race is not a mere epiphenomenon of class. It has its own autonomous origin and unique character and is not amenable to a reductionist analysis. There is therefore no reason to believe that racial inequalities and injustice do not survive in a non-capitalist society. Besides the overthrow of capitalism is such a distant prospect that it makes no moral or practical sense to prolong the current black predicament. What is more, it is wholly non-dialectical to view revolution as the antithesis of reform. Reforms are necessary moments of, and culminate in, radical and qualitative changes. For others, the racial question is about ending racism or changing racist attitudes and eradicating racial prejudices. Attitudes do, of course, matter for they can hurt and are potential sources of action. However they are largely derivative in nature and cannot be changed by concentrating on the attitudes themselves. They do not spring up and survive in a vacuum, but grow out of, and are continually sustained by, the structure of social relations of which they are largely psychological reflections. As a rule, we consider inferior those who in fact occupy lowly positions in economic and political life. The way to change attitudes is therefore to change the social soil that generates and nourishes them. Attitudes, further, become socially relevant and harm, as distinct from hurt, others only when they result in conduct. And that only happens when their behavioural expression is not blocked by the law, public opinion, social pressure or the fear of retaliation. It is, therefore, far more effective to change the social context of action so that an individual does not find it in his interest to act on his prejudices. This generally has the additional advantage that the inoperative prejudices have a habit of becoming weaker and even atrophying over time.

The racial question ultimately is about restructuring the pattern of relationships between blacks and whites on the basis of equality and justice. Racial equality implies many things. Briefly it implies that all operative rules and practices should be *applied* in a non-discriminatory manner. It implies also that they should be non-discriminatory in their *content*. A rule or a practice is so discriminatory when its requirements are irrelevant to its intended purpose and it has the consequences of adversely affecting all or most blacks. Thus the rule that a policeman should be at least five foot nine is discriminatory because height is not materially relevant to effective policing, and excludes racial groups with less than average height and in no position to do anything about it. At a different level, a rule that requires clerks, typists, train drivers and airline pilots to be college graduates imposes a gratuitous and irrelevant requirement, and discriminates against racial groups with lower educational standards. Racial equality implies, further, that even when justified, if the requirement of a rule bears particularly heavily upon the blacks in such a way that blacks, by and large, cannot meet it, then ways need to be found to help them remedy the deficit.

Racial equality, however, is hardly enough. Blacks who have suffered deprivation for centuries lack some of the basic psychological, moral, economic and political conditions necessary to compete as equals with whites. Their pride has been wounded, their personality scarred, and their self-confidence shaken. Having fewer and less definitive role models, their intellectual and social horizons are often limited, and their motivation, drive and energy adversely affected as compared with whites. People cannot set up goals and exert themselves to realise them unless they have motives to do so. And motives, unlike the anatomical features, are not inherent in people. They are responses to and developed in the context of the range of possibilities available to the agent, and are socially derived. Again the social and economic conditions of the blacks impose hurdles that only the most determined among them venture, let alone manage, to surmount.

A just society needs to take active steps to encourage and help them extricate themselves from the vicious and self-perpetuating cycle of deprivation and the debilitating mood of diffidence and despondency. White society needs to see that it is in its own best interests to rid itself and the white-dominated social system of the cancer of racism. Only when this perception comes about is change likely to occur. Such changes as ensue are likely to benefit both whites and blacks.

The story of how Britain and especially America have gone about tackling the task of reducing racial inequalities and injustices has been a subject of considerable research in recent years, and the present volume is an important contribution to it. I cannot discuss the research here and would only like to highlight its three important lessons.

[handwritten marginal annotations, left margin:] this is / unsive to / a prove / are q

[handwritten marginal annotations, right margin:] Not true— / white people / are fundamentaf- / ally immoral + / have perpetuated / immoral acts / across time / & history e.g / slavery is an / immoral + / barbaric / act!

First, no reform has been *secured* without powerful and constant black pressure. Successive American governments launched reformist programmes because of the growing black unrest both in such sensitive institutions as the army and in society at large. It is true that Kennedy and Johnson had expressed strong commitments to the black cause, and an influential body of liberal opinion had pleaded for action. However some of the earlier presidents too had shared the commitment and the liberal opinion was not new; yet nothing was done. It was the black agitation, initially the non-violent civil rights campaigns and later the riots, that activated the moral impulse, energised and mobilised the liberals, provided a political counterweight to the highly influential racist lobby, threatened disorder, changed the equations of white self-interest and resulted in reforms. In Britain too the race riots of 1958, social unrest and the general worsening of the relations between the black immigrants and the indigenous population played an important part, although, of course, the influence of the strong moral commitment of several sections of the two major parties and the sense of post-imperial obligation must not be ignored.

Second, no reform is *secure* unless black organisations and their leaders are able to consolidate, defend and build on it. As the American experience clearly demonstrates, reforms secured in the teeth of opposition by vested interests were fragile, vulnerable to subversion, lacked the resources to implement them and needed to be jealously guarded and zealously followed through. Black organisations and leaders had to monitor them, ensure their implementation, identify and overcome the subtle ways of blocking them and encourage their communities to take full advantage of them. This meant that having hitherto attacked the political system *from the outside,* they now had to *enter* it, master its complexities and learn to use its resources. Agitation may secure a reform, but it cannot make it secure. The two processes call for different skills and attitudes and require very different rhetoric. Until such time as the basic inequalities and injustices are eliminated, political action has to take place *both* inside and outside the system, and requires both agitational and organisational skills. The black Americans learnt the lesson in the early seventies. Their British counterparts are beginning to learn it a decade and half later.

Third, reforms are unlikely to be fruitful and achieve the desired goal unless they are carefully formulated and part of a well-conceived strategy. 'Eliminate racism', 'remove racial discrimination', 'create equality of opportunity' or 'introduce anti-racist education' are empty slogans meaning nothing and incapable either of guiding those who genuinely wish to help or of restraining those determined to resist them. Racial inequalities operate and perpetuate themselves differently in such different areas of life as education, employment and housing, and one needs to identify their specific and distinctive structures. One needs also to show what inequalities are significant, how they are embedded in specific rules and practices, how the latter discriminate against the blacks, and what new rules and practices should replace them. Without a carefully planned, detailed and programmatic strategy, action lacks focus and direction, and the painfully secured reforms may turn out to be empty or even counterproductive.

While the British and American political systems share several features in common, it is important to bear in mind that there are also significant differences, and the experiences of one cannot be easily extended to the other. The blacks in America constitute over eleven per cent of the total population, are relatively homogenous and wield considerable electoral power. They are not immigrants, do not have to justify their existence and are not haunted by the fear of induced or forced repatriation. Thanks to their long history of struggle, collective memories of common suffering articulated and immortalised in a powerful body of literature and their energetic participation in recent years in the American political system, the blacks have developed powerful organisations and thrown up politically sophisticated leaders of national stature. Thanks, further, to the civil rights struggles of the sixties, firm presidential commitments, crucial supreme court decisions, influential government commissions and widely discussed academic researches, America has a well-developed tradition of discourse on racial issues. Racial questions are articulated in autonomous and non-reductionist terms; there is a widespread agreement on how to conceptualise and debate them, and the crucial terms of the debate are clearly defined.

As for the American society itself, it largely sees itself as a nation of immigrants. The Anglo-Saxons do, of course, feel possessive about the country and wield considerable power. However, after decades of resistance they too have accepted, albeit for their own ideological reasons, the view that everyone save the native Indian is an immigrant. Not only the cultural and linguistic but also ethnic pluralism is thus an integral part of American self-consciousness. Far from being seen as inimical to common culture and common citizenship, ethnic pluralism is woven into their very definition. The American political tradition, further, is orientated towards social engineering and accepts federal initiative and action as perfectly legitimate. The language of 'national goals' arouses no collectivist fears, and the policies deemed necessary to realise them are formulated and implemented with considerable zeal and energy.

In almost all these respects Britain presents a remarkably different picture. Although not statistically insignificant, the blacks constitute only four per cent of the population. Well over half of them are first generation immigrants, and their British-born children have not fully overcome the consciousness of being immigrants either. The blacks, further, are a heterogenous group consisting of communities with distinct history, culture and mutual suspicions. They have little experience of common struggle and lack strong organisations and national leadership. Indeed there is not a single national organisation uniting and speaking for the bulk of the blacks. Britain, further, is a relatively homogenous society, is not a nation of immigrants, has never accepted ethnic pluralism as an integral part of its self-conception, and has rather rigid and narrow view of what constitutes common culture.

Britain also lacks a tradition of discourse on racial matters. There is no agreement even on the language of debate. The term black is rejected by the bulk of the Asians; such terms as race and racism arouse hostility; and such concepts as positive discrimination, affirmative action and the quota system are all sysematically confused and little understood. The earlier national consituency on racial matters, which sponsored race relations legislation, has disintegrated and a new one has not yet taken its place. Race no longer occupies a distinct terrain and is fragmented into a cluster of dimensions of different areas of social life. There are therefore different sub-constituencies for different 'race-related' but not 'racial' issues, such as immigration, law and order, relations with the police, education, employment and housing. Both the right and the left, further, have conspired for their own different reasons to bury race into either good community relations or class-conflict, and hampered the reemergence of an autonomous realm of debate with a national constituency.

The collection of papers that follows should be read in the context of the remarks made above. The papers are concerned to describe the process of reducing racial inequalities and injustices in different areas of social life. The authors are all involved in changing the racial culture and climate of different organisations, and describe in vivid detail how the demand for change arises, the problems it encounters and the different ways in which different organisations tackle them. While rightly emphasising that the struggles for racial equality and justice in Britain and the United States are similar in several respects and Britain has much to learn from the American experience, the authors and the editors are fully aware of the differences in the social structures and political traditions of the two countries.

Being essentially concerned to do things rather than merely talk about them, the authors wisely avoid irrelevant ideological rhetoric and concentrate on the unglamorous but very important question of how to change organisations. The result is a rich harvest of sensible and shrewd practical suggestions collected from the crucible of experience. In matters affecting the life-chances of millions of men and women, one good practical suggestion is often worth more than a bookful of rhetoric. The collection should prove invaluable to those actively engaged in bringing about organisational changes in different areas of life. Moreover, everyone who is interested in this vital subject will find something of value in these chapters.

BHIKHU PAREKH

Professor of Political Theory, University of Hull
and Deputy Chairman, Commission for Racial Equality

Acknowledgements

The Editors wish to acknowledge that without the support of many individuals and organisations, the training and other projects described and discussed in the following chapters could not have taken place.

In particular, from the British side, the support of the Home Office and its Staff, particularly those of the Police, and Prison Departments is gratefully acknowledged. We wish to acknowledge also the special encouragement of the past and present Race Relations Advisers to that Ministry, Miss Nadine Peppard and Mr. Trevor Hall. The support of the Commission for Racial Equality, its Chairman, Mr. Peter Newsam and Deputy Chairman, Professor Bhikhu Parekh, have been greatly valued. The support of local Community Relations Councils and their Staff, especially those at Leeds and Manchester, in providing learning experiences, is acknowledged.

On the American side, we would like to acknowledge the pioneering roles of the U.S. Department of the Army, The National Institute of Mental Health, Center for Minority Group Mental Health Programs and the Department of Health and Human Services.

The view of contributors are entirely their own. Nevertheless, without the commitment of the above mentioned people and organisations, and others not specifically mentioned, to equity and fairness of treatment in our great social organisations, and in society itself, the endeavours described below would not have been possible.

JOHN W. SHAW
PETER G. NORDLIE
RICHARD M. SHAPIRO

1

Introduction: rationale and overview

This book was prompted by the question 'What have we learned so far?' from the several years, both in Britain and the U.S.A. in which attempts have been made to deal with prejudice, discrimination and racism against minority group members both in organisations and in society as a whole.

There has been over a decade of experimenting, largely in the dark, with how to bring about significant behavioural, cognitive and organisational changes in various sectors through training and other methods in race and community relations. The record of success, both in the U.S.A. and the U.K. has been pretty patchy, but the practitioners involved have learned a lot. It should, therefore, be worthwhile to document the learning experiences from these efforts.

We have chosen participants from both countries. The preponderance of American over British contributors reflects the greater involvement of the U.S.A. in tackling these problems by training and related means. Making allowance for the social differences between the two countries, the American experience should be the most instructive because of its greater scope.

The informed reader will know that there are important differences between the situation in the U.K. and the U.S.A. The development of a multi-ethnic society in Britain is a more recent occurrence than in America. The size of the ethnic minorities within the population as a whole and their presence within the main social organisations, such as the police, is considerably smaller in Britain than in the U.S.A. The history of immigration and settlement in Britain is quite different from the longstanding presence of the American black minority. Different ethnic minorities preponderate in the two countries, as several chapters will show. Also, the legal situation in the U.S. is immeasurably stronger, and the public and social commitment to equal opportunity is, or at least has been, much greater than in Britian. Nevertheless, we believe that the problems of race training and organisational change are similar, in that the same methodological issues are encountered.

The general social climate in which interventions now take place has changed since the late sixties. These changes have affected, for example, the nature of training activities. Emphasis has changed from changing individuals to changing institutions. The purpose of this text is to describe and assess the strategies and methods which have evolved. The intended audience are the individuals who decide whether and the method by which a change programme will be implemented and the practitioner who plans, executes and assesses it. It is not an academic treatise but a practical guidebook. Contributors were chosen for their practical involvement in the various strategies for improving race relations. They were asked not only to describe what they have done, but also to assess the progress made so far and to make, where possible, considered judgments as to the best way forward. The topics chosen reflect differences both in methodology and in the types of organisation concerned.

In order to give the reader some structure for approaching this text, the remainder of this chapter will be devoted to an explanation of the order of presentation and brief comments on the contribution made by each writer. In this way, the reader will be able to identify those chapters likely to be of most interest and of most practical relevance.

Chapters two, three and four focus mainly on the police service which, owing to the nature of its face-to-face contact with the public, has often been the first social agency in any community to be required to put its house in order. In chapter two, Raymond Hunt describes and assesses a major long-term programme of action-research designed to reduce institutional racism in six dissimilar police agencies in the U.S.A. He draws procedural and philosophical conclusions. In chapter three, John Shaw describes and assesses the impact of a series of senior executive seminars designed for police officers in command positions in England and Wales which ran on an annual basis throughout the late sixties and the seventies. In the eighties the original purpose has been maintained, while the concept has been extended to include similar ranks within the British prison service and other public bodies.

In chapter four, Guy Cumberbatch and Metasebia Tadesse communicate the main findings of their research into the most ambitious British experiment to date in community policing, namely, the Lozells Project, which takes its name from an area of Handsworth in the city of Birmingham. The authors include a consideration of the tragic events of 9 September 1985 when Handsworth erupted in civil disorder and relate these events to the aims of the Project itself.

Chapters five and six are devoted to two developments which have taken place in the U.S. military forces. In chapter five, Peter Nordlie reviews what is probably the largest ever single organisational effort, namely, the U.S. army experience with race relations policies and training programmes from 1969 until the early 1980s. He concludes his review with a balance sheet of profits and losses so far as the outcomes of these efforts are concerned. He emphasises the importance of thoroughgoing research into outcomes and effects. In chapter six, Richard Hope describes the work of a major institution for the training of race relations or equal opportunity specialists for the U.S. armed forces. He shows how changes in the training objectives of the institute reflect the changing policies and needs of the military throughout the period under consideration.

Chapters seven, eight, nine and ten focus on training and organisational change programmes in several types of public sector organisation. In chapter seven, Richard Shapiro describes and assesses the impact of a drive for organisational change in the area of equal employment in a major U.S. public health organisation. He shows how policy commitment, structural change and race training can be dovetailed so as to produce an effective vehicle for change. The changes in minority employment profiles within the organisation include data on women and minority ethnic groups.

In chapter eight, John Coffey, from the background of an extensive training experience in federal and state agencies, gives an overview of race training from the fifties to the eighties in the U.S.A. He indentifies the main training objectives and how they can be achieved by various training methods. In chapter nine Angela Rodriguez describes a federally funded project to promote the reduction of insitutional racism in a major hospital in Dade County, Florida. The areas examined include recruitment, selection, promotion, payment, training, affirmative action policies and procedures and employee satisfaction.

In chapter ten, Wendy Taylor describes developments in equal opportunity and race relations in the West Midlands Probation and After-care Service, in the U.K., from the perspective of a practitioner/specialist. She describes the total strategy followed, including needs assessment, communication initiatives, meeting special needs of ethnic minority offenders, staff training, community liaison, and the issue of corporate responsibility.

The final chapters, eleven, twelve and thirteen, address methodological, theoretical and strategic issues in general. In chapter eleven, Peter Smith reviews the evidence for the usefulness of small group training methods in race relations training, offers an analysis of racism awareness training and enunciates some basic principles of training design for race relations workshops. In chapter twelve, Mark

Chesler and Hector Delgado discuss the relationship between training for individuals and the accomplishment of organisational change. They argue that training systems can be supportive of 'creative and far-reaching policy changes'. Essentially, however, they believe that new behavioural norms need to be institutionalised within organisations.

In chapter thirteen, the editors delineate the key features of successful organisational change to combat personal and institutional racism. Drawing upon the models collected in this volume, they point out some of the blockages, pitfalls and derailments which can befall many schemes. In general, both editors and contributors share the view that to improve race relations in our social institutions, planned systemic change is called for.

However, the actual plan which is formulated depends upon the goals being sought and on the situation as it confronts the change-agent at the start of his intervention in the organisational or training process. The following chapters, (excepting chapters eleven to thirteen) describe unique situations, how the teams of change-agents or trainers tackled the problems facing them and with what measure of success or failure.

Coping with racism: lessons from institutional change in police departments

Race relations remain the major question about the future of American cities. Whatever understanding exists across race lines is fragile at best in some of our cities. This makes the whole of the police officer's world equally fragile in those cities.

from *The Future of Policing*

The Brixton riots of England during the Spring of 1981 make it clear, if it wasn't already, that race and police–community relations are hardly less fragile in Britain than in the U.S. Indeed, from the perspective of his official Brixton inquiry, Lord Scarman was moved to observe that:

... a significant cause of the hostility of young blacks toward the police was loss of confidence by significant sections. ... Whatever the reason for this loss of confidence ... it produced the attitudes and beliefs which underlay the disturbances, providing the tinder ready to blaze into violence on the least provocation, fancied or real, offered by the police. (p. 46)

Scarman went on in his report to offer a number of proposals and recommendations for improving the quality of policing in the U.K., stressing the idea that 'there is scope for a more coherent and better directed response ... to the challenge of policing modern multi-racial society' (p. 76). Noting the existence of 'widespread agreement that the composition of our police forces must reflect the make-up of the society they serve', Scarman pointed out, however, that 'it does not do so'. Accordingly he made recruitment of minority officers a priority for the British police.

Such recommendations have become commonplace in the U.S., of course. Action proposals and plans are easier to state than they are to implement, however. Impediments exist that make recruiting (and retaining) minority police officers difficult. Some of these impediments are to be found in the attitudes of individual white police officers and members of local communities toward minority persons. Others reside, as Scarman recognised, in negative perceptions of police roles among minority people that may make police work an unattractive career choice for them. Still other impediments, more subtle than personal prejudice and reactive antipathy, reside in the invidious effects of basic belief systems, social practices, and institutional structures of policing. Because it is tacit and woven into the social fabric, this so-called 'institutional racism' is difficult to detect, hard to ferret out, and extremely resistive to change. This chapter reviews one effort to confront and deal with institutional racism, not only in recruiting minority police officers but in internal police operations generally.

A PROBLEM-SOLVING APPROACH TO INSTITUTIONAL RACISM

In 1976, the William O. Douglas Institute began a multi-year action-research effort against institutional racism in several U.S. law enforcement agencies. The project progressed in phases from fact-finding, through planning, to implementation.[1]

Institutional racism was construed in terms of the comparative consequences of organisational policies and practices for racial minorities and non-minorities. The definition of institutional racism encompassed two types of 'errors'.

1 *Errors of commission* – which are organisational policies and practices that, regardless of their motivation are directly or indirectly disadvantageous to racial minorities (e.g. height minima, assignment of black police officers only to black neighbourhoods); and
2 *Errors of omission* – which are chronic manifestations of individual racism to which there is no serious organisational response (e.g. verbal racial slurs, discriminatory acts by individual supervisors).

The 'institutional racism in law enforcement' project was conducted in three phases: Phase I – Organising and fact-finding; Phase II – Developing prescriptive packages for change and planning for implementation; Phase III – Monitoring change tactics, providing technical assistance, and disseminating findings and recommendations. There was no formal evaluation phase. Some short-term assessment was done during Phase III. More resulted simply from the experience of performing the project. Other evaluative impressions were gained from follow-up visits in 1982 to certain of the participating agencies.

Phase I: Fact-finding

1 The strategy for *fact-finding* – indeed, for the project as a whole – was premised on an idea that action-oriented research must generate *managerially* useful information. This requires that one 'bring together [researchers], decision-makers, and information users in an

active-reactive-adaptive process where all participants share responsibility for creatively shaping and rigorously implementing an evaluation that is both useful and of high quality' (Patton, 1979, p. 289).
Obviously an investigator or consultant alone cannot decide the
usefulness of particular kinds of information. One depends upon
managers and information users for those assessments. We relied
heavily on both the chief and a Minority Representative in each
participating police department and on each department's project
Task Force (which I shall describe presently). We kept no secrets
from them and interacted with them not just at the beginning and end
of the project, but continuously. Thus we treated the police administrators and officers with whom we interacted as 'co-producers' of
the evaluation as well as ultimate users of the information it yielded
(cf. Whitaker, 1980). We felt we first needed to help those decision-
makers define the problems they needed to solve and then look
together for ways of solving them.

This interactionist joint management (J—) model approach to
programme development and implementation is a strategy for social
problem-solving that avoids unilateral decision-making in favour of
discussion, negotiation, mutual accommodation, and compromise
among the parties (Hunt, 1983). It presumes that evaluation questions framed at the outset of a project have to be seen as provisional
and subject to change as work progresses. Initial formulations of
evaluation questions can do little more than suggest obvious places to
begin gathering information. Other questions are always possible;
and, in any case, the final test of any evaluation information must be
its utility to its users, not its 'interest value' to the evaluator (or
others).

I do not suggest, however, that third-party evaluators act as passive
agents of established organisational interests. We certainly did not
work this way. Instead, we played an active advocacy role, but we did
it in what Patton (1979) calls a utilisation-focused framework. Our
aim was to initiate a *process* that would (a) yield evaluation information
of high utilisation potential during the project, and (b) also continue
working in each department after we had gone.

In each department a 'Task Force' of members was formed as the
project's 'agent' in the department. Each Task Force included minority and non-minority officers, some of whom were command officers and others not, except in one department where there was no
minority officer having a rank above sergeant.

The Task Force was crucial to the project's operations. It was the
project's 'eyes and ears' in a department and was responsible for
continuity of operations during and beyond the project. It was a
major source of information and procedural guidance for project

staff. It was a 'consultant' for reviewing judgments of project staff about institutional racism in a department. It was an affirmative action planning body. It was an instrument for certain affirmative action initiatives. And it was a forum for evaluating the effectiveness of the project as a whole. The membership of each department's Task Force was, therefore, carefully chosen (in consultation with the chief and Minority Rep.) to reflect political and social realities within the department as well as the goals of the project.

2 *Data collection* relied heavily on the Task Force and Minority Rep. Examples of racist behaviour were reviewed and argued about in group discussions. These discussions were generally organised around 'critical incidents' of racism experienced by minority members of the Task Force, or known to them. Where agreement was reached that the incidents were institutional phenomena, certain ones were selected for investigation. Usually this began with *interviews* with individual members of the Task Force and then with other key informants in the police department or outside it, including relevant personages of city/county government (e.g. city managers, personnel directors, affirmative action officers), and, when it seemed desirable, community figures.

Document files dealing with operating policies and procedures, affirmative action plans, and hire–fire and discipline records (including selection methods) were searched, both in the police departments and other city offices, for information suggesting patterns of discrimination. And a self-administering *Opinion Survey* was given to all members of each department. It asked about job and racial attitudes, concepts of the police role in society, and perceptions of community characteristics. The survey was intended to collect information, obviously, but also to provide a means of universal participation in the project by members of the subject organisations.

Data gathering was thus a mixed-method process of 'triangulation' (Jick, 1979) on possible qualitative and quantitive indicators of institutional discrimination (racism). It mingled elements of self-study with consultant input and sought to rule problems in or out by a preponderance of evidence. Apparent contradictions among indicators were treated as pointers to areas where more information was needed. Unfortunately, it wasn't always available. Consequently the 'facts' were sometimes vague; and the 'diagnoses' of institutional racism could not always be straightforward. This equivocal reality shaped the final step of fact-finding.

3 Using a *survey feedback* method, written diagnostic reports were prepared and forwarded to the chief, Minority Rep., and Task Force members in each department. The project director then visited each department for detailed review and critique of the staff 'diagnoses'.

This process deliberately resembled a courtroom-like adversary proceeding where evidence was offered and argued (see Levine, 1974). It was repeated one or more times – sometimes with further factfinding intervening – as we sought consensus on a set of indicators of institutional racism that could serve in each department as a basis for planning affirmative action and organisational change programmes during Phase II.

Phase II

Like fact-finding, developing prescriptive change packages and planning their implementation also moved in three distinct steps.

1 *Development of prescriptions for change* began with staff-developed briefs or diagnoses of institutional racism. These documents typically pointed to more problems in a department than could be dealt with at once. Hence, a consensus was sought on which ones could be change 'targets'. Priorities were attached to particular targets as part of a 'need assessment' that took into account both the inherent significance of a potential target and the feasibility of affecting it with the resources at hand in a particular place.
2 It remained next to *devise ways of achieving them.* The result was variable by department, both as to the form and scope of change.
3 The last step in planning was to allocate tactical responsibilities: *who does what?* Clarification of roles and expectations, and coordination of the efforts of the Task Force, Minority Rep., chief, and project staff was a complex part of this organisational operation. Because the characteristics of the departments differed, so did its results.

Phase III

This part of the project had somewhat different meanings for the departments and the project staff. For the former it was a period of action – implementing change. For the staff it was a period of monitoring this implementation, commenting on and urging progress, and, occasionally, evaluating results. During Phase III, project staff mainly provided technical assistance to the departments, either directly or by obtaining outside consultants. The change efforts themselves, however, were the department's own. They designed them and they ran them (when they did).

Problems

So much for methodology. What of the problems that fact-finding revealed as potential targets for remedy? Space allows only the following brief summary of them; and the reader is to understand that not all of them were found in each department.

1   Affirmative action planning/programming

None of the police departments in our study operated under a visibly coherent plan to encourage, organise, or evaluate affirmative action achievements. The written affirmative action plans under which the five departments operated were typically platitudinous, vague and confined mainly to statements of broad objectives. They uniformly lacked implementation plans (i.e. explicit prescriptions for how to get from where they were to where they wanted to be in some time period). And they never included provisions for evaluating accomplishment of their objectives. Moreover, departmental affirmative action plans were only loosely integrated with city/county plans or with departmental manpower policies and programmes (if there were any). At most, affirmative action planning was abstract and pro forma. In no sense did it produce useful management tools. Furthermore, public commitment to affirmative action as department policy was not evident – not that it was avoided, it just wasn't evident.

Small wonder, then, that few specific race-related problems had been identified by the departments in their planning process and fewer solutions found. Small wonder, too, that what actual affirmative action existed was mostly compelled by agencies outside the police departments (e.g. courts) and was reduced to 'numbers games'. And small wonder that rank-and-file cynicism about affirmative action was widespread. (*Opinion Survey* respondents, for example, described the ways affirmative action was practiced in their departments as both 'ineffective' and 'phony' (Hunt and McCadden, 1980).)

2   Recruitment

Recruitment was a major problem. No police department in our study had a complement of minority employees close to parity with any reasonable community population or workforce criterion. Some did show signs of progress in this direction; but others showed none. For the most part, minority recruiting efforts were passive and pro forma. Recruiting budgets were uniformly low; and there was weak minority involvement in the process despite the well-known facts that police recruitment is very much a matter of one-on-one persuasion, and that recruitment of minority individuals (blacks especially) into police work is difficult at best. Furthermore, department recruiting was poorly integrated with the activities of city or county personnel departments.

3   Selection and hiring

Procedures inimical to the prospects of minority persons being hired were found in each department in the study. In addition to poor preparation for examinations, there were signs of prejudice and discrimination by interviewers in oral examinations and in background investigations. There was also failure to make imaginative use of alternative entry mechanisms (e.g. police cadet programmes) to further affirmative action objectives; and there were frequent indications of 'cultural racism' (Jones, 1972) in the selection/hiring process. For instance, one internal affairs officer (responsible for pre-hiring background investigations) commented to me that blacks 'have a problem' when they come to the department and try to 'act the way they always did' (i.e. according to black folkways), and are unwilling to change toward closer conformity to the standards of behaviour preferred by the department. Obviously these standards of behaviour are not simply 'police standards', they are white standards.

4   Training

Blatant racism – prejudice and discrimination – still exists in police academies, but it wasn't prevalent in the places where we worked. As with most other modern manifestations of racism, its appearance in the training of minority police officers tends to be subtle and hard to pin down. But disproportionate weeding-out of minority rookies during probation is obvious and appears to be the result of a combination of factors. One is fall-out from playing numbers games during recruitment: poorly qualified minority persons are recruited to satisfy 'quotas' and appearances, sometimes with full expectation that they will fail and, in the process, 'prove' the argument that minorities (and women) are unsuited to police work. In one case, vitually the entire minority contingent of one recruit class 'washed-out' during probation or shortly after it.

A second factor contributing to failures by minorities during probationary periods is incompetent and insensitive supervision of field training. The difficulties facing a minority recruit are many. Early socialisation of rookies by their fellow officers is crucial. But probation and field training is an especially difficult time for minority recruits. Often, as a price of acceptance, they must demonstrate exceptional competence and avoid any appearance of 'trouble-making'. Many minority rookies experience real inner conflict over going to work for 'the man'. The position of the minority rookies is therefore exceptionally delicate. Plainly the situation calls for supervisory skill and compassion. Both are commonly lacking. In no department was field training carefully supervised; nor were field training supervisors thoughtfully selected or trained to perform their tasks. In one department, for example, field training officers were selected by vote of their fellow officers. It was a frivolous custom in this department to elect only 'odd balls' to the position. Open acts of prejudice and discrimination aside, training and probationary practices in police departments generally took no serious account of differences in the circumstances of white and minority rookies.

5   *Evaluation and promotion*

Somewhat surprising to us was the absence of career development planning or programming from the police departments we studied. In most of them, standards and methods for making decisions about promotion (and assignment) tended toward the mysterious and commonly lacked credibility among white as well as minority officers. Informality and cronyism was widespread; casual judgment by supervisors was the consistent rule of performance evaluation.

In certain departments seniority-related structural impediments to minority promotion existed. However, promotional prospects for minority officers were dimmed more by ineffective or discriminatory work assignment patterns and supervisory evaluations than by clear institutional barriers. Minority officers tended to be assigned to staff positions in 'community relations', not to 'detective bureaus'. When they received the 'special assignments' important for promotion, they tended to be exploitatively assigned to 'keeping the lid' on minority communities. Not only doesn't this help much toward diversifying their experience and in advancing their police careers, it often exposes them to inordinately hazardous duty, for which they commonly receive neither recompense nor even thanks.

6   *Organisational climate*

Many of the problems already mentioned suggest something about the atmospheres of police departments as workplaces. In addition, we found cases of de facto segregation: blacks were not invited to membership in one police benevolent association, for instance; and frequently there was poor control by management of such individual acts of racism as racial slurs, jokes, discriminatory acts, off-the-job harassment, and the like. In some places, minority solidarity was deliberately made tenuous, even when it might have been desirable as a stimulus to action against discrimination, by threats and selective acts of favouritism. Complaints by white officers of 'reverse discrimination' added to the tensions of departmental life. Police departments tend not to be comfortable work environments for minority (and female) persons. The implications of this for turnover and retention hardly need pointing out.

Problem-solving

Turn now to some of the remedies developed for these problems, which will be summarised under the same headings used for the problems.

1   Affirmative action planning programme

In two instances, temporary project task forces were institutionalised as standing departmental Affirmative Action Committees responsible for planning and monitoring affirmative action and related efforts. In two cases, departmental affirmative action officers, who had been found to be neither effective nor committed to affirmative action principles, were replaced. And also in two cases, possibilities for better coordination between the police agency and other relevant city/county offices, personnel in particular, were increased by the establishment of interdepartmental liaison.

2   Recruitment

Among the efforts undertaken on the recruitment front was extension of abstract affirmative action planning to include the planning of concrete implementation tactics. This resulted in broadened recruitment efforts and in their reorientation. New means were devised for identifying minority candidates for police appointment and for 'supporting' them through the selection period (e.g. via a 'buddy' system in which minority police officers shepherded individual candidates through the selection process, making sure they got to examinations, kept appointments, etc.).

3   Selection and hiring

Where it was indicated, oral examination boards were recomposed to assure minority representation; minority participation in the background investigation of candidates was enhanced; and 'prep' programmes were initiated to orient candidates to the often unfamiliar and anxiety-provoking examination and selection procedures they would encounter. Of particular interest was renewed use of alternative entry routes to police work (e.g. cadet programmes which agressively recruited minority high school students).

4   Training

Group discussion of the role and responsibility of field training officers was initiated in certain departments. Increased care in the selection and supervision of these officers was also initiated; and practices such as electing them were terminated.

5   Evaluation and promotion

In one department, major overhaul of personnel evaluation and career development programming was undertaken to make it more systematic and 'visible' as a process, and, to increase the accountability of supervisory personnel in their evaluations of subordinates. In other departments, less sweeping but still consequential changes in personnel practices were made; and in most of them, provisions were introduced to make the use of special assignments a more planned process that took into account the career development of individual officers. Mostly, these changes had equal potential for benefiting white and non-white or male and female officers, and usually had police union support.

6   *Organisational climate*

Executive orders were issued, together with admonitions that command officers enforce them, in order to improve managerial control over expressions of individual racism in certain departments. In some places measures were taken to encourage communication between departmental management and representatives of minority interests; and, in one case, a major department-wide programme of human relations training was undertaken to combat racism.

Outcomes

So what was the impact of these remedies? Are minorities now better represented in the departments? Well, yes, in some cases they are; but they might have been anyway. Furthermore, in some cases, minority representation has declined. The outcomes of projects like this one are hard to gauge because cause–effect linkages of project 'inputs' and departmental 'outputs' are hard to demonstrate. The success of such things as recruitment efforts is subject to many influences besides conscientous affirmative action (e.g. competition from other employers, to name one); and well-laid plans sometimes are unhappily overtaken by events. In any case, we were frankly more concerned with initiating a programme planning *process* within the cooperating departments than in producing particular measurable short-run results. On this count, we were well satisfied with some aspects of our experience, but not at all satisfied with other aspects of it.

A review of the dissatisfactions and why they occurred is instructive. But before getting to it, it is necessary for perspective to note that I am concerned not just with organisational 'change' in some disinterested spiritless sense of the term but with literal reform of the institutions of society. This is a moral as well as a technical task. Hence, dismantling the process of discrimination cannot be free of passion. That's one reason why there is organisational resistance to it. Emotion is dissonant with the iron rule of bureaucratic rationalism.

Eradicating discrimination also threatens established interests; indeed, it may well question their legitimacy – their morality. This generates passion, too, regardless of how 'cool' its expression may be.

Anyway, obstacles to implementing programmes for eradicating institutional racism are numerous, as of course we know, and hard to overcome. Some that we experienced were these:

– *Denial of a problem.* This was manifest in quibbling about the evidence for institutional racism, discrediting witnesses to it, victim-blaming, and characterisations of the carriers of 'bad news' as subversive trouble-makers.

– *Professions of helplessness.* Financial exigencies and appeals to insurmountable external barriers (unions, city personnel policies, etc.) were frequently offered to explain or justify inaction even in the face of acknowledged 'problems'.

– *Displacements of responsibility for devising remedies.* Whites want blacks to do it, and blacks think it's up to whites to be better people.

– *Organisational inertia.* Organisations – large ones especially – have heavy 'sunk costs' in their existing structures and ways of doing things. Moreover, they are complex systems with many interdependent elements. They are hard to understand and control. Hence, they are difficult to change even when they want to do it.

– *Ambiguous alternatives.* When alternatives to a familiar course of action are ill-defined and equivocal as to their outcomes, the way solutions to social problems usually are, they tend not to be welcomed.

– *Risk aversion.* This is a reason for avoiding ambiguous alternatives. Organisations, like people, vary but, by and large, they avoid uncertainty and risk. They tend to prefer the devil they know, especially if that devil seems benign as far as the personal careers and social interests of their dominant members are concerned.

– *Excessive and inappropriate expectations.* The frustrations and disappointments that result from expecting too much from change efforts, or the wrong things, has disastrous effects on the motivation necessary to sustain long-term programmes in the face of the resistances already enumerated.

Some kinds of resistance to change, like the ones above, are common to virtually all organisations. Others are peculiar to certain kinds of organisations. In the case of police departments, our experience suggests that these include:

The feudal nature of police organisation

It is only somewhat exaggerated to compare modern American police departments with the manorial fiefdoms of Europe in the Middle Ages. The central figure of the local chief looms uncommonly large in the highly decentralised context of U.S. policing. The quasi-military command structure, customs of obedience to the chief, and traditions of reciprocal loyalty, encourage an analogy between police organisations and feudal systems of vassalage. The point is that police agencies in the U.S. exhibit concentration of power but in a framework of still more powerful local custom. This marks the character even of the 17,000 or so modern-day metropolitan police agencies in the U.S. The power of the local chief is *within* a system. It does not include a licence to change that system, quite the opposite.

Instead of feudal analogies, one might prefer to think of police in Weberian terms: as a species of 'traditional' bureaucracy. Unlike more familiar rational-legal bureaucracies, where individual loyalty attaches to a system of formal rules (e.g. a constitution), police organisations attach loyalty to the person of a leader who serves and is guided by 'ancient' traditions. But whether feudal or traditional bureaucracy, the point is that police departments are comparatively closed systems, markedly resistive to outside influence or change. Moreover, the power of the chief to control them is less than it may seem, for it depends upon his consistent conformity with expectations of his 'vassals' that he preserve a status quo and the 'faith' that sustains it. Local custom, in short, is more powerful than chiefs.

Professionalisation of the police

This in some ways clouds the organisational case I've just argued. It suggests bureacratisation in the rational-legal sense. Emphasis on professional self-regulation helps to further close the boundaries of police organisations to external influence. Converting customs into formal professional standards that control entry to police organisations and the practice of police work helps institutionalise an organisational status quo. It (the status quo) then no longer needs to be legitimised merely by tradition and the crass preferences of its incumbent members; it can be justified by its consonance with more universal 'professional standards'. At the same time, the normal internal political interests of the police themselves can be screened or idealised by the same 'professional standards'.

Militant unionism

In many police organisations the rank-and-file has taken effective command. To some extent this has come about because of mounting rank-and-file concern with compensation, benefits, working conditions and the like; but it also, and more importantly, reflects an attempt by police practitioners to control redefinitions of the police role in society and, with it, the instruments of its practice. This is at once a defensive response – a closing of ranks in reaction to threats against established interests – and a proactive attempt to control the future course of events.

The basic nature of the police role

Two features at least of the traditional police officer's role warrant mention in this discussion because they, too, constrain against change. One is the suspiciousness required of the police officer who must be ever watchful for signs of transgression and personal danger, and award his trust carefully. This tends to isolate him from the citizenry while promoting solidarity with a brotherhood of officers who share a common fate and tradition.

Quite different, but also working to buffer police organisations against outside influence and change, is their concept of themselves as neutral, apolitical guardians of the public's safety, the thin margin between civility and anarchy. This idea argues strongly against the propriety of intrusions by external 'political' forces (e.g. affirmative action) into policing. By definition this is an inappropriate intrusion, because of the ostensible neutral even-handedness of police practice.

The technocratic orientation of police departments

There are two aspects of this, too. Police departments stress efficiency and rationality. They de-emphasise non-technical issues in their operations, training and system of values. Despite their function as 'human service delivery systems', police departments give relatively short shrift to human relations issues and skills. Second, the police lack managerial traditions and the skills one associates with them. Traditional bureaucracies, their role models are individualistic and charismatic. Police agencies cannot easily be brought to grips with social problems (other than crime, which anyway they are disinclined to think of as a social problem), or made easily responsive to collective solutions to such problems as institutional discrimination.

The influence of local circumstances

This is the last impediment to change I shall mention here. It underscores the fact that policing in the U.S. is a local enterprise.[2] The character of American policing is shaped by local contexts and the network of influences embedded in them. The problems of American police departments vary greatly with these contexts. Universal remedies for them are hard to find.

Some lessons learned

A serious programme for organisational development should include provision not only for the identification of problems of institutional discrimination and the formulation of remedies for them, but provision as well for anticipating impediments to the application of these remedies and the formulation of remedies for those impediments. In our own work we handled some of these diffiulties reasonably well, but others poorly if at all. In the process we learned (or re-learned) some lessons that have general utility. Four in particular have relevance to action-research. They have to do with institutionalising change-making processes; avoiding technical traps; the perils of rationalism; and requirements for external leverage to sustain change programmes.

Insufficient institutionalisation

A change effort of any scope takes time. During this time a variety of forces opposed to it may surface. Management is needed to overcome these forces and maintain programme continuity. Administrative and problem-solving structures are needed for programme follow-through. We anticipated that the departmental task forces would play this role and, together with the chief, would manage the change process. This strategy involved certain implicit and, as it proved, problematic assumptions: 1. that basic managerial skills existed in the host organisations and were represented in the task forces responsible for implementing remedial programmes; 2. that there would be continuity of commitment to the goals of these programmes in the departments; and 3. that the instruments of change and hence the change process itself would be institutionalised within the host organisation. We cannot take the space here to discuss these problematics, except to say that we overestimated both the commitment to change and the managerial skills available to direct it in the cooperating departments. Turnover of key people, chiefs in particular, complicated the problem. For instance, among the five departments in the study, we worked with a total of nine different chiefs. Each succeeding chief had views about the project different from his predecessor, as well as different ideas about its methodology and commitment to it. Programmes were implemented under auspices different from those under which they were designed. A continuing process of negotiation and adjustment was therefore essential to sustain the thrust of programmatic change over time and emerging circumstances. Sometimes this proved impossible. We went away from three of the five police departments dissatisfied with the extent to which either their task forces or organisational change processes had become effectively institutionalised.

Technical traps

The fact-finding part of action research requires collection of data. Most social data are subject to interpretation; and some of it is apt to be inconsistent with other of it. Two unfortunate things happen as a result. One is that fact-finders become preoccupied with the details of data, their specific interpretation and their inter-relations. They begin to treat the problem as an abstruse social scientific or legalistic exercise. In the process they lose sight of the forest of discrimination problems for the trees of their indicators.

A second thing that happens is that opponents of change concentrate on the 'facts of the matter' and literally nitpick a fledgling programme to death. Plainly, data are important in designing constructive change efforts. But, in most circumstances, the 'facts' are rarely definitive in themselves, and are ambiguous in detail – we're not yet very good at social measurement, unfortu-nately. Little good can come of particularistic debates on the meaning of data. The purpose of diagnostic data is to inform not determine thoughtful planning. Suggestive indication of problems and possible remedies is about all that can be asked of most social data. The experiences that come from acting on plans probably does more to clarify a situation than most before-the-fact data gathering (see Weick, 1979).

The perils of rationalism

Americans are a rational people, as our attraction to data-based, planned strategies for social change attests. The managers of American organisations are especially rational; and police officers are rational people among rational people. Such at least are the images. Whether the images are true or not, people act on them. They *intend* to be rational; and they accept evaluation on norms of rationality (see Thompson, 1967). In the affairs of rational men emotion and conflict are thought to be dysfunctional. But eradicating racism cannot be done dispassionately. Conflict and emotion *must* be accepted as a *functional* part of it. One may wish to minimise its more destructive features, but trying to avoid it altogether simply means avoiding coming to grips with the substances of racism and its human consequences. These are emotional subjects. Confrontation with the 'irrationalities' of emotion and conflict is an inescapable and, really, a modest price that must be paid for progress toward social justice.

Requirements for external leverage

Organisations and institutions are hard to change. It follows from this truism that there are limits to organisational self-reform.

External power often needs to be applied in order to change them, or to help direct change, and surely to sustain it. Leverage can come from the courts, from unions, community action organisations, consultants, and a variety of other sources. In our work with police departments we often found the help of individual elected officials, minority organisations, and private agencies helpful in keeping reform on track. But, in the end, it is government which generally has the decisive role here. Its agencies, the U.S. Commission on Civil Rights, for instance, are responsible for imbuing society with a moral tone, and for holding individuals and organisations accountable to the public interest. It is imperative that governments maintain an active and aggressive role in moving the United States and other nations toward social justice and equality of opportunity for their citizens.

There is a practical side-benefit to be gained from providing organisations with outside leverage toward change. It gives an excuse for changing things that may be more convenient to managers than moral argument – 'it's not really me who wants this fellas, it's them; what can I do?' This diffuses reponsibility for unpopular changes, and allows managers to preserve their personal occupational interests and friendships, and yet to press ahead with reform. Without the opportunity to shift some blame to powerful 'outsiders' (the courts, Title VII, the mayor, E.E.O.C., etc.) even a sympathetic executive might shrink from actions prejudicial to her or his job or long-standing personal affiliations.

Conclusions

When I look back over the attempts by my colleagues and me to reform institutional racism in police departments, I am led to a couple of conclusions. One of them is procedural; the second is philosophical.

First conclusion

In 1974, I described a strategy of organic change based on the idea that planned organisational change consists mostly of helping organisations to move in directions essentially consistent with their *existing* dispositions (Hunt, 1974). In addition to that notion, I argued: 'that [organisational] change and development are calculated to be gradual, fitful, agonisingly slow at times, and certainly piecemeal. Sensational results are the exception, not the rule. One must be wary of simplistic and excessive expectations for change in complex social systems'. (Hunt, 1974, p. 71). Furthermore, I suggested that:

Organisational effectiveness has to do with how well a social system

mobilizes resources to achieve its goals. But complex organisations have a multiplicity of goals. . . . This not only makes it hard to define goals; it also makes it hard to know which resources are important. . . . As one moves closer to operational levels, goals become ever more specific, practical, occupational, and segmental. Executive-level organizational goals probably mean next to nothing to personnel at working levels. . . . [But it] should always be possible to reconcile lower-level goals with higher-level goals.
(Hunt, 1974, p. 71)

I conclude from these propositions that rational programmes to dismantle racism and discrimination will work best when they translate their goals into specific operational terms – into concrete tasks that can be done by someone who can be identified. 'Goals' themselves can be restated as specific indicators or criteria of accomplishment of the tasks allocated to these actors. For example, one may wish to increase minority membership in the sworn ranks of police agencies, because fact-finding shows under-representation. In order for this to happen, however, minorities must get on the civil service lists from which employees are chosen; and to do that they must take an examination. One can translate an affirmative action goal, the way one department in our study did, into the specific task of identifying minority candidates and getting them to the examination; and then assign responsibility for performing this task to specific individuals. Effectiveness of performance of the task can eventually be tested by the proportions of minority candidates taking the examination, compared with some baseline.

Task-oriented approaches to changing organisations have the advantage of organising it in relation to tangible activities. This helps to get things started. People have something they can do. Once they start, they also have a way of getting feedback that can lead them to a better understanding of their problems, and to more effective remedies for them. It helps, too, if a sense of proportion guides the selection of change targets (tasks); and if they are acted upon selectively so as not to dissipate scarce resources (time, money, energy, etc.) in trying to do too many things at once.

Working this way husbands resources and helps initiate action by relating it to tasks that are 'possible'. It provides a sense of achievement to the performers of the tasks, or, if not achievement, then at least a kind of data-driven basis for re-thinking programmes and re-defining the tasks by which they are implemented. And it provides a sustaining sense of being in control of events rather than being helpless in their face, something that is especially important to voluntary change efforts.

A related idea suggested by an organic strategy of problem-solving is that it go forth step-by-step, in stages or phases, as well as task-by-task.

Phasing [change] efforts, like the concept of organic development, is a more or less direct extension of the system perspective on organisation. By introducing change [progressively] and purposefully, opportunities for planning and thoughtful selection of change targets and tactics are increased. Furthermore, chances of detecting both signs and sources of resistance to change and unanticipated consequences are improved, as are prospects for finding timely solutions to them. Most importantly, phasing provides for the progressive development of structures and feedback loops that can support planning and change in successive organisational subsystems. (Hunt, 1978, p. 75)

Taking the task of increasing the number of minority police officers, phasing effort to focus successively on recruitment (as described above) and then, for instance, on selection is a constructive way of proceeding. It conserves resources and provides a base of experience for planning specific, differently oriented tasks at later times.

Phased change efforts are, of course, by no means unfamiliar among desegregation programmes and other attacks on institutionalised discrimination. I think, for one example, of the federal court-ordered school desegregation process in Buffalo, New York, where I live. Still it is worth mentioning the concepts again, whether or not they are familiar. My experience has confirmed me in my belief in their worth. Indeed, had we followed them more assiduously our particular project might have benefited from it. Yet, I perceive a dilemma. Ideas about planned organisational change with which I am familiar assume that organisations have at least some general notions about where they would like to go, and just need orderly ways of getting there. Planned change technologies are intended to satisfy this instrumental need. The problem with change strategies in affirmative action environments, however, is that the organisational problems there may not be entirely tactical. Assumptions of organisational purpose may not hold. If they don't, planned change methodologies may, at best, be impotent as ways of dismantling insitutional discrimination. Many American organisations, both public and private, have yet to embrace genuine affirmative action as a part of their missions; and organisational development (OD) procedures are not well-adapted to helping them do it.

What is more, organisational change strategies are fundamentally 'local' in their orientations. They focus on organisations one at a time, and seek accommodation of change programmes to the novel features of individual organisations. But, if social change is sought local organisation by local organisation, then at societal levels it may be dismayingly slow in coming. A few local success stories may suggest unwarranted promise for this approach as a way of achieving national purposes. Engaging as OD strategies may be – and effective as they may sometimes prove – one must, I think, hesitate to advertise them as solutions to national problems of institutional racism. Individual psychotherapy, for example, may be effective for individual sufferers from mental illness, or it may not be. Either way, however, individual psychotherapy is infeasible as a solution to the *social* problem of mental illness because it takes too long and costs too much. One wonders if the same might not be true of organisational development approaches to social justice, and hence whether an alternative strategy might not be superior.

Toward a Public Health Model for eliminating racism. OD strategies for social change are expressly individualistic. They locate the critical elements of social systems and their problems among the attitudes and sentiments of the separate members of society; and they seek to accomplish social change via the instrument of aggregated individual attitude or motivational change. The psychotherapeutic model, perhaps in its group manifestations, is prototypical of this orientation to social change and betterment.

Speaking of Lord Scarman's inquiry and report on the 1981 Brixton riots, Henriques (1984) notes how Scarman admits police racism as at least one reason for the disorder. Scarman's report, however, follows a traditional individualistic line, firmly resisting any acceptance of racism as a social (structural) phenomenon. According to Scarman, only a few British police officers are prejudiced – the 'immature and ill-considered'. Furthermore, British society, Scarman thinks, is not itself and cannot be racist. Racial prejudice and discriminatory behaviour by British police can only be attributed to the occasional presence of a few 'rotten apples' who, moreover, are confined to the *lower* ranks. (Scarman never met a racist senior officer!) 'Thus', Henriques observes, 'prejudice [racism] is constituted as an individualised, exceptional phenomenon, automatically exonerating society as a whole' (p. 62). Prejudice (racism) is an irrational response of only a comparative few deviant individuals, resulting perhaps from ignorance or another unhappy mental state. Hence, the solution to racism in the social body is two-faceted: 1. treatment (education, training, etc.) of the afflicted minions (by their superiors?); and 2. surgery, which is to say, removal (dismissal) of refractory cases.

Little evidence exists, however, to show that treatment or training programmes focused on the racial attitudes and motivations (or ignorance) of individual police officers have produced significant, positive and durable effects on the racial attitudes of police officers, or on overall police behaviour toward minority citizens and groups. In a more general context, Thomas Pettigrew has commented as follows on this fact:

> Proponents of remedies [for racism] fashioned on older medical models of a doctor, a patient, and a couch, or on newer ideological models that assume the profound 'sickness' of all bigots, will simply overlook the most significant and easiest-to-change segment of White American racism. This model, then, maintains that we do not need 'to cure' bigots so much as we need to erode the bases of institutional racism which condition the bigot's attitudes and behaviour.
>
> (Pettigrew, 1981, p. 118)

Pettigrew's judgment is grounded in careful review of the literature on relations between indicators of racism and of mental health and thoughtful consideration of its social policy implications. This led him to conclude that, in fact, racism may not be so compellingly rooted in white individual psychology as has commonly been supposed. Instead, much of it may directly and indirectly reflect simple conformity with immediate social environmental influences. This idea directs attention to the props and behavioural incentives in the structures and customs of institutional life. It leads as well to a non-individualistic social or 'public health' strategy for eradicating racism that would act on its social environmental supports – much as one might act to eliminate fevers by draining swamps where insects breed.

A public health strategy for anti-racist action emphasises, on the one hand, eliminating situational supports for racist actions (e.g. by 'delegitimising' racial slurs in organisational settings, or by making discrimination illegal), and, on the other hand, introducing incentives for non-racist behaviour (e.g. by taking citizen complaints and other indicators of the pattern of police officer behaviour into account in performance evaluation, promotion, duty assignment, etc.). Incentive methods of reducing racist behaviour have not been used very much, perhaps; but be that as it may, the essential thesis of a public health model for eliminating racism is that 'the only [or at least the most efficient] means to counter institutional racism is to create new and powerful anti-racism mechanisms' (Sabshin et al., 1970, p. 792). These mechanisms are ones that concentrate chiefly on controlling the overt *behaviour* of people, including police officers, rather than on modifying their covert mental makeup. Incidentally, it follows from this that, contrary to Scarman, anti-racism efforts such as race relations training for police personnel would, as a matter of priority, best and most efficiently concentrate *not* on lower ranks – the numerous operatives who interact regularly with citizens and whose behaviour most needs controlling – but on command and supervisory officers who directly or indirectly (via policy) do that controlling.

A public health model of change accepts the proposition that a social system may itself be racist and, hence, may induce 'error' in the behaviour of individuals irrespective of their personal intentions. Effective anti-racist action, therefore, begins with recognition of this social reality and the task of structural remodelling it implies. Failure to do so not only precludes the prospect of eradicating racism, it may aggravate the problem. For ironically, as Henriques (1984) advises us, 'the racist *status quo* is maintained to a large extent not only through coercive and blatantly racist practices, but through the [well-intentioned] liberal position which criticises them as aberrations' (p. 88).

There is, of course, a tension between these methodological and strategical concepts and some basic aspects of Western thought about race relations (and other things) that I have so far mentioned only in passing. Hence to my second conclusion.

Second conclusion

Rationalist approaches to change, of the phased-organic or problem-remedy (U.S. Commission on Civil Rights, 1981) varieties, run a risk of not fully comprehending the realities of racism and institutional discrimination. I've sought to emphasise that these are not entirely rational phenomena, and will come back again to the point. First I want to consider a procedural matter related to it.

Deliberate planned change runs up against 'irrational' human emotions. It also runs up against the impatience of its eventual beneficiaries. The victims of institutional discrimination want relief from it now, not in phase 4. Who can blame them? And who can ask them to wait while we figure out what to do, particularly when they believe they already know. Anyway, why should they trust white planners ever to do anything? Whites have not historically shown enthusiasm for the job of eliminating institutional discrimination. And often in the past, the invocation of 'technical problems' has only been a code word for 'going slow'.

The whole rationist problem-solving apparatus runs a risk of converting the enterprise of dismantling institutional racism from a hopeful human social-political reform into an abstract technical or legalistic exercise. If it does that, it will have done a profound disservice to the cause of social justice in civilised society. The root values of human social equality cannot be dissolved in some technocratic potion without weakening them. Affirmative action programmes, whether phased, organic, or what have you, are instruments in the specific service of equity values. This fundamental fact – and the values themselves – must be kept prominent in the processes of reform. They define the reasons for the programmes, and they innervate them. Without a moral reference there are no criteria for equity decisions. Without a compelling moral force to counter vested interests, organic development is merely a synonym for no change at all.

Racism is both ideology and manifestation. Institutional discrimination may be racism's most visibly signicant manifestation; but ideology is the tacit network of beliefs and values that encourages and justifies these (and other) discriminatory manifestations. Ideas about white supremacy epitomise American racist ideology. Benjamin Bowser and I have spoken on this point as follows:

> Racism is multi-dimensional – individual, structural, and cultural. To describe it or combat it along any one dimension may not comprehend or reduce it on another. It spills over from any of these levels into the others. . . . A social order acts out racism. It does this because it is influenced by economic and political interests which benefit from racism either as an intended condition or unintended consequence of pursuing those interests. . . . [But] at bottom racism is a cultural phenomenon. . . . Cultural racism has been necessary to the acting out and reinforcement of racism, both in social structure and individual behavior . . . Racism generated through culture is self-generative and, consequently, hard to change. One can believe that real changes have occurred when in fact only appearances have altered.
>
> (Bowser and Hunt, 1981)

I certainly have no wish, obviously, to minimise the importance of correcting institutional racial bias. But I do wish to sound cautionary and admonitory notes. At the base of institutional discrimination is racism and white supremacist ideology. If our purpose is to 'create a climate of equality that supports all efforts to break down the structural, organisational, and personal barriers that perpetuate injustice' (U.S. Commission on Civil Rights, 1981, p. 42), then we shall have to consider carefully George Fredrickson's (1981) warning that 'equality and fraternity do not result automatically from the elimination of Jim Crow laws and practices'.

Values and ideologies sustain discrimination. We must take seriously James Jones' (1972; 1981) arguments on the cultural basis of racism. This is the hard-to-crack nub of the matter: invidious institutional systems rooted in white European values that, mostly subconsciously, lead to a devaluing by Western whites of Third World cultures and to consequent disadvantages for their people.

Obviously, as I have argued, we need to move aggressively to devise and set in place administrative and other remedies for institutional discrimination. But, affirmative action is a moral as well as, or more than, an administrative remedy. And if we are to use administrative remedies well, and remove racist barriers to a truly just society, we will need to become more self-conscious about the difficult ideological and value premises of discriminatory social systems.

NOTES

1 Principals in this undertaking, in addition to the writer, were Hubert G. Locke, Calvin W. Humphrey, and Franklin W. Zweig. The project was supported by funds from the National Institute of Mental Health, Center for Minority Group Mental Health Programs (see the volume edited by Locke and Walker [1980] for a general description of it). This present chapter is essentially a revision and extension of a presentation by the writer during Consultations on the Affirmative Action Statement of the U.S. Commission on Civil Rights, March 10–11, 1981, in Washington, D.C.
2 There are something like 40,000 *public* police organisations in the U.S., 17,000 of which are 'large', and no national or even statewide constabulary.

REFERENCES

- Bowser, B. P. and Hunt, R. G. (1981). 'The impact of racism on white Americans: Afterthoughts and reflections.' In B. P. Bowser and R. G. Hunt (eds.), *The Impact of Racism on White Americans.* ch. 13, Beverly Hills, CA. Sage Publications
- Fredrickson, G. M. (1981), *White Supremacy: A Comparative Study of American and South African History.* Oxford, New York
- Henriques, J. (1984), 'Social psychology and the politics of racism'. In J. Henriques *et al., Changing the Subject: Psychology, Social Regulation, and Subjectivity*, pp. 60–89, London, Methuen
- Hunt, R. G. (1974), *Interpersonal Strategies for System Management.* Monterey, CA., Brooks/Cole
- Hunt, R. G. (1983), 'Coping with institutional racism: A model for social problem-solving'. In R. H. Kilmann *et al., Producing Useful Knowledge for Organisations*, pp. 521–51, New York, Praeger
- Hunt, R. G. and McCadden, K. S. (1980), 'Race-related attitudes and beliefs of police personnel'. *Social Development Issues*, 4, pp. 31–49
- Jick, T. D. (1979), 'Mixing qualitative and quantitative methods: Triangulation in action'. *Administrative Science Quarterly*, 24: 602–12
- Jones, J. A. (1972), *Prejudice and Racism.* Reading, MA., Addison-Wesley
- Jones, J. A. (1981), 'The concept of racism and its changing reality'. In B. P. Bowser and R. G. Hunt (eds.), *The Impact of Racism on White Americans.* ch. 1, Beverly Hills, CA., Sage Publications
- Levine, M. (1974), 'Scientific method and the adversary model: Some preliminary thoughts'. *American Psychologist*, 29: 661–77
- Locke, H. G. and Walker, S. E. (1980), 'Institutional racism and American policing'. *Social Development Issues*, 4 (1)
- Patton, M. Q. (1979), *Utilisation-focused evaluation*, Beverly Hills, CA., Sage Publications
- Pettigrew, T. F. (1981), 'The mental health impact'. In B. P. Bowser and R. G. Hunt (eds.), *The Impact of Racism on White Americans.* ch. 5, Beverly Hills, CA., Sage Publications
- Sabshin, M., Diesenhaus, G. and Wilkerson, R. (1970), 'Dimensions of institutional racism in psychiatry'. *American Journal of Psychiatry*, 127: 787–93
- Scarman, Lord. (1981), The Brixton disorders 10–12 April, Cmnd 8427
- *The Future of Policing: A Panel Report* (1984). Seattle, WA., William O. Douglas Institute for the Study of Social Problems
- Thompson, J. D. (1967), *Organisations in Action.* New York, McGraw-Hill
- U.S. Commission on Civil Rights (1981), 'Affirmative action in the 1980s: Dismantling the process of discrimination – a proposed statement'. U.S. Commission on Civil Rights Clearinghouse Publication 65, January
- Weick, K. E. (1979), *The Social Psychology of Organising,* 2nd ed, Reading, MA., Addison-Wesley
- Whitaker, G. P. (1980), 'Co-production: Citizen participation in service delivery'. *Public Administration Review*, 40, May/June

Planning and implementing race relations seminars: the Holly Royde experience[1]

This chapter will elucidate the lessons to be learned from the University of Manchester's long-standing involvement in management seminars in race and community relations. Originally devised for the police service, they developed to meet the needs of other management groups in the public service, notably, prison governors. Inter-agency seminars were also held for several years. Currently, the emphasis is on team-building seminars, with the aim of facilitating the formation of Action Plans to combat personal and institutional discrimination in specific penal institutions. All the seminars described took place at the Holly Royde Conference Centre.

A senior executive police seminar, necessarily, has different objectives from training devised for staff of lower ranks, whether full-time in race relations as a specialism or performing normal duties. An awareness of the difficulties of policing a multiracial inner-city area 'at the sharp end' and the ability to make effective yet sensitive decisions in such contexts are among the relevant goals for such seminars (see, for example, Scarman, 1981, para 8.32). As to training methodology, the following sections show that the 'conference method' (Utgaard and Dawis, 1970), the 'case study' method (Patten, 1971) and extensive use of small group discussion and projects (Smith and Willson, 1975) can be successfully employed to facilitate emotional and behavioural learning. The need for activity-based learning methods grows as the objectives of the seminars change from primarily appreciation, awareness and sensitivity to include training in better day-to-day decision-making and more effective forward planning. Scarman (paras 4.69 to 4.80) is particularly critical of senior management's attitudes and methods and regards them as causative factors in the Brixton disorders of April 1981.

THE LATE SIXTIES: BEGINNINGS

Holly Royde's involvement in race training goes back to the time in the sixties when Sir John McKay was Chief Constable of Manchester and approached the University for help with training in the then burgeoning field of race relations. National interest in this experiment followed and an annual national seminar for the police service began in 1968.

Initially, the police personnel whom the seminar recruited were either Community Liaison Officers or officers in operational command positions, mainly (but not exclusively) in divisions with high numbers of ethnic minorities. (A 'Community Liaison Officer' is a specialist whose role was first developed in the sixties. These officers, of varying ranks, act as a bridge between a police commander and the various communities in that division or district.) When the author became involved with the seminar, he discovered that they often had had no specific training for the task but usually had considerable first-hand knowledge of ethnic minorities and some sympathy with their special situation in society.

In order to direct the seminar effectively, one needed to identify the training needs. The author's personal contacts with the police had been minimal and previous professional contacts nil. With limited time resources available, the 'needs assessment' programme originally consisted of spending several days with the metropolitan police in 1969, talking to certain C.L.O.s about their role and its associated problems and attending a divisional one-day seminar in race relations. This informal 'research' provided one with important insights into the C.L.O. role and into community relations as seen by the police service in London. One rapidly learned also that metropolitan attitudes and arrangements were not always shared by the members of the provincial police forces who constituted the majority of the seminar participants.

The other pressing training need was to evaluate the effectiveness of the content and method of the existing seminar provision and to assess, if possible, its impact upon the attitudes and behaviour of those officers who attended. Of necessity, one's approach to this problem was to treat the first seminar one directed as a 'pilot', to be revised as and where necessary next time around. The author's first seminar was planned in 1969, and took place in residence at Holly Royde in early 1970, being entitled 'The Police and the Immigrant Community'. Thirty-one police officers were enrolled and attended the five days' seminar.

Subsequent observation of the events which took place seemed to support Allport's statement that while preaching and exhortation may play a part in the process (of reducing prejudice) the lessons cannot be learned at the verbal level alone (Allport, 1958). For although the programme included the best political, academic and practical speakers currently available nationally and the opportunity to question them, the course format permitted little participative learning. As observer of the process, one was shaken by the excessive amount of defensiveness generated by the topic and saw unmistakeable proof that even a well-planned programme could be largely counterproductive if necessary confrontation was not put to constructive use. The post-seminar participant evaluation underlined the frustration endemic in a situation in which the experience of the participants was not constructively utilised. This led one to consider what the criteria of effectiveness were for such a seminar. (Shaw, 1971).

First, it was essential to provide the conditions for an open dialogue, free from defensiveness. Such conditions are best achieved in small group discussions with guidance by experienced group facilitators.

Second, it was necessary to see the seminar as a developmental process, with each successive stage mirrored in the group behaviour (see Tuckman, 1965). Thus, it was to be expected that resistance would be expressed early on. On the other hand, performance of group tasks would be expected to improve as the process reached its peak in the later stages of the week.

Third, it was advisable, where possible, to use practitioners as speakers more than academics so that the connection between information and its relation to practical situations always remained a central feature of the ensuing debate. One had concluded, after the pilot year, that academics at that time had low credibility for many serving policemen in the U.K.

Fourth, for similar reasons, race relations should be placed in a wider social and police context so that its complementarity with other aspects of policing, such as enforcing the law, the constable's discretion and his generally accepted role, be clearly established.

Fifth, the officers' own professional experiences must be related, analysed and reconstructed where necessary. This would probably be best done through the medium of case material provided in advance by participants. (See Batten, 1965: Patten, 1971).

Sixth, informal social contact between ethnic minorities and seminar participants should be arranged as an essential part of the seminar experience.

Accordingly, the following year, a seminar programme was devised incorporating all the aforementioned criteria. It followed what is known as the 'conference-discussion' method (Utgaard and Dawis, 1970) which incorporates a lecture–small group–plenary discussion pattern. The author was influenced in his seminar design by the leadership conferences organised by the Tavistock Institute (Rice,

1965) which contained a judicious mixture of study groups, lectures and application groups.

In the author's brief paper of 1971, he wrote:

The basic daily pattern is as follows: the day starts with the presentation of a topic by one or more speakers. Often one speaker is enough, but on one occasion this year when the subject was Police Discretion there were three speakers to cover the various aspects of a complex theme. After this, small groups explore the theme with the assistance of a tutor. These groups are small enough for total group participation to take place. The groups report back to the plenary and a general discussion ensues in which the original speakers are involved.

(1971, p. 277)

The evaluation carried out at the close of this seminar showed overwhelming support for the method, with particular approval being expressed about the value of the small groups. So far as its impact upon the attitudes of the participants was concerned, I reported at the time that between one third and one half gave indications of some positive attitude modification.

However, there was still some lingering suspicion among officers at that time of the 'new-fangled' subject of community relations, which was regarded by a minority as a political ploy designed to weaken the law-enforcement role of the police service. Nevertheless, there was such a clear improvement in member motivation and in the general atmosphere of the seminar over the previous year's that the methodology used became the norm in succeeding years.

The participants were still disturbed by some of the facts and opinions presented to them and were confronted over aspects of their roles and behaviour, as they had been before. However, the use of small discussion groups to handle this material meant that dialogue and constructive conflict, rather than mere confrontation, ensued given the right discussion and group facilitation methods.

The effectiveness of the approach increased as the ethos of the police service *vis-à-vis* community relations changed and the academic staff gained more experience in the techniques required by the methodology.

THE SEVENTIES: CONSOLIDATION

Several governmental policy changes were made during this period which significantly affected the nature of the annual police seminar. First, as the need for greater race and community expertise grew in the police service, the C.L.O. had to be given a more extended period of training. For him or her, a week's intensive seminar was no longer seen to be enough and Holly Royde was, henceforth, to be used solely for 'senior officers with command responsibilities'. Second, as other professions in the criminal justice system became more aware of the racial dimension, the seminar's member composition was modified to allow for a dialogue between police, the prison service and the probation service to take place.

Chesler (1976), in his analysis of race relations training, drew a distinction between 'attitudinal or cultural racism' and 'behavioural racism' and added that each may be either individual or institutional in its expression.[2] Since as Chesler assumed, race training was about heightening people's consciousness of racism, then it followed that each training programme should focus attention on the several dimensions of racism. So far as this training programme was concerned, it took several years for a satisfactory balance of the elements to be achieved. Thus the year-by-year programmes throughout the seventies show a gradual but sustained movement towards a concept of training that did justice both to the complexity of the issues and to the emotional and professional needs of the participants.

Gradually, a pattern developed in which the first half of the week was taken up with an overall analysis of the state of race relations in society and in the service itself: minority speakers put their own points of view; community visits were made; police speakers defined the policing issues; and discussion of the political and social policies likely to enhance good race relations took place. The second half, by contrast, concentrated on remedies. These included effective selection and training, practical examples of good community policing, and the encouragement of appropriate strategies at divisional level by means of small group projects.

Chesler (1976) in discussing the 'programmatic goals' of organisations distinguishes between 'root change' and 'system maintenance' as the possible bases of organisations' self-interest in generating race training programmes. It must be plainly admitted that 'system maintenance', in the sense of adjusting the police service to meet the demands of a changing society, was the summit of governments' ambition during this period. This limited objective, unsatisfactory as it may be to the radical, was pursued with sincerity by governments of both political complexions throughout this period.

In such circumstances, as Chesler has also pointed out, the best way to avoid irrelevant planning is to 'direct race education to the internal issues potent in an organisation' (1976). Thus, as well as the perpetual need to raise the general level of awareness of participants so far as race is concerned, the annual programmes reflected many changes in these 'potent issues'. These included impending changes in legislation, matters of public concern such as racial attacks, public disorder and policing styles, and issues internal to the service but affecting public confidence, such as equal opportunity in recruitment and promotion.

THE EARLY EIGHTIES: EXPANSION INTO PRISON SERVICE AND OTHER AGENCIES

A number of events in the early eighties, for example, the public disorders in various cities in 1980, 1981 and 1982 and the Scarman Inquiry, along with other inquiries such as the Hytner Report, raised the level of debate about racism in British society to a new peak. At the same time, the criminal justice system, in particular the prison and probation services, consciously grasped race relations and equal opportunity as important issues which had to be tackled if the system were not to break down under the pressure of events. The varying strategies adopted by these services necessarily included training at various levels. Thus, within the space of a year or two, prison governors' seminars as well as inter-agency seminars had been added to the original police seminars at Holly Royde and all based on a broadly similar approach.

It has been asserted elsewhere (Shaw, 1981), that it is not known whether any large organisation in Britain has attempted to transform its attitudes, behaviour and practices completely, in recognition of the fact that it is now required to function in a multi-ethnic society.[3] To make such root and branch changes, it helps if an organisation has strong central direction, clear accountability at all levels, also a well-developed system of rewards and sanctions for compliance or non-compliance with organisational policy. On these grounds alone, the prison service is well placed to attempt such organisational development. The seminars for governors began in 1982 and were seen as part of an overall strategy for change in the service. This strategy also included the issuing of detailed policy documents, the appointment and training of race relations specialists, as well as appropriate input into refresher training for all ranks.

The governors' seminars were designed to meet the following attitudinal, behavioural and organisational objectives and although each seminar touched on 'potent issues', this was done within the framework of the stated objectives.

1 Governors will be thoroughly acquainted with departmental Race Relations policy.
2 They will be aware of historical trends in Britain since the war regarding immigration and settlement.
3 They will be aware of the nature and incidence of personal and institutional discrimination in penal institutions.

4 They will start to think practically about the implementation of departmental policy.

5 They will be given the opportunity to meet and communicate with ethnic minority members of self-help groups, community associations, churches and clubs.

Throughout these five-day seminars governors met in small groups at least once every day and usually more frequently. The group facilitator sought at the first meeting to draw out members' motivations and to be non-judgmental when negative feelings about the seminar were expressed. Every major formal presentation by a speaker was followed by a group meeting in which the ideas were fully explored and discussed. The facilitator tried to ensure a balanced and positive discussion and was alert to the possibility that prejudices can be reinforced through discussion. As group cohesiveness developed throughout the week, the group work switched from discussion *per se* to task performance, including problem-solving exercises. A facilitator was always assisted by a member of a Prison Board of Visitors from one of the ethnic minorities to ensure a black perspective on the service was available in all discussions and decision-making.

Other techniques used were: inter-group exercises such as Star Power (in which the behaviour of powerful elites is explored) (Shirts, 1969); group experiential exercises, such as role plays, run by a group facilitator; community visits designed to overcome white ignorance of day-to-day life in ethnic minority communities; and the use of film and television material. It was regarded as essential that all experiences of the above kind were fully debriefed so that the learning derived could be generalised and applied to future situations. The group facilitator had to enable the process of 'meaning attribution' to take place (Lieberman, Yalom and Miles, 1973).

From 1980 to 1984 an inter-agency seminar was held annually, bringing together participants from six disciplines with an interest in the criminal justice system. As mentioned above, the police seminars had allowed in members of other disciplines and the concept of a mixed seminar developed from there. The six disciplines invited to the first seminar were the police service, the prison service, the probation and after-care service, the social services, the education service and the magistracy. Equal representation from all these groups was sought. The proceedings of the first seminar were published in full (Peppard and Shaw (eds.), 1980).

All small groups were themselves inter-agency, enabling a topic under discussion to be viewed from several angles. There was an 'awareness-raising' component but the overall aim was to encourage inter-agency action, ensuring fairer delivery of services and alleviating misunderstanding and conflict in the community. In support of this goal, we might invite a team from a local authority which was developing an inter-professional strategy; or a police authority which was collaborating closely with other social agencies. The final task of the small groups was to prepare a paper on effective inter-agency cooperation. In this way, we believed, minds would be turned towards the back-home situation and the practical application of the ideas learned in the seminar.

The most recent development has been the prison service 'generic' seminars to bring together in one training experience, people of varying ranks and functions within penal institutions. The concept as originally developed was for a seminar of thirty-six participants, made up of threesomes[4] drawn from twelve institutions. Each threesome had to include a governor grade, a uniform grade and a specialist such as psychologist, chaplain or education officer. Among these three would be the person with the role of race relations liaison officer in that institution. Team-building and action-planning were the key objectives of the seminar, whose content was devised in close collaboration with Capt. M. J. Marriott, U.S.N. (Ret.), formerly director of Equal Opportunity Management Institute, Patrick A.F.B., Florida, who had lectured to the Holly Royde seminars over a number of years.

ANALYSIS AND ASSESSMENT

Several analysts (e.g. Chesler, 1976; Hunt, 1981; Shaw, 1981) have warned against expecting too much from race relations training. Even, it is said, where such training is effective in changing individuals, it is doubtful whether much consequent change in their organisations will be achieved. This attitude has been heightened by current distinctions between personal and institutional racism. As Chesler trenchantly remarks, 'Individual change is, from my point of view, simply not a sufficient goal in a society rife with institutional racism and injustice. It may be a necessary goal, a first step on the road to greater organisational and institutional change; or it may be a useful outcome of institutional changes. But the racism embedded firmly in institutional mechanisms and ideologies will not be countered by a few enlightened individuals. . . .' (1976, p. 45). Hunt adopts a similar stance when he states that 'strategies for eradicating institutional racism or ameliorating its effects must necessarily orient to structural reform and not to individual attitude change, although the latter may be a welcome by-product of the former'. (1981, p. 1).

As has been pointed out elsewhere, 'pressure for change can be directed either at the people within an organisation, or at the working groups within an organisation, or at the total organisation itself' (Shaw, 1981, p. 437). Training interventions are typically directed at the first two levels i.e. people, and, in some cases, work groups or teams. Strictly speaking, then, effective training for organisational personnel ought, if the above analyses are correct, to be planned in conjunction with simultaneous changes in policies, norms and practices in the organisation itself. Judged according to this criterion, the seminars discussed in this chapter must have varied significantly in their overall effectiveness, since the organisational factor has not always been attended to.

For example, the seminars for prison governors were planned as part of an overall organisational strategy. The senior police seminars, on the other hand, were made up of participants from different police forces, which are all at different stages so far as the development of race relations and equal opportunity policies are concerned. By definition, the inter-professional seminars (which ended in 1984) were not part of a concerted organisational strategy, being made up of personnel from several organisations. The crucial fact, however, from the evaluation point of view, is that the prison department's strategy, although the most comprehensive, does not as yet include a thoroughgoing monitoring of their total programme's effectiveness. Thus, in order to assess our effectiveness, we had to make do with participant evaluation of the governors' seminars themselves and some self-reports of attitudes.

Training, despite the reservations mentioned above (p. 35), occupies a central place in the attempts made by organisations to eliminate racism and to develop personal and professional skills in race relations. The importance of this place is well brought out in the Fiman Report (1977), which is probably the most comprehensive analysis of race relations training ever carried out anywhere. After a most thorough investigation of the effects of race training on army personnel at the Defence Race Relations Institute (see chapter 5) the author concludes that 'there is evidence that . . . training serves important functions and has a high value for the Army in that it is providing a group of individuals highly motivated and generally more qualified than personnel who have not received the training to deal with the problem of reducing discrimination in the activities of the Army'. (p. iv). However, given that sponsoring organisations in Britain are not usually prepared to put resources into training evaluation, then the trainer's best bet is to follow those models which research elsewhere has shown to be effective and which his own experience has confirmed. The situation is all too often as Hinrichs describes it, 'trainers are usually under pressure to do something.

Hence there is little research into effectiveness. Most courses are sold and accepted on faith.' (1976, p. 831).

At the very least, however, good training practice demands that the trainee be asked to evaluate the various components of the training experience and that the trainer systematically analyse such feedback as he receives by this method. Where possible, also, pre- and post-seminar measures of relevant opinions and attitudes should also be taken. Whatever success has been achieved at Holly Royde has been so because evaluational feedback has always been elicited and examined carefully. Participants have always been asked to respond anonymously to make it more likely that true feelings are expressed.

In general, immediate post-seminar evaluations have tended to confirm that participants place a higher value on participative learning than on didactic presentations. Although, where an individual presenter made his case with clarity, humour and vividness, the general trend could be overturned. Generally speaking, however, the outside visits, the discussion groups, case studies and practical projects have tended to be evaluated more highly than the essential lectures which were always included in the programmes.

The beneficial effect of a participative experience, in this case a face-to-face dialogue between police and black youth, can be judged by the following statement volunteered by a senior police officer. He said the experience 'was a revelation, for me at any rate, that ethnic minorities . . . have a definite mistrust of the police, a fear of the police and no wish to recognise the police as a potential friend'. Undoubtedly, given this senior officer's lack of awareness of minority attitudes, no lecture, however brilliant, would have achieved with equal effect the heightened awareness which he gained through face-to-face dialogue with black youths.

However, more important than awareness-raising, which is the most commonly reported outcome of the seminar, is the effect, if any, on the post-seminar behaviour of the participants. Mere figures may be misleading here, since police officers are not selected for the seminar solely on the basis of the degree of community relations problems in their divisions. Hence, some returning participants have greater scope than others for implementing changes in community policing and related matters. In a recent follow-up evaluation, carried out just under a year after the seminar ended, thirty senior officers were asked to indentify any practical innovations resulting from their attendance at the seminar. Seven (twenty-three per cent) of the respondents cited specific decisions or initiatives. Several cited more than one. Respondents were required to provide specific information to back up their claims to have made changes. Of the remaining twenty-three (seventy-seven per cent), fifteen (fifty per cent) either cited enhancement of pre-existing commitment to good race relations because of the attitude-reinforcement and increased awareness derived from the seminar or said that they were contemplating changes in method or approach. Eight (twenty-seven per cent) were unable to specify any new initiatives nor to claim attitude reinforcement.

The new initiatives taken included the following example: one commander reported many changes in the way a division with a multi-ethnic population was policed, including the identification of 'drop-in' points on each beat where officers may call and be involved in the self-help activities of various communities, the better use of special constables, the provision of 'hot lines' to community leaders for use in emergencies or times of tension, and better liaison with other service agencies, especially where the physical environment is concerned. Other innovations cited were – more attention being paid to the selection of community beat constables for sensitive areas; establishing a police–minority group dialogue where none had existed before; better training in behaviour and attitudes for police representatives on police–community forums; and the placement of probationer constables in the offices of a Community Relations Council to give the officer firsthand experience of the work they do in the community.

An analysis of those respondents (twenty-seven per cent) who made no subsequent changes in their community policing strategy or tactics led me to draw the following conclusions regarding their inactivity. Some officers, it is clear, were satisfied, one might even say complacent, about what their forces are doing already in the field of community relations. While there were usually some grounds for satisfaction, the complacency was probably due in some measure to the isolation of the senior officer from the realities of day-to-day life among the alienated and oppressed. Sometimes, but not always, a face-to-face encounter with, say a group of unemployed youth in a deprived urban environment could dispel the ignorance and create a realisation of the gap between the two which somehow had to be bridged.

On the other hand, some officers from the county (i.e. mainly rural) constabularies said that the seminar did not specifically cater for their needs, since the focus tended to be predominantly on ethnic minorities of whom they often have few. While one could argue that problems in the field of race relations have their counterparts in the area of general community relations and that officers should be able to spot these comparisons and draw the necessary conclusions for their own practice, the evaluations showed that greater effort needed to be made to assist them to make these connections. Other officers from county forces, however, while seeing the relevance of the cases studied for policing in general, said that because they had little opportunity to practise what they had learned, the learning remained at an essentially theoretical level. Yet another group felt that while they had sizeable populations of ethnic minorities, there was a greater feeling of trust and understanding between those minorities and the police than was to be found in the larger inner cities. They believe this was due to the quality of the relationships that had been allowed to develop and that the seminar encouraged them to strengthen and deepen these relationships. Perhaps further research would show that such a perceived difference in the nature of police–minority group relationships was indeed a fact. Or perhaps it would not.[5]

From the point of view of organisational change, an extremely important group were the fifty per cent who, while not making changes or denying the need for change, claimed that the seminar had had a reinforcing or galvanising effect, hence they would probably make changes in the near future. A logical and comprehensive organisational development policy (towards the enhancement of police–community relations) would direct the attention of its follow-up mechanisms to this group particularly, for they are the ones, presumably, who with some more encouragement, assistance and stimulation would be most likely to repay any such follow-up efforts. It seems clear that follow-up would more likely pay off in these cases than they would either in the case of the innovators, on the one hand, or the non-innovators on the other.

The size of this middle group was swollen by the inclusion of those who because they had attended other seminars and were subject to other influences, were reluctant to specifically attribute any particular community policing initiative that they have made to any particular source. It is only fair to say that the difficulty of evaluating the long-term effects of Holly Royde upon senior police officers is increased by the number of local, regional and national training courses, the amount of public debate and the publication of research material on this topic. Moreover, this plethora of efforts makes it difficult for trainers to avoid overlap, repetition and redundancy in their courses. The situation calls for greater coordination of the efforts of all those involved, whether within the service or in academe or in consultancy and training firms, so that a more systematic programme of training and development may be devised.

To turn to attitude-measurement, Nadine Peppard has written of the difficulty of 'assessing whether attitudes have shifted in any permanent way or have merely been impinged upon in the heat of the moment, so to speak, and will revert to their previous level with the passage of time'. (Peppard, 1984, p. 315) Such uncertainty is inherent in all post-seminar assessment. That possibility acknowledged, in 1984 the seminar directors administered an attitude measurement instrument to the Holly Royde inter-agency seminar on a pre- and post-training basis to assess what, if any, change had taken place in attitudes during the seminar. The findings revealed that in several of the dimensions tested some positive movement occurred.

Summarising this data, one can say that participants left the training experience with greater awareness of their responsibility as senior executives for implementing race relations and equal opportunity policy; with greater appreciation of useful managerial strategies for so doing; with increased awareness of the need for public authorities and organisations to give a lead in this area; with greater awareness of their own prejudices; and a greater realisation that Britain is a multi-racial society. The pre-seminar averages for the above attitudes were moderately positive to start with and the post-seminar scores showed increases ranging from 0.5 to 1.3 points on a ten-point scale. Analysis of variance of these figures shows that these increases in the executives' anti-racist posture should be regarded as encouraging tendencies rather than statistically significant ones.

Virtually no movement at all was found on four of the dimensions measured. Included in this group was the degree of the participants' acceptance of the reality of racial disadvantage in Britain today. The before and after scores being relatively static may be explained by the fact that pre-seminar awareness of this phenomenon was already high. Also showing little improvement over the original average was the predicted likelihood of their taking new initiatives in race relations and equal opportunity. This is an interesting finding in view of the improvement, already noted, in their awareness of their managerial responsibility *vis-à-vis* good race relations, their awareness of new strategies and of the importance of an anti-racist commitment if public authorities are to have credibility in the eyes of minorities. Perhaps they were merely being realistic or sceptical about the opportunities they would have for putting theory into practice. On the other hand, the reason was probably to be found in the inherent shortcomings of a brief seminar which was able to raise the level of awareness but lacked the time to get to grips with translating ideas into action. The later sessions were devoted to this task, but clearly more time was needed.

Another data source for evaluating these seminars was to be found in the group facilitators' reports. The processes of attitude modification could be seen 'in close-up' in these group meetings. One group leader reported on the effect upon his group of a decision-making exercise in which they had to place in rank order a number of candidates, drawn both from the ethnic majority and from the ethnic minority communities, for a post in the public service. In debriefing this exercise some members expressed the view that the civil service had a good record in the recruitment and promotion of minorities. Others in the group demurred, citing cases of discrimination which went to industrial tribunal. These cases included recruitment, unfair treatment of minorities and discriminatory delivery of services. The discussion later widened into a discussion of the record of the public service generally, including housing provision. As the facilitator said, 'The exercise served its purpose of bringing to light latent issues slumbering below the surface of our previously rather urbane discussion.' This example showed how ignorance could be challenged in a constructive manner, informing the minds and changing the attitudes of participants, the mixed nature of the group being crucial to its success.

Next, some references to the results of the evaluation of the prison service seminars for governors and other personnel. As we had found with the police, the participative and experiential items in seminar programmes ranked, in general, highest in post-seminar participant evaluation. For example, taking the top of the rank orders of programme items from four different seminars, based on participant ratings of their value, no fewer than twelve out of twenty top choices were of experiential and participative items. This was an encouraging pointer since as Coleman has said, 'a property of experiential learning is that it appears to be less easily forgotten than learning through information assimilation'. (Coleman, 1976, p. 58).

Smith has emphasised (see chapter 11 below) the importance of making it easier for workshop participants to export changes after it is over. He stresses the need for formulating plans while it is still in progress. All governors' seminars have required projects of this kind to be carried out by small work groups of governors. These projects, on such topics as local management strategy, codes of practice for establishments and training programmes, have produced many fine papers, trenchant criticisms of the service and high level commitment to harmonious race relations in the future. There is evidence to show, moreover, that returning governors, newly sensitised to the importance of harmonious race relations, have implemented some changes in institutional practice and training courses, and given greater thought to the appointment of race relations liaison officers. However, the time has probably come for these returning participants to be followed up more assiduously than may have happened in the past. This process is already beginning (see The Annual Report of H.M. Chief Inspector of Prisons, 1983) and can only be to the good of the service for, as the old business adage has it, 'management gets what it inspects'.

Finally, reference was made above to the 'generic' seminars, devised to bring together people of different ranks and functions in prisons and youth custody centres. Pre- and post-seminar attitude measures were carried out during this exercise, items were evaluated for relevance and personal impressions were also collected. The attitude measures showed the greatest movement in those very areas where our efforts were largely directed, namely, developing togetherness among teams from specific institutions and promoting post-seminar action to improve race relations and equal opportunity in institutions. The items 'likely initiatives after return' and 'feeling of group cohesiveness' both showed more than one point increase on a five-point scale. Other attitudes showed impressive improvement even though not reaching these levels. The sense of achievement and satisfaction among participants was most marked, summed up in the comment that the seminar was 'invaluable to an increased awareness of the interdependence of all who work within penal establishments'.

CONCLUSIONS

In recent years, long after the Holly Royde seminars first began, the community relations dimension of the work of the law-enforcement bodies and other criminal justice agencies has come under close scrutiny as a result of social unrest and public disorder. This scrutiny has served to underline the need for seminars such as this chapter describes. Lord Scarman, for example, in discussing the shortcomings of the senior police command of 'L' District of the Metropolitan Police in April 1981 asserted the principle that 'community relations are central, not peripheral, to the police function'. (1981, para. 4.80). He added later, 'training courses designed to develop the understanding that good community relations are not only necessary but essential to good policing should, I recommend, be compulsory from time to time in a police officer's career up to and including the rank of Superintendent'. (Para. 5.28). The Police Training Council Working Party Report (1983) also emphasised the need for in-service training for senior officers.

On the other hand, many incidents in penal institutions, with serious implications for the preservation of racial harmony, have caused that service to examine carefully its own policy and behaviour in the field of race relations. Two circular instructions (28/1981 and 56/1983) and the 1983 Report of Her Majesty's Chief Inspector of Prisons have focused particularly on these issues. While recognising the importance of training, they said that it was not, however, a substitute for an active professional approach within the individual establishment. (56/83/Sect. 5). Local authorities, too, as incontrovertible evidence of discrimination in housing allocation (see C.R.E., 1984) and other services has come to light, have scrutinised their own record. In all official policy statements, designed to counter these disturbing trends, training, including racism awareness training, was usually accorded a central place.

As academic providers of training, Holly Royde can only applaud these official opinions. But such applause will have to be tempered by the realisation that training, however well done, is only part of the solution to the racism which manifests itself, in attitudes and behaviour, in our great social institutions. Elsewhere in this volume (see chapter 12), certain principles of effective training design and practice are enunciated and with these we agree, since our experience bears them out. To these principles, however, two other important but obvious ones should be added. First, that all training objectives need to be evolutionary in nature. Which means that however carefully a seminar is devised at a given time, it will not be totally appropriate in succeeding years. As new issues come to the forefront in society, so the informational content of the seminar is affected. While a seminar may have a settled methodology, content, case material and issues can and will change. It follows, therefore, that evaluation, review of objectives and implementation needs to take place on an ongoing basis.

Secondly, while participative or experiential learning is a vital aspect of race relations training methodology, its implications should always be brought out not left implicit. Included in this prescription are role-playing exercises, community visits, simulations, case studies, inter-ethnic discussion groups and self-assessment exercises. Reference has already been made to the group facilitators' key role in fostering 'meaning attribution', namely, helping the significance of a learning experience to be understood, generalised and its potential applications to be appreciated. Without this the learning cycle remains incomplete; incomprehension and frustration may reign and the trainer's efforts be nullified. Research shows this to be so and experience bears it out.

Finally, one must refer to two policy and strategy issues that could have significant implications for race relations. First, there is the need to see senior executive seminars as merely a part of the total training effort that goes on within the respective agencies, so that a coordinated and overlapping training strategy may be devised. The occasion of the Scarman Inquiry into the Brixton Disorders gave the opportunity to make these points so far as the police service is concerned. In a written submission (Shaw and Luckham, 1981), it was argued that 'it is imperative that some body or committee at national or regional level should monitor what is happening, identifying examples of good practice and keeping under review changing requirements in this field'. (Para. 3, p. 4). This is especially necessary, it was argued, in Britain where the police service is organised locally rather than nationally and needs a central research and development group for race relations training, quite independent of the service itself. Fortunately, an official body, The Police Training Council Working Party also came up with a similar idea (1983, pp. 23–4) and subsequently government has set up such a centre at Brunel University in 1984. This might well lead in due course to the coordination, between the police and other agencies, that is also necessary.

Secondly, in the same submission to Scarman, the question was raised of the effectiveness of training *per se* to solve the problems which the police service, and other agencies, face in race relations. It was argued that, 'course attendance . . . is not the panacea. The experience needs to be fed back and diffused through a division or force which will itself have to change structurally to cope with modern conditions'. (p. 6). Then, advocating that a 'a force, or division of a force, be chosen for an experiment of this kind' (*ibid*) a scheme of organisational development was set out, including the human and financial resources needed. Such a scheme would have as its objective the elimination of personal and institutional racism in the division and the acquisition of the professional attitudes and skills essential to effective policing in a multiracial society. In this development, training would have its part to play, but structural change would be crucial. The lessons learned here would be exportable to similar units in the service.

Such a solution remains the ideal. Meantime, as has been specified, much can be achieved by influencing the personal attitudes and behaviour of senior officers, changing their motivation or reinforcing it where appropriate and providing assistance with their managerial functions, through the executive seminar method. That such a programme works well at the personal level we have ample evidence, both from police and penal participants. As one governor said after attending an inter-agency seminar, 'The personal value of contacting so wide a range of people was immeasurable; working out the implications for our institutions is the difficult but essential follow-up.' (Capel, 1981, p. 15).

NOTES

1 I am grateful to Angela Rodriguez and Bryan Luckham for their comments on an earlier draft of this chapter.
2 See also the diagram in Chapter Twelve (p. 185) for a diagrammatic depiction of Chesler's analysis of racism.

3 See Chapter Ten for a discussion of such an attempt in the West Midlands Probation Service, Birmingham, England.
4 Later amended to four-person groups.
5 Police Department, Home Office, sponsored the Seminars and collected the follow-up dates on my behalf.

REFERENCES

- Allport, G. W. (1958), *The Nature of Prejudice*. New York, Doubleday Anchor
- Batten, E. R. with Batten, M. (1965), *The Human Factor in Community Work*. London, Oxford University Press
- Capel, J. (1981), 'Personal Impressions of a Conference: Criminal Justice and the Social Services in the Multi-Racial Society'. *Prison Service Journal*, July 1981: 13–15
- Chesler, M. A. (1976), 'Dilemmas and Designs in Race Education/Training'. Paper presented at second National Symposium on Race Relations Education and Training, Washington D.C., 15–17 September
- Coleman, J. S. (1976), 'Differences between experiential and classroom learning.' In Keeton, Morris T. (ed.) *Experiential Learning: Rationale, Characteristics and Assessment.* San Francisco, Jossey-Bass
- Commission for Racial Equality (1984), *Race and Council Housing in Hackney*. London, C.R.E.
- Fiman, B. G. (1977), *Analysis of the Training of Army Personnel at the Defence Race Relations Institute*. Alexandria, Va., U.S. Army Research Institute for the Behavioural and Social Sciences
- Hinrichs, J. R. (1976), 'Personnel Training.' In Dunnette, M. (ed.), *Handbook of Industrial and Organisational Psychology*. Chicago, Rand McNally
- Hunt, R. G. (1981), *Coping with Institutional Racism: A Model for Social Problem-Solving*. mimeograph, State University of New York at Buffalo and Institute for the Study of Contempory Social Problems
- Hytner, B. (1981), *Report on the Moss Side Disturbances*, Manchester City Council
- Lieberman, M. A., Yalom, I. D. and Miles, M. B. (1973), *Encounter Groups: First Facts*. New York, Basic Books
- Patten, T. H., Jr. (1971), *Manpower Planning and the Development of Human Resources*, New York, Wiley
- Peppard, N. (1984), 'Race relations training: the Patrick experiment.' *New Community*. 11: 312–16
- Peppard, N. and Shaw, J. (eds.), (1980), *Criminal Justice and the Social Services in the Multi-Racial Society; Report of an interdisciplinary seminar*. London, Community Programmes and Equal Opportunity Dept., Home Office
- Police Training Council Working Party (1983), *Community and Race Relations Training for the Police*. London, Home Office
- *Report of Her Majesty's Chief Inspector of Prisons 1983*. London, H.M.S.O., 618
- Rice, A. K. (1965), *Learning for Leadership: Interpersonal and Intergroup Relations*. London, Tavistock
- Scarman, Lord (1981), *The Brixton Disorders 10–12 April 1981*. London, Home Office/H.M.S.O.
- Shaw, J. (August 1971), 'Attitude change among the police.' *Race Today*, pp. 277–9
- Shaw, J. and Luckham, B. L. G. (1981), *Submission to the Brixton Enquiry*, mimeograph, Manchester University
- Shaw, J. (1981), 'Training methods in race relations within organisations: an analysis and assessment.' *New Community*, 9: 437–46
- Shirts, R. G. (1969), *Starpower: Directors' Instructions*. La Jolla, Western Behavioural Sciences Institute
- Smith, P. B., and Willson, M. J. (1975), 'The use of group training methods within multi-racial settings.' *New Community*, 4: 1–14.
- Tuckman, B. W. (1965), 'Developmental sequences in small groups.' *Psychological Bulletin*, 63, pp. 384–99
- Utgaard, S. B. and Dawis, R. V. (1970), 'The most frequently used training techniques.' *Training and Development Journal*, 24: 40–43

Community policing
in crisis[1]

INTRODUCTION

This chapter examines some of the problems with inter-agency collaboration and community policing in multi-ethnic inner-city areas. The focus of this contribution is provided by a case history of what seems to have been the largest British experiment attempted to date in community policing. It took place in Lozells which is on the edge of Handsworth in Birmingham – Britain's second largest city. It ran from 1979–85 and we were able to monitor its progress with a research team funded by the Home Office. Shortly after the experiment ended, on 9 September 1985 Lozells erupted in the worst night of rioting in our post-war history. It left two people dead and forty shops destroyed. Estimates of the damage currently vary from £15 m. to £30 m.

What went wrong? Were the police to blame? What is the future of inner-city areas like Lozells or community policing in them in these troubled times? These questions represent legitimate concerns which will be addressed in this chapter. However, they can all too easily narrow the arena of debate into simply apportioning blame rather than expanding our understanding of the problems. The recent spate of riots which began in Lozells have stimulated a blizzard of 'solutions' offered by the complete political spectrum. The criticism of these is not that they are all wrong or indeed irrelevant. However, they seem without exception either individually inadequate or inherently ineffective. Perhaps at the end of the day the real danger is that defensive postures will be adopted by all concerned, that the ideological hobby horses of commentators will draw attention away from the need for more analysis. In all of this, community policing is most vulnerable. Thus the evidence in this chapter could be used (superficially and wrongly) to support the simple statement made by one commentator that 'community policing has been tried and it's failed'. However, concluding this would involve throwing out with the bathwater some precious babies that no civilised society can afford to lose.

Before describing Lozells, the community policing experiment, the riot and the unhappy legacy which this created, it is worth noting the context in which such events must be considered.

COMMUNITY POLICING

Visitors from Mars might be forgiven for thinking that Britain had only just invented the police. Hardly a day goes by without the news media questioning the police role. Even the most unlikely events seem to provide a catalyst for further debate on what the police should or should not do. For example, it is an astonishing fact that the recent miners' strike (March 1984–March 1985) raised more issues on television news about the police than it did about either coal board or government policy (Cumberbatch, McGregor, Brown and Morrison, 1985).

Of course the police role in riots is a little more obvious. Nevertheless unlike the press of other European countries, the British mass media are more inclined to consider the police role to be essential to the causes of riot (Cumberbatch, McGregor, Jones and Brown, 1985). This is best illustrated by reference to the discussions on the Scarman Report. This inquiry into the 1981 disorders in Britain by Lord Scarman was generally very well received. The *Daily Mirror* described it as 'one of the great social documents of our time', while the *Guardian* affirmed 'Lord Scarman has created a watershed in policing policy' (see Venner, 1981). One of the most cited conclusions to the inquiry was offered in its review of the police: 'their role is critical. If their policing is such that it can be seen as the application to our new society of the traditional principles of British policing, the risk of unrest will diminish . . .' (Scarman, 1982, p. 135).

After Scarman, community policing came to be seen as the panacea. Chief constables in almost everyone of Britain's forty-three separate regional police forces proclaimed a commitment to community policing. More than this, as one extensive series of interviews with chief constables concluded: 'So chief constables do not so much say that community policing is a fresh answer to their problems as that it *is* British policing and has been for a century and a half.' (Leighton, 1982, p. 50).

The kind of message reiterated in the post-Scarman debates was that a return to traditional policing would mean a return to public tranquillity. The introduction of mobile patrols (unit beat policing) in the late 1960s was now seen as a mistake; a minor and temporary aberration in fact which isolated our beloved village bobbies from their devoted public. Now that the lesson had been learned, now that bobbies would be put back on the beat and community policing restored, all would be well again.

There is little doubt that this optimism has been severely shaken by the riots of 1985. Clearly something has gone wrong but the question is what? As will be argued later, far too much was expected of the police. They responded quickly to Scarman's recommendations but community policing never really had the chance it deserved. In any case, to place the responsibility for the cause of riots entirely on the police is manifestly unfair. Other factors must be considered by even the most bigoted of commentators.

It would also be unfair to suggest that Scarman himself either exaggerated the importance of the police or ignored other precipitating factors in the riots of 1981. Unlike the Kerner commission (1968) in the United States, the brief given to Scarman was to examine the events of the 1981 Brixton riot and its immediate causes and to assess the 'underlying reasons for the disturbances, focusing in particular on the policing of multi racial communities' (Scarman, 1982, p. 223). More than this, Scarman was encouraged to make 'recommendations' about policing but in other areas of social policy – unemployment, housing, racism, education and so on, he was instructed to restrict himself to 'suggestions'.

When the riots returned to Britain in 1985, almost all of Scarman's recommendations about policing had been implemented for some time whereas none of his suggestions about other areas of social policy had been followed up other than by other inquiries. Although the significance of this point is open to various possible interpretations the result of this imbalance in policy implementation has encouraged critics of community policing to argue that it has been tried and failed. A popular view among police officers now is that community policing in inner cities means soft policing and simply stirs up trouble. Thus at a recent meeting of the London branch of the Police Federation, the chairman received enthusiastic applause when he said: 'there are particular sections of our community who do not want to be policed. Their aim is to create areas . . . free of legal constraint and totally outside the laws of the land. The police have known this for years but have accepted the political pressures put upon us and government by Scarman's one sided report.'

Critics of community policing who wished to see tougher approaches to law enforcement were quick to seize on the 'failure' of community policing in Handsworth as witnessed by the recent riots there. In this the irony of Lord Scarman's praise of Handsworth's community policing was not lost. Scarman had commented: 'Future historians may well say that the nation's battle for policing a multi

racial society by consent was won on Soho Road and on the back-
streets of Handsworth.' (Brown, 1982).

A few police officers would still agree with this. Most would not.
Tony Judge of the Police Federation writing in *Police* October 1985
opened his article on Handsworth with a quote from the Labour
member of parliament for the area: 'Community policing
undoubtedly failed the people of Handsworth', and concluded
'whilst some anxious advocates of community policing still insist that
the key to peace keeping in the inner city remains 'flexibility', others
say that this really means weakness, and in the end leads to escalating
crime rates'. This magazine *Police* which is the Police Federation's
mouthpiece, rarely publishes anonymous correspondence, but
nevertheless gave prominence to a lengthy unsigned letter entitled
' "An utter shambles" – A Handsworth officer's view of the riot'. In
this the writer complained that in recent years there had been a
'decline of firm policing'. He went on: 'Gradually more and more
restrictions were placed on officers policing the area – their hands
being virtually tied, having to turn a blind eye to certain matters.'

Clearly community policing is no longer the flavour of the month.
It isn't so much that attitudes have changed very dramatically in
police circles but that the critics are now more outspoken and there
are now even fewer people around to speak up in its defence.
However as suggested earlier, community policing never really had
the chance it deserved. Even in Lozells it hardly got off the ground.
As the following account will show, the Lozells community policing
project was a marginal experience for most people living in the area.
It faced resistance at all levels not the least by a deeply ingrained
public passivity. It aroused suspicion in the minds of many community leaders about whether the police were really concerned with
being friends to the community or were continuing their role as
agents of the state. Finally it co-existed uneasily with different styles
of policing that were essentially coercive and thus was the most
serious challenge of all. At the end of the day the conclusion must be
that community policing is fundamentally incompatible with the
organisational philosophy and structure of policing. Those who pre-
ach 'policing by consent' ignore the realities of police experience – it
would be nice if we could all be reasonable but we're not, it would be
nice if we could all agree on what we wanted the police to do, but we
can't.

THE AREA

Handsworth is as much a romantic concept as a geographic reality. It
symbolises many things, but most of all multi-ethnic Birmingham

and indeed for some even multi-ethnic Britain (Rex and Tomlinson, 1979). However unlike many other areas described as multi-ethnic – for example Brixton – it is genuinely so. Popular mythology has it that Handsworth is roughly one-third 'black' (Afro-Caribbean), one-third Asian (Indian/Pakistani) and one-third white (many of whom are Irish). However this description glosses over the cultural diversity within these ethnic groups and disguises the dynamics of a changing population. In the last ten years there has been a notable decline in the 'white' population and a dramatic increase in the 'Asian' population – fairly easily explained by the age profiles of these groups. The white population contains a disproportionate number of older people who are dying off whereas the new commonwealth immigrants are younger and reproducing.

More than anything Handsworth has become an attractive focus for commerce which is creating for some of the Asian community at least, a comparative oasis of wealth amidst the severe recession of the West Midlands as a whole. Traditional relatively wealthy white middle class pockets of Handsworth have shown the most dramatic change in population most visibly indexed by the large vans of Asian commerce which commute from them.

The challenge of policing such an area is not easily summarised by such a description of cultural diversity. In many ways the challenge is less in the diversity than in the streetwise sophistication and political sensitivity of the various groups. For example among young blacks there exists an unusual degree of ethnic identity demonstrated by the visible symbols of Rastafari – such as 'dreadlocks' (uncut hair), the 'colours' (red, green and gold of the Ethiopian flag) and smoking 'ganja' (marijuana, a drug which is of course illegal in Britain). In one detailed observational study we carried out in 1982, over three-quarters of black youths on the streets of Handsworth either had dreadlocks or wore 'tams' (hats) which hid them. While policing problems are hardly located entirely amongst this group, the culture gap between them and white police officers is probably wider than anywhere else and seems a persistent source of conflict. As one police officer put it – 'How can I even talk to someone who calls me "Babylon" and won't even recognise the legitimacy of my authority in law?'

While the cult of Rastafari has declined somewhat in the last two years, the sheer numbers of youths hanging around on the streets – 'dossing' as many of them call it – has increased considerably with growing unemployment. This is a more general almost endemic problem now to an inner city born of the industrial revolution and dependent for its wealth on the now declining heavy manufacturing sector. As with ethnicity, the change within Birmingham is probably

as important as any statistics relative to other parts of the co
Thus fifteen years ago, the West Midlands as a region h
highest wages and the lowest unemployment in Britain wherea
it has the worst long-term unemployment on record. The Bir
ham Partnership Area which includes Handsworth has the highest
unemployment rate of any inner-city area in the country. Overall the
unemployment rate for adult men in Handsworth is more than forty
per cent but for the young especially for ethnic minorities the position
is even worse running at over eighty per cent. For them the labour
market has virtually collapsed. Moreover only one in four work
placement schemes for young people is actually run by an employer
thus long-term prospects seem very bleak. Even on these schemes
ethnic minorities are twice as unlikely to obtain a place as white
youths while outside of them the prime facie evidence for discrimination seems even higher echoing the recent Policy Studies Institute's
figures on national trends (Brown and Gay, 1985).

Of course unemployment is simply one measure of the multiple
deprivation which blights the area. Whatever the effects on attitudes
and values of the various specific deprivations, unemployment has
the simple effect of producing large populations of young people on
the streets. In June 1981 we interviewed over a hundred youths who
were 'dossing' around Handsworth and the city centre. Mindful of
the recent riots in other cities we asked them what they would do if
they saw a riot starting. Over eighty-five per cent said they would join
in. The reasons were primarily for the fun or for some material gain
through looting rather than any deep-seated antagonism towards the
police. Of course it would be wrong to read too much into the
answers to hypothetical questions, but this does give some indication
of the potential for riot which has existed for some time.

Although the riots have stimulated some furious debates, concern
over urban deprivation did not begin with the riots of 1981. Successive governments especially since 1967 have attempted to grapple
with the problem (see for example Hall, 1981). Notably in 1977
following a government white paper – *Policy for the Inner Cities*
(Department of the Environment 1977), a 'one off' sum of £100 m.
was made available for a new inner-city partnership programme.
Birmingham received some £11m. of this and Handsworth was one
of four priority areas identified for support. The funds were intended
especially for improving the built environment, however requests for
support were invited from any interested groups within the priority
areas. Thus a wide variety of projects were funded.

Handsworth visibly benefited from this source of urban renewal.
Especially visible were the consequences of the housing 'enveloping'
schemes which concentrated on the facades of houses. New garden

walls were built, roofs retiled, windows replaced across an extensive area without destroying whatever community might exist. Cosmetic? Perhaps so but the area visibly improved and most residents appreciated this. Unfortunately such activity did not create much in the way of jobs– most building contractors seem to have come from outside the area having submitted the most attractive tenders for the work. Moreover more generally, the Inner City Partnership funding did not seem to do anything much to help the plight of urban black youths in finding work. Thus while a number of firms received direct assistance under the partnership schemes, some three-quarters of those surveyed suggested that these schemes had not any effect on their employment levels (Public Sector Management Research Unit, 1985).

However it is far from being the case that the Partnership programme was a flop. Some early reviews (e.g. Cross, 1982) based on the first year's activities expressed concern that ethnic minorities were relatively unsuccessful in their applications for funding. However race *per se* was not a focus of the programme and in any case, later and more comprehensive analyses of the first two years of the Partnership paint a different picture. Taking what seems a more valid perspective of the *beneficiaries* of funding (rather than the applicants) it appears that ethnic minorities were well served. Thus it is claimed that overall sixty per cent of the funding directly benefited these groups. Afro-Caribbeans benefited most (forty-one per cent of total funding against nineteen per cent for Asians). Moreover the pattern observed in the first year (where ethnic minority groups received only thirteen per cent of the funding) was not continued: over the full five years in cases where the Afro-Caribbean sector benefited, over half the funding actually went to Afro-Caribbean organisations (Public Sector Management Research Unit, 1985).

The Inner City Partnership programme was undoubtedly a boon for the area. However the sheer scale of unemployment and deprivation meant that its impact was probably more to arrest some aspects of urban deterioration than to ameliorate things. Additionally, with hindsight, few adventurous projects were funded. Among the more interesting was the Lozells Community Policing Project.

THE LOZELLS PROJECT

In late 1978 soon after the Partnership was launched, the statutory agencies, including West Midlands Police, met and endorsed the idea of applying for funds to support a community policing project. This application was successful and initially £30,000 per annum over three years (later rising to £50,000 per annum over five years) was allocated. This funding was on the basis of a 1:4 split between West Midlands Police and the Inner City Partnership.

In January 1979 the Public Liaison Department of West Midlands Police suggested that the project should focus on the Lozells area, this being of reasonable size (23,000 inhabitants) and suffering from multiple deprivation including high crime rates, high unemployment, and additionally contained thirty-four per cent new commonwealth people. It's worth nothing here that British census data still does not include race as such but merely place of birth of the head of the household. Moreover the above figures were based on the 1971 census. When the 1981 census data became available even this conservative estimate of ethnic minorities showed forty-seven per cent new commonwealth peoples in the project area. Our own estimates to include those born here – mainly Afro-Caribbean – put the figure at nearer sixty per cent and rising.

The Lozells Project effectively commenced in April 1979 with the establishment of a steering committee to administer its funds. This committee was made up of two representatives from each of the statutory agencies: education, social services, probation and after care and West Midlands Police. The local Handsworth Police division ('C' Division) was also well represented with the Chief Superintendent acting as chairman of the committee which usually met monthly with fourteen to twenty people attending.

The project had three main stated aims:

1. to develop closer links between the police and the community;
2. to encourage people living in the area to participate with local agencies in solving problems within the community;
3. to give support to the numerous groups and agencies working within the community who strive to improve the quality of life.

The way in which the project developed revealed numerous problems which provided salutary lessons for all. However before discussing these, let us look at the achievements of the project.

The range of activities embraced by the Lozells Project during its five years was impressive and can only be briefly summarised here. The focal point for the project and the main source of expenditure was a community centre which opened in September 1980 with a police-run youth club on two evenings a week. This building – the Wallace Lawler Centre – had been largely unused until obtained by the project. Over the years since then, mainly due to the enthusiasm and energy of the project's warden Mike Dobson, it became a very active resource for the area. Apart from being a place where various groups could meet it became the base for camping and outward bound type activities using project equipment – especially the four mini buses which were available free of charge to groups in the area.

Apart from the community centre, the project financially supported a wide range of groups and agencies in the area, provided intensive police input to the local secondary school, organised regular swimming and football events (using the centre's transport), supported an intermediate treatment group for young offenders and later opened a second youth club.

In terms of activities the Lozells Project was undoubtedly successful. Without police support the activities might never have been available. However in evaluating the experiment, our concern was to assess the value of the police input to the project and gauge how far this provided benefits beyond what might be expected had they not been involved. Thus, we turn to our evaluation of the police input which is best illustrated by reference to the youth club and the activities in the local secondary school.

POLICE–JUVENILE LIAISON

The youth club began well. Attendance built up rapidly to over 100 in the senior club (6.30 p.m. – 9.30 p.m. Mondays and Thursdays) and to sixty odd in the junior club (eight to thirteen year olds, 4.30 p.m. – 6.30 p.m. Mondays and Thursdays). The staff were expected to be three permanent beat officers with a rota of one beat officer and two police constables from one of the units, plus police cadets as helpers on their six-week placements. In practice attendance was far less than this and police input declined markedly over the first two years. When the club first opened the children viewed both researchers and police with some suspicion but within months they became assured of our independence and soon began to see the police officers as less of a threat. Possibly this was because the police officers in the main rarely interacted with the children. Thus over one sample of eighty hours recorded, interaction duration between even two of the more enthusiastic officers and children amounted to only six per cent of the time available.

Initially the senior club showed a good racial mix and fairly equal numbers of white and black and a good proportion of girls (forty per cent). This was quite unusual for the area where black youths tend to predominate in the youth clubs. One other encouraging point was that when we spot mapped the addresses of children, we found that eighty-five per cent of them lived within the immediate vicinity (travelling less than half a mile). However it soon became apparent that the club had a rolling membership with only a small percentage of children attending regularly. Additionally most of the girls soon dropped out followed by the white youths so that by Easter 1981 the ratio of blacks and whites was 70:30 and by the summer it was almost entirely black (Afro-Caribbean). Very few Asians ever attended.

To try and find out what was happening and why children dropped out we interviewed fifty children who had stopped attending the club and asked them why. None claimed to be attending any other club – the most popular activity, mentioned by forty-one per cent, – was 'just dossing around with my mates' while a further thirty-four per cent said they went to friends' houses. The main reasons for not attending were that it was boring/not enough variety (sixty-eight per cent). However other spontaneous mentions of reasons for not attending also included not liking the police (twelve per cent), not liking so many blacks (twelve per cent), or not liking some of the other kids (seven per cent). We received many useful suggestions as to how to make the club more attractive such as more discos but these need not concern us here.

In these interviews with non-attenders we asked 'What are the police at the Wallace Lawler like?' Over forty per cent made positive comments such as 'cheerful', 'helpful', 'friendly' and so on whereas only ten per cent made negative comments such as 'they just mean trouble'. Interestingly when interviewed in the youth club the children's comments were overwhelmingly neutral – only twenty per cent made positive comments – the club did not seem a setting which allowed useful interviews.

More importantly for projects such as this, is the question of whether such positive experiences generalise in any way. Thus we interviewed over 150 children away from the centre (both youth club attenders and non-attenders) about whether they thought the police at the Wallace Lawler were different from other police. Although forty per cent would not say or did not know, the remainder overwhelmingly said they were different – better: e.g. 'they're nicer' (twenty-six per cent), 'they're big headed in uniform' (ten per cent) and so on. No child thought police on the streets were nicer than those in the youth club.

The importance of this distinction between different types of police is best illustrated by reference to other data on school children receiving the police input. At the time of our evaluation this police input to the local secondary school covered six classes of fourteen to fifteen year olds per annum each of which involved one hour per week over thirteen weeks. Most of these meetings were structured to allow a film or talk for up to half an hour with half an hour for role play, discussion or debate in small groups of six or so children. Topics included the Criminal Investigation Department, magistrates courts, dog handling, the diving unit, identification procedure, the drug squad, juvenile crime, the Birmingham Consolidation Act (which covered the 'sus' law), the police and the press. In most respects the syllabus was an excellent one having been refashioned from earlier initiatives taken by the local permanent beat sergeant Ted Schuck.

While most children rated the course as interesting and indeed probably learned valuable information in these classes, our evidence showed that it did not change attitudes to the police. We gave 'before' and 'after' questionnaires to children in five classes to tap children's perceptions of the police in general and the police involved in the school input. The results were clear – in the 'before' study on every single item of a seventeen item rating scale the school input officers were *expected* to be 'better' than police in general (less sneaky, more honest, better trained, kinder, fairer etc.). Moreover *after* the course the school input officers were seen as less intelligent, less friendly and less educated than they had expected.

Given that children did not expect to meet typical police officers in the school, it is hardly surprising that attitudes to the police in general did not change (there was a weak trend for police in general to be seen as less bullying but also less intelligent after the course). Similar non-significant results were found in all our other measures such as attitudes to various kinds of police work, how well the police did these jobs and willingness to report various crimes to the police (after Belson, 1977).

We thus conclude that this kind of community policing at least seems largely ineffective in changing attitudes and is not an economical use of police resources. However other data from larger surveys of 600 school children both in Lozells and in two control areas within the city both confirmed the above findings and extended them. In these larger surveys we asked children about contact with the police and what the experience was like. Here almost half of the children had had some contact with the police. However while positive experiences seemed largely unrelated to most of the measures we took of attitudes to the police, negative experiences were significantly correlated with anti-police attitudes. Thus while positive experiences do not seem to change attitudes, negative ones look as if they might, and serious attention needs to be paid to the source of these negative experiences – most of which as mentioned earlier seem to arise on the streets when kids are 'dossing' around or 'just messing about'. It should be stressed here that most of our survey data is obtained from fourteen to fifteen year old school children who were a few years younger than the 'dossers' we interviewed on the streets and thus may not share the same experiences. However something in the order of half the negative experiences which described police demeanour referred to rudeness or discourtesy in some form or another – possibly all trivial and certainly unnecessary.

PROJECT MANAGEMENT

The administration of the Lozells Project via the steering committee brought middle and senior management of the statutory agencies into regular contact with the police and this was, in itself, a useful exercise in the eyes of most of the committee. Although the gains from this were seen as largely intangible and heuristic, the dynamics of the committee's deliberations proved interesting. Thus no one – especially the police – wanted the project to be simply a police project but by default it became police dominated. It is difficult to describe the process of this in the brief space available here but the absence of specific project objectives was central (the project's stated aims were vague goals).

The Lozells Project was surrounded by considerable ambiguity from its inception. This ambiguity was in part deliberate to allow the project to develop. In part it was necessary since it was new and no one involved had prior experience of anything similar. In part too it was inevitable given the nature of the organisations involved.

When research funds became available one of our first tasks was to trace the development of the project by interviewing all those involved in the steering committee. This proved an interesting exercise since no one really knew where the idea had come from (except 'from above') or what it was meant to achieve or how. They were even less able to say how the success or failure of the project might be judged. We were somewhat surprised by the candour of our interviewees but soon began to appreciate that their genuine concern for the project to be successful had been somewhat frustrated by the ambiguity surrounding it. As one original member of the committee anticipated of all our later interviews: 'if you were to go to half a dozen members of the steering committee and ask them what the objectives were, they would not be able to tell you . . . no one has come from the top and said (anything) . . . there is no directive that I have encountered'.

Thus in the absence of guidance from above, the steering committee were cautious. They were especially cautious in their relations with local groups and agencies as we shall see. For guidance they looked to the police on the committee. The police by the very nature of their work are used to dealing with almost any contingency. However in this case the police chairman was due for retirement and in this uncharted territory was especially cautious not to blot his copy book before leaving the force. Suggestions for action were often prudently handled by the reminder 'we must move carefully on this one'.

LOCAL GROUPS AND AGENCIES

The consequence of all this was that local groups and agencies were kept at arm's length for over a year after the project started. It is true that a number of these were given financial support by the project, but these were almost entirely groups either in or closely allied to the statutory sector. Thus, in the first year, of the twenty-one groups or agencies receiving funding via the Lozells Project, only six were outside the statutory sector and of these four already had a statutory agency worker attached to them. In fairness to the Lozells Project this imbalance was redressed in later years (echoing the general pattern of the Inner City Partnership schemes noted earlier). However in the meantime considerable damage was done.

When the project commenced many community leaders naturally heard of it 'on the grapevine' and expressed their interest in becoming involved. The caution of the steering committee in accepting this involvement must be understood in the context of the steering committee members. Most of them were middle management and knew virtually nothing about the specific Lozells area and the bewildering array of community leaders that exist there. Social services' listings suggest fifty-two groups and organisations in the area but if private agencies were included such as Lucas who had a large factory nearby and used the centre for their retirement club – the number could easily double. If the project boundary were extended half a mile or so in each direction (which happened with mini bus hire) then the number could easily rise to two-hundred and fifty or so. Caution at accepting offers of help prevailed until things could be sorted out.

It was not until August 1980 that a public meeting was held to launch a local Lozells Project Advisory Committee. This meeting was attended by thirty people who represented only eleven of the local groups and agencies who could have potentially benefited from funding. Nevertheless a committee was formed and in November 1980 members were elected. They were enthusiastic and had a clear idea of their potential role and spent some time drafting a constitution defining their role as policy decision makers. This was rejected by the steering committee who could neither see the need for a constitution nor the desirability of the advisory committee being anything other than advisory. Monthly meetings of this advisory committee continued until March 1981 but attendances dropped to half a dozen people and became more and more sporadic until by the end of the year it had virtually collapsed in frustration at its impotence.

In fairness to the steering committee, most members did not quite appreciate the problems with the advisory committee since they never met each other formally. The advisory committee met in the evening after work, the steering committee met in the day time during work. Additionally the advisory committee listed as its membership all those on its *mailing* list and then ignored actual attendance. Whatever the explanation, the problem of community involvement dogged the project. In February 1983 a new attempt was made to launch an advisory committee. It was well published – 6,000 leaflets were dropped in the project area. However only two dozen people turned up and this included a television camera crew, police and researchers. *Post hoc* explanations were offered – it was a cold windy night, leaflets had gone out late and so on. However even though a new advisory committee was eventually launched, the above point indicates the serious lack of community interest and involvement in the project. The resistance occurred at many levels but principally at the level of public passivity rather than at the level of ideological resistance.

This is not to suggest that ideological opposition to the Lozells Project was entirely absent. Indeed, following the attempts by the steering committee to keep local involvement at arms length until the project was well under way, this resistance grew.

COMMUNITY LEADERS AND COMMUNITY GROUPS

Over the first two years of the project (1979–81) we interviewed a reasonable sample of community leaders (fifty) and local groups and agencies (forty-two). The distinction between these two was made primarily in terms of how people described themselves: either as representing sections *of* the community or as representing a service provided *to* the community. A sample of these various people (twenty-five) were re-interviewed during the final year of the project (1984–85). The results of our surveys can now be summarised:

First of all ninety per cent of the community leaders were generally favourably disposed towards the idea of the Lozells Project but while seventy-six per cent of them claimed to have heard of it when it was first launched, few had detailed knowledge of what it entailed. Indeed a number had quite serious misconceptions about it. Thus two well established and generally well informed community leaders seemed to believe that the new sports centre in Handsworth Park was part of the same police organised project. While the project was generally welcomed, some seventy per cent of community leaders went on spontaneously to question whether the police could play both the role of law enforcer and that of social worker. Attitudes in this group did not seem to change much over time. Almost all (ninety per cent) felt police community relations had improved since the mid

1970s. All but one of the black (Afro-Caribbean) community leaders claimed police harassment still took place even though it was less common than it used to be. This compares with forty per cent of Asian community leaders who claimed that clients did not report this problem. In part this difference is explained by the focus of most black organisations on youth problems and youth clients whereas the Asian organisation tend to serve a broader community with very few specialising in youth work. It's worth recording in passing that black community leaders were unanimous in saying that black youths would not go to a police run youth club. Just over half the Asian community leaders thought that Asian youths might attend. Ironically no Asian youths (apart from Vietnamese) ever attended whereas the club soon became almost entirely dominated by black youths.

Attitudes among local groups and agencies were essentially similar. Here two-thirds of those interviewed questioned whether the police were trying to help the community or help themselves. Suspicions as to what the police were really up to increased when a number of agencies tried to become involved in the project but were discouraged from doing so 'until the project gets going'. Over three-quarters of the agencies interviewed felt that they had been quite deliberately ignored when the project was set up. More importantly most felt that the project had been foisted on to the area without any consideration given to community needs. The location of the project community centre was often cited as an example of this 'I don't suppose they even realise it isn't in Lozells, do they?' (The centre is in fact just outside Lozells proper in Newtown.)

A number of groups claimed that the Lozells Project had adversely affected area funding while two groups claimed that when they applied for additional funds from the Inner City Partnership they were told 'you have the Lozells Project now'. Three of the main agencies in the area: WELD, The Asian Resource Centre and the Handsworth Law Centre flatly refused to have anything to do with what they called 'The Police Project'.

With hindsight these reactions were predictable as a problem – the most active agencies tend to be the most radical in their political orientations and the most suspicious of the police. Indeed in many ways it is almost axiomatic with their role as grass roots agencies. The kind of work which law/advice centres engage in often involves them assisting clients in cases brought against the statutory agencies (the police, the council and so on). Thus their particular experiences, their professional ethic and their political sensitivities make them unlikely bedfellows with the police.

This lack of affection for the police was quite generously reciprocated by police officers whom we asked about their attitudes to these legal/advice agencies. Comments were all dismissive: 'they're troublemakers', 'they've no real power', 'they're so left they don't have a right foot between them' and so on.

Although the police were correct in the assumption that these more active agencies would not want to take part in the project, in talking to the agencies it was possible to detect a potentially charitable attitude. Most indicated they *could* have been persuaded to take part in a police linked project but not a police dominated one. Although many of the concerns expressed earlier had dissipated by last year, by then it was really too late to woo the majority of the more radical and important agencies back and little effort was made to do so. This is a great pity when the Lozells Project promised to attempt something unique. Without grass roots support it is still possible to justify the project for its various successes but it cannot be considered to have achieved fully one of its declared aims 'to give support to the numerous groups and agencies working within the community who strive to improve the quality of life'.

LEADERS AND FOLLOWERS

After the riots, one of the most striking phenomena was the appearance of 'community leaders' who claimed to represent community interests. In various surveys of 350 people in the Lozells community we presented people with a list of problems that they might have faced and asked them what they would do if these problems happened and who might help them These were problems where we hoped people might spontaneously mention community leaders or local voluntary and statutory agencies. In fact these were very rarely mentioned so we asked directly: 'We are particularly interested in community organisations and community leaders in your area. Do you know of any around here? Who are they, What do they do?'

Only half of the people we surveyed were able to mention any community leaders or organisations at all. In 1981 for example those mentioned covered twenty-six different leaders or agencies but only six per cent of people mentioned the Wallace Lawler Centre/Lozells Project and even in 1983 it was mentioned by only ten per cent of the sample. This indicates something of the problem in an area apparently bristling with aid agencies. Most people remain quite ignorant of the services available to them.

In order to investigate further public attitudes towards community leaders we carried out two other small surveys of seventy-five youths on the streets and of a quota sample of eighty households in the Lozells area. In these we asked for the names of community leaders and agencies. If none were mentioned, we said 'what about . . . ?' and then read a list of four selected randomly from a more lengthy list. This proved a fascinating exercise. Most of the community leaders were apparently quite unknown other than 'sounding familiar', but where respondents knew of them they were more likely to provoke negative comments than positive ones.' 'He doesn't lead me mate' was one of the more benign comments – most were quite slanderous. Without wishing to impugn the integrity of all community leaders we seem to have exposed a rather serious community problem in this research which merits more attention than we have had the resources to investigate.

Unfortunately ignorance of or lack of faith in community leaders or organisations is not compensated for by any community spirit engendered by good neighbours. In one survey nearly half of the sample (forty-two per cent) did not know their neighbours well enough to 'borrow a pint of milk or ask favours like this'. Moreover when asked: 'If someone attacked you outside your house, how many of your neighbours would investigate the noise and do something to help', fifty-nine per cent said 'none' or 'only one'. This is not a problem unique to the area. Our own survey data in Lozells has been essentially replicated elsewhere and we may quote the conclusions on a large survey in Leicester carried out by Sills, Taylor and Golding (1983): 'Many people living in the priority zone identified other people in their area as being one of the major problems. Thus there were complaints about problem families, vandals, prostitutes, the coloured. With the exceptions of Braunstone, few people saw their neighbours as a source of help or support.' The authors add – 'what is "community"; a planner's romance, a genuine resource or has the silent materialism of the working class, the result of economic pressures, placed a barrier to genuine community?'

The idea of community based schemes is a fine notion in principle but we must recognise that the term 'community' disguises enormous apathy and deep divisions in most of them. These seem especially powerful aspects of inner city life. Problems of unemployment, poor education, inferior housing, high crime, lack of transport and so on form an idea of multiple deprivation but these are not the sole source of conflict. They aggravate other tensions which exist due to different world views, social habits and conflicting interests. If one adds to this the fact that some people are thoroughly nasty anyway, then the idea of policing by consent becomes something of a Utopian dream. However it is a dream shared by almost all shades of the political spectrum from radical marxist to hard-nosed conservative.

All of the above is not to deny the validity of unemployment as a source of conflict or racism as a source of conflict or poor housing as a

source of conflict, or to suggest that amelioration of all the deprivations so evident in our inner cities would not help matters enor-
mously. However just putting bobbies back on the beat does not
change the nature of the communities that they are required to
police. With or without foot patrols, with or without community
policing problems of crime and disorder exist to which the police will
be asked to respond. The fact that society *requires* them to respond is
in some ways less important than the fact that most police actions
follow a *request* by the general public for the police to respond to an
incident. Thus numerous studies now show that the police do not
really define their work for themselves – more correctly it is defined
for them by the general public – usually by telephone. Thus over
eighty-five per cent of police deployments are reactive to public calls
for assistance rather than proactive at the initiative of the police
(Ekblom and Heal, 1983; Cumberbatch and Morgan, 1984). Unfortunately, given the varieties of publics which exist, this cannot be
taken to imply that 'the public' all agree on what they want the police
to do. Indeed in police circles there is fairly profound pessimism that
they are 'damned if they do and damned if they don't'. This is well
captured in a statement made by the Handsworth Police 'commander' – Superintendent David Love – soon after the riots. He
reflected: 'I'm not trying to duck the issue, but if I'm being attacked
from all sides I can't be doing too badly. I must be steering the middle
ground.'

Although quite a few people who have attempted to steer their way
through the choppy waters of Handsworth might endorse this as a
sentiment, rather self-evidently, catching flak from all sides doesn't
guarantee that one is on the right course. Indeed if the middle ground
results in the appalling violence of September 1985, then it is hardly a
safe one to be recommended.

Nevertheless the riots and the background to them well illustrate
some of the problems with policing the area and are worth describing.

THE LOZELLS RIOTS

After the riots, a few commentators made self congratulatory 'I told
you it would happen' statements. However, the outbreak of riots on
Monday 9 September took most people completely by surprise.
Since 1981 the West Midlands Police have monitored 'tension indicators' the details of which are transmitted from local senior police
management on a weekly basis to the force headquarters. In the
period prior to the riots these were fairly stable with some encouraging signs. Thus complaints against the police showed an overall

reduction since 1980–82 while in the period up until the end of September 1985, the Handsworth Division was the second lowest among the twelve divisions in the force area (West Midlands Police, 1985).

More than this, the day before the riots started the local park had entertained 50,000 revellers at the Handsworth Carnival without disturbances. Indeed the *Birmingham Evening Mail* on 9 September reported a local black councillor, James Hunte, as praising the police (although in the next edition of the paper after the riots he was able to condemn them for 'insensitive policing').

The criticism of 'insensitive policing' is a common one in the recent history of riots but is as ambiguous as the often proposed solution of 'community policing'. The incident which is generally taken as the trigger to the riots took place at around 16.45 on Monday 9 September. This involved attempting to enforce parking restrictions near the junction of Villa Road and Lozells Road. The driver of one vehicle which did not have an excise ('road tax') licence on display gave a false address and when questioned further became aggressive and called on bystanders to help him. Soon the incident escalated with a large number of black youths attacking the police with stones, bottles and staves. Eleven police officers were injured and seven police vehicles damaged. A number of arrests were made and in order to de-escalate the situation the officer in charge ordered all police personnel to be removed from the vicinity of the incident. Given the location this was prudent. The incident took place outside two establishments popular with black youths – the Acapulco cafe and the Villa Cross public house. Both establishments had become centres for drug trafficking (mainly cannabis) and despite a number of police raids on them earlier in the year remained active and protected by the large number of youths congregating both inside and outside the premises. Typically at that time of day these might number a hundred or more.

Particularly during 1985 local residents had repeatedly expressed concern over the drug trafficking at these establishments. The 'community' newspaper (*The Soho Star*) carried a lead story on the problem to coincide with a public meeting held on 5 September where demands were made that the police should act to clean up the area. The local residents' committee (mainly white) were particularly vociferous over this as they had been before over crime generally. For example, in October 1982, long after the Lozells Project started, they organised a 1,000 signature petition calling for 'more bobbies on the beat, more Panda patrols and the re-opening of a police station on the Lozells Road'. Their demands were carried in a newspaper article entitled 'Brum's streets of fear' (*Birmingham Evening Mail, 6 October*

1982). Although traffic offences were a less serious concern, these seem to have become a growing problem with cars parked antisocially to impede traffic flow along the busy through roads of Handsworth. One local resident complained: 'the arrogant bastards just stop in the middle of the road. The police are just soft.'

Thus the build up to the incident of 9 September in a sense was very predictable. However the timing and the ferocity of events were not. In the next few hours following the trigger incident a number of false emergency calls were made but the next real incident was when a fire was started in a disused Bingo Hall between the Acapulco cafe and the Villa Cross pub. At 19.35 hours fire crews attending reported being under attack from stones and bottles. As soon as police officers arrived to assist they were attacked with petrol bombs and other missiles. Not having either a protected vehicle or protective equipment, they too were forced to withdraw and the riot got underway with 200 youths petrol bombing and looting the immediate area and up to 500 rampaging the neighbourhood.

It is worth noting that at the time of the second incident only thirty-three officers were available for deployment. By 21.00 hours this had grown to ninety, by 22.00 hours the manpower stood at 260 and had doubled before midnight when some 600 officers were present at the scene and some control could be attempted. In the meantime considerable damage was done – mainly to property. In retrospect it seems almost miraculous that only two people died and only 122 were injured (seventy-nine of whom were police officers).

A series of incidents took place the following day, notably when the Home Secretary and journalists arrived to survey the scene. They were greeted with some of the antagonism that had earlier been reserved for the police. Indeed one of the features of the riot is that few citizens were attacked or threatened (unless they appeared to be journalists).

In the aftermath of the riot some of the existing tensions in the community came to a head. A number of Asian community leaders criticised the police for not acting quickly enough. Emergency calls for assistance during the riot had been unproductive. The two Indians who died in their post office had made repeated calls for help but police resources were not adequate to penetrate the riot area to give any assistance. A number of Asian shopkeepers suggested that the arson attacks and lootings were racist – West Indian commerce had escaped unscathed. They called on West Indian community leaders to condemn the violence and control their youth. When this satisfaction was not given the city's Community Relations Council suffered the mass resignation of the Asian representatives (*Birmingham Evening Mail,* 16 September 1985). To add to the problems

Birmingham's Irish community declared itself an ethnic minority too which should be eligible for special grant assistance (*Birmingham Evening Mail*, 15 October 1985).

Below the surface of this public quarrel between the ethnic minorities was the same one that the local (white) residents' committee had raised – black youth and crime. Those who were arrested in the riots were mainly black (189). Some were white (seventy-two) while a few were Asian (thirty-five). Debates over what these figures meant resurrected earlier ones about robberies and assaults where in the larger Handsworth area up to the end of August 1985 descriptions of assailants gave 224 black, twenty-seven white and fourteen Asian, while thefts from the person described offenders as 153 black, seventeen Asian and seven white. More than this almost half of all victims were Asian (West Midlands Police, 1985).

While the above figures are part of the source of conflict, perhaps the crucial factor is the differing perceptions about police attitudes to them. Thus many Asians and some whites believed that the police were doing too little about black youths (as witnessed by the low clear-up rate for thefts, assaults and robberies – at less than seventeen per cent), while at least some blacks felt that the police were doing far too much.

In this conflict of opinion, one incident at the end of the riots was most unfortunate. A black youth appeared on television news as he was released from police custody wearing a police helmet and claiming that he had done a deal with the police. Although this seems untrue, reactions were predictable. The *Birmingham Post* headline was 'Asians hit out at Rasta deal'. The *Express and Star* newspaper concluded 'agreements between thugs and police cannot be tolerated, it's a licence for tomorrow's criminals to hold any community at ransom' (13 September 1985).

The legacy of the riots is not a happy one. The anger and the sadness which are all too evident are no doubt relatively transitory emotions which will tend to evaporate with time and the warmth of some positive actions which are promised. However 'getting back to normal' which is the desire of many in the aftermath of the riots is hardly the kind of modest ambition which should be lauded. Normality is something of an uneasy peace between antipathy and passivity in an environment suffering from multiple deprivation. The Ebeneezer Bible Institute just across the road from Villa Cross has a little plaque reading "Hope for better things'. Even that seems a little ambitious for some. Yet Lozells is something of a Pandora's box and has its lessons which should be salutary ones.

LESSONS FROM LOZELLS

In this chapter a number of important concepts have been used without definition. 'Insensitive policing' and 'community policing' are but two terms which have a powerful appeal that disguises the range of meanings that they can have. Other portmanteau terms are 'the police', 'blacks' and 'riots'. The problem with all of these terms is that while there are indeed common elements in the instances they embrace, the differences that they contain are probably even more important. The increasing use of the term 'black' for instance in the literature on race relations to refer to both Asian and Afro-Carribean peoples crudely expresses certain similar features (such as not being white and probably being the victim of various discriminations). However, this apart, other features place the two groups at the polar opposites of white culture. For example in the success of the work ethic in Asian commerce and in the hedonism (such as in music) of the Afro-Caribbean peoples. Of course these are in themselves crude stereotypes which some find offensive but they are part of a reality that 'communities' in consensus are illusory. Events such as the assassination of Indira Gandhi can quickly expose some quite profound antipathies between even those people who ostensibly share common cultures.

An area like Handsworth is normally remarkably free from tension, but this is not because it is a community of shared interests and values where a consensus exists on what the police should or should not do. This of course presents the enormous problems which 'the police' have. They as a group share many common characteristics but are hardly the homogenous brotherhood of some stereotypes.

In looking for lessons from Lozells, the first point is that journalists who arrive like visitors from Mars to ask 'take me to your leader' are likely to miss the point about the area.

The second point is that while the riots were a sad conclusion to the Lozells Project, they had very little to do with it – or indeed police –community relations in a general sense. This is indicated by earlier research commissioned by the Home Office (Southgate, 1982) following the 1981 disturbances in Handsworth. This research asked residents what they thought caused the riot. Only nine per cent of those surveyed mentioned police harassment. Whites and blacks rated this higher (fifteen per cent and fourteen per cent respectively) than Asians did (three per cent). The most popular view was unemployment, mentioned by forty-three per cent. Although we have not had the resources to carry out a similarly large survey, the research we have done would suggest that little has changed since 1981 in Handsworth. However, knowing how many people think police harassment caused a riot does not tell us how many people might riot due to police harassment. The hypothetical question we asked youths about their willingness to get involved in the riot is probably a better indicator. Most of those we interviewed said they would – mainly for looting or just for fun. Perhaps the question about riots is more meaningfully asked by 'why not riot? Here Cashmore's description of the hopeless situation for black youth in *No Future* (1985) has a depressing ring of truth.

The literature on inner cities, on riots and on policing is a good example of how commentators allow their own Utopian dreams to blur their visions of the problems and their solutions (e.g. Benyon, 1984; Kettle and Hodges, 1982; Lea and Young, 1984; Scratton and Gordon, 1984). Given the disagreements between the various commentators, how on earth can they expect communities to arrive at consensus?

As Harrison (1985) wisely comments, there is a need for holistic solutions to the inner city. It is most unfortunate that inner cities are not represented by Conservative members of parliament since this unnecessarily politicises the problems of inner cities.

A whole host of different solutions need to be adopted. As regards the police, the lack of ethnic minorities among them is a serious one in symbolising a perceived problem. There are some obvious barriers to a career in policing for ethnic minority groups. Racial prejudice is clearly one of them. However this is more a problem for recruitment and relationships at work than a problem of policing behaviour since racial prejudice in law enforcement is generally accepted as unprofessional conduct even though it probably does not receive the priority it should have as a specific disciplinary offence.

The Lozells Project itself was a valuable learning experience in many ways. It was described as the 'icing on the cake' by one senior police officer who was very committed to community policing. Unfortunately this is exactly what the project remained rather than being an essential ingredient of police work in the area. Thus one of the original aims included increased foot patrols which were never forthcoming. Doubtlessly lack of manpower was the main reason for this. The West Midlands Police has an authorised establishment of 6,684 officers and an actual strength of 6,524 despite a recommendation in 1980 from the Establishment Review endorsed by the Police Authority that a further 1,042 officers were needed.

It is of course a matter of priorities where budgeting cuts fall, but Handsworth seems to have been particularly unlucky in this in having only 187 officers to police such a difficult area – roughly equivalent to that which most other subdivisions in the force area have.

Debates about policing tend to revolve around vague labels of styles of policing, 'insensitive' versus 'soft' or 'firm' versus 'consensus'. These labels obfuscate the problems. The priorities of policing can only be determined by a much clearer understanding of police work and its effectiveness. The problems with the Lozells Project were in no small part due to the existence of similarly vague notions about what it should be attempting to do or why and how.

Current developments in the literature on policing by objectives (e.g. Butler, 1985; Lubans and Edgar, 1979) seem to promise the best generic solution to many difficulties the police currently face. Disagreements seem inevitable where means are not distinguished from ends and where vague goals exist instead of specific objectives and action plans. In such a system of management, evaluation and feedback on performance in terms of effectiveness and public satisfaction are part and parcel of the organisation. The ideas contained in policing by objectives can allow a genuinely comprehensive theory of policing to develop where the rationale of police action is a matter of public knowledge and indeed could be communicated in day-to-day law enforcement. At the end of the day we probably wouldn't all agree on policing priorities and certainly are not likely to become 'a community' of publics but at least the police would have a clearer mandate to get on with their job.

NOTES

1 The assistance of Errol Walker, Robin McGregor, Nishat Rahman and Gill King is gratefully acknowledged.

REFERENCES

- Belson, W. A. (1977), *Public and Police*. London, Harper and Row
- Benyon, J. (1984), *Scarman and After*. Oxford, Pergamon Press
- Brown, C. (1984), *Black and White Britain. The Third PSI Survey*. London, Heineman
- Brown, J. (1982), *Policing by Multiracial Consent: the Handsworth Experience*. London, Bedford Square Press
- Brown, C. and Gay, P. (1985), *Racial Discrimination Seventeen Years After The Act*. London, Policy Studies Institute
- Butler, A. J. P. (1984), *Police Management*. Aldershot, Hants., Gower Press
- Cashmore, E. (1985), *No Future*. London, Heineman
- Cross, M. (1982), The Manufacture of Marginality. In E. Cashmore and B. Troyner, *Black Youths in Crisis*. pp. 35–52, London, Allen and Unwin
- Cumberbatch, M. G. (1984), 'Community Policing.' In D. J. Muller, D. E. Blackman, A. J. Chapman (eds.), *Psychology and Law*. New York, Wiley
- Cumberbatch, G. and Morgan, B. (1984), The Police Officer: Myths and Realities, The Study of Real Skills, Vol. 4: *Social Skills* pp. 141–55, Lancaster, MTP Press
- Cumberbatch, G., McGregor, R., Brown, J. and Morrison, D. (1985), *Television News and the Miners' Strike*. London, Broadcasting Research Unit
- Cumberbatch, G., McGregor, R., Jones, I. and Brown, J. (1985), *British Riots: the French and German View*, in preparation
- Department of Environment (1977), *Policy for the Inner City*. London, H.M.S.O.
- Ekblom, P. and Heal, K. (1983), *The Police Response*. H.O.R.U. Paper 9, London, H.M.S.O.
- Hall, P. (1981), *The Inner City in Context*. London, S.S.R.C.

- Harrison, P. (1985), *Inside the Inner City. Life under the Cutting Edge.* Harmondsworth, Penguin Books
- Kerner, O. *et al.* (1968), *The Report of the National Advisory Commission on Civil Disorder.* U.S. Government Printing Office
- Kettle, M. and Hodges, L. (1982), *The Police, the People and the Riots in Britain's Inner Cities.* London, Pan Books
- Lea, J. and Young, J. (1984), *What is To Be Done About Law and Order?* Harmondsworth, Penguin Books
- Leighton, M. (1982), 'The Men We Have To Trust.' *The Sunday Times Magazine*, 26th September
- Lubens, V. A. and Edgar, J. M. (1979), *Policing by Objectives.* Hartford, Conn., The Social Development Corporation
- Public Sector Management Research Unit, Aston University (1985), *Five Year Review of the Birmingham Inner City Partnership.* Department of Environment
- Rex, J. and Tomlinson, S. (1979), *Colonial Immigrants in a British City.* London, Routledge, Kegan and Paul
- Scarman, Lord (1982), *The Scarman Report.* Harmondsworth, Penguin Books
- Scratton, P. and Gordon, P. (1984), *Causes for Concern.* Harmondsworth, Penguin Books
- Sills, A., Taylor, G. and Golding, P. (1983), *Policy for the Inner Cities.* Centre for Mass Communication Research, University of Leicester
- Southgate, P. (1982), *Public Disorder.* Home Office Research Study no. 72
- Venner, M. (1981), 'What the Papers Said about Scarman.' *New Comunity*, 9, (3): 354–63
- West Midlands Police (1985), *Handsworth/Lozells September 1985*, West Midlands Police, Birmingham

The evolution
of race relations
training in
the U.S. Army

In the decade of the seventies, the U.S. Army wrote a critical chapter in the history of race relations and equal opportunity in American society. Although it entered the lists belatedly, given the racial turbulence in the U.S. in the mid to late sixties, the Army ultimately undertook the most massive effort ever mounted by any organisation to eliminate discriminatory practices and to create equality of opportunity for all its members.

That the Army stumbled and wavered at times in this effort and that some of its undertakings may have been ill-advised or less than effective should occasion no surprise. The fact is that there was no precedent, no blueprint, no firm body of knowledge upon which to draw for what the Army sought to do. No organisation comparable to the Army had ever tried to do it. None the less, without a tested plan of battle and in the face of all the normal cultural and organisational resistances to real change, the Army undertook to change itself from what was, historically, an openly racist and discriminatory organisation into one in which discrimination is expressly forbidden and equal opportunity and affirmative action are actively promulgated as keystones of Army personnel policy.

While the Army cannot claim total success in this endeavour, and the process of change which it initiated is continuously evolving, none the less it would be difficult to name another comparable organisation in all history which can lay greater claim to having transformed itself from a racist to a non-racist organisation. It may be instructive, therefore, for those with an interest in how to achieve organisational change toward greater equality of opportunity, to review the experiences of the U.S. Army during the 1970s as it struggled to implement programmes intended to achieve such change.

The Army Race Relations and Equal Opportunity Programs of the 1970s were the fruition of processes which could be said to have begun in 1948 (although, indeed, they did have earlier roots). Until 1948, the U.S. Army was formally, legally, and explicitly segregated with blacks relegated to a formally-prescribed second class status. By law, by custom, and by practice, there was no equality of opportunity in the Army and blacks (the only significant minority at the time) were relegated to labour and service roles. Thus, the Army, as was most of American society, was segregated and discriminatory with respect to skin colour. Army leadership was exclusively white.

In 1948, President Truman issued a landmark Executive Order which declared, in part, that: 'There shall be equality of treatment and opportunity for all persons in the Armed Forces without regard to race, color, religion or national origin.' (Executive Order 9981, 1948) Although it was quickly noted that the order did not specifically outlaw segregation and many Army leaders, such as General Omar Bradley, stated their opinion that segregation would continue, none the less that Executive Order came to mark the beginning of a momentous change process still unfolding in the Army today.

The then Secretary of Defense, Louis B. Johnson, interpreted the Order broadly and directed the individual military services to draw up detailed plans for ending racial segregation. However, progress was sporadic and slow. Normal organisational inertia was an effective deterrent to change. The exigencies of the expanding Korean conflict however, soon outstripped the reluctant pace of military leadership on this issue. Recruits began pouring in to Army training camps so quickly that there was no time to form units by colour. In August of 1950, at Fort Jackson, S.C. (an Army basic training post), the first order was issued to form draftees into platoons as they arrived without regard to colour. At the same time, the extreme need for replacements in all-white line units in Korea led to 'on-the-spot integration' as replacements were assigned to units without regard to colour. (Stillman, 1968) Desegregation, therefore, became a fact in the Army more because of the practical demands of war than because of a diligent pursuit of desegregation policy. But, a fact it became, and policy, eventually, would come to endorse the fact. In time, that policy was to evolve into a strong organisational commitment to equality of opportunity, non-discrimination and affirmative action. In terms of enunciated policy, the U.S. Army has completely rejected its formally discriminatory past and embraced a policy of equal opportunity.

In civil society during the 1950s and 1960s, school integration became an intense national issue and the civil rights movement grew into a potent force pressing for social change. During this period, the widespread racial conflict and civil strife was generally not reflected within the Army, at least overtly, until 1969. But several significant events in the ongoing social change process were occurring. A broadening of the role of the Armed Services as agents of social change was formalised in the Department of Defense Directive of July, 1963, which stated in part: 'Every military commander has the responsibility to oppose discriminatory practices affecting these men and their dependents and to foster equal opportunity for them, not only in areas under his immediate control, but also in nearby communities where they may live or gather in off-duty hours.' (DOD Directive 5120.35, 1963) That represented a decided change from pre-1948 policy language. As racial conflict spread north in 1964, Congress responded by passing the broadest Civil Rights Act in history. On the same day, the Army issued AR–600–21 (Department of the Army, 1964) implementing the above-cited DOD Directive. This regulation, which has been expanded and modified over the years, is the Army's basic regulation promulgating equal opportunity policy. It specifically sets forth the Army's requirements for education and training in this area.

EQUAL OPPORTUNITY (EO) TRAINING IN THE ARMY OVER THE PAST TEN YEARS[1]

In September 1969, the Department of the Army directed that race relations instruction be incorporated into the Army educational system, and the infantry school at Fort Benning was designated the proponent agency. By September 1970, a four-hour block of instruction entitled, 'Leadership Aspects of Race Relations' had been developed which was incorporated into non-commissioned officer education system courses. Shortly thereafter, a similar course entitled, 'Race Relations' was included in basic combat training. These were among the Army's first efforts to educate and train both leaders and troops in areas thought to be relevant to the maintenance of a good racial climate. In addition to the blocks of instruction incorporated into the various schools, by 1971, the Army had initiated *unit training* in EO which came to be the largest component of the total education and training programme. By early 1972, an annual eighteen hours of unit training in EO became mandatory for all Army units.

Another important event in the history of EO training in the Army was the establishment of the Defense Race Relations Institute (DRRI) at Patrick Air Force Base in 1971. This school was to train EO specialists for the Army, Navy and Air Force. At DRRI, a programme of instruction was developed which was to have far-reaching impact on the design and conduct of race relations education and training in the Army. The original mandatory unit training undertaken in the Army was based on a curriculum and on materials developed at DRRI and the training was to be conducted by DRRI trained instructors. Because of the shaping influence DRRI has had on the Army programme, it may be useful to examine briefly some of the characteristics of the early DRRI curriculum. Richard Hope, in chapter five, describes the DRRI experience in detail.

The original eleven-week programme of instruction for DRRI students encompassed four major areas (U.S. Department of Defense, 1971): (1) American ethnic studies; (2) behavioural sciences; (3) community involvement; and (4) group leadership practicum. The emphasis of this original programme was on knowledge, awareness, understanding and intergroup communications. At that time, there was no content dealing with how organisations function or specifically with how organisational mechanisms in the Army continue to perpetuate discrimination. The implicit assumption underlying this curriculum seemed to be that an increased awareness and understanding of minority history and culture and some of the psychological dynamics of racial prejudice would lead to decreased racial prejudice. A decrease in racial prejudice would, in turn, lead to better intergroup communication and less intergroup tension and conflict. There is little or no evidence that such a model is valid. But valid or not, it clearly identified improved communications and the reduction of intergroup conflict as goals. There is, however, no indication, in this early period, that helping to eliminate *racial discrimination* was an *explicit* goal of the training.

Between 1972 and 1974, the mandatory unit training in the Army was based on an eighteen-hour Core Curriculum, developed by DRRI and which was organised around six themes or phases which again emphasised knowledge, awareness and communications.

In February 1974, the Department of the Army issued AR 600–42, which again modified policy for race relations education in the Army. (U.S. Army, Secretary, 1974) The basic objective of race relations education was 'to maintain the highest degree of organisational and combat readiness by fostering harmonious relations among all military personnel.' This statement of policy emphasised that:

1 . . . commanders will be alert to the continuing need for promoting racial harmony;
2 . . . emphasis of the race relations program will be on the development of the teamwork and comradeship that builds pride in unit;
3 education will include specific efforts to . . . stimulate interracial communication in units; and
4 . . . instruction will focus on the history, background, lifestyle, contributions, and interactions among ethnic and racial groups.

Three elements of the Army race relations programme were

identified in AR 600–42; 1. *Individual training* which is formal race relations instruction in basic combat training and professional development courses taught in Army service schools and USAR schools; 2. *Unit training* which is a comprehensive racial awareness programme designed to stimulate interracial communications and to promote racial harmony in units; and 3. *Special training* for leaders and managers which is formal instruction in race relations conducted in Army colleges and in special courses. This new approach to unit training which was to be substituted for the old Core Curriculum was a series of mandatory seminars to be held not less than once monthly during prime training time in every unit on a continuing basis. The seminars were to be conducted in platoon-sized groups and were to be led by the unit chain of command. The course outline for the Unit Racial Awareness Program (RAP) was organised into six blocks of instruction:

1 Introduction;
2 Personal racism;
3 Interracial and interethnic communication;
4 Minorities in American life;
5 Institutional racism;
6 Racial and ethnic awareness.

The content of the first four blocks was generally similar to the content of the Core Curriculum which they superseded. The last two blocks, however, dealt with institutional discrimination and actions required to eliminate discrimination. These constituted new major themes in the content of race relations instruction.

The RAP seminars were the heart of Army EO unit training from early 1974 until September 1977 when the programme was again modified by the issue of a revised regulation (AR 600–21) which restated Army policy on equal opportunity programmes and provided new guidelines for the equal opportunity education and training programme. The new guidance specified four components of the education and training programme and detailed minimum requirements in each. These four were: 1. Entry level training; 2. Individual education for Army leaders, managers, and supervisors; 3. Unit training; and 4. Unit discussion leader training. Major commands were given considerably broader latitude than they had before in tailoring the programme to their own needs and supplementing the regulation. No requirement for minimum numbers of hours of training was specified. A set of guidelines for unit EO training was provided as an appendix to the regulation. These guidelines specified four learning objectives:

1 to facilitate and improve the soldier's understanding of the entire Equal Opportunity Program for the United States Army;

2 to inform unit members about potential sources of minority/gen-
   der dissatisfaction and interracial/intersexual tension in the Army
   and about what the Army is doing to remove any grounds for
   dissatisfaction and tension in specific areas;
3 to increase the soldier's understanding and acceptance of different
   cultural models; and
4 to provide the chain of command with contemporary information
   and feedback on the status and progress of the Equal Opportunity
   Program.

The guidelines then suggested a procedure wherein the commander first determines the needs of personnel in his unit for equal
opportunity information and then selects the methods and content of
the training needed based on the initial survey results. As an aid to
this process, materials were developed which provided outlines for
thirteen suggested equal opportunity topics which commanders
might wish to consider using. Once the commander determined the
topic and method of presentation, he was to select the instructor and
establish the time and place of the training. The commander was to
ensure that the training was scheduled, that attendance was mandatory for all unit personnel and that there was maximum participation
of all members of the command. The guidelines further specified a
list of training tasks required to achieve each of the learning
objectives noted above.

There were other developments occurring in the mid 1970s to
1980 as the programme continued to evolve. A growing emphasis on
institutional as opposed to *individual* discrimination appeared in
training programmes throughout the Army. Considerable effort was
spent developing quantitative indicators of the differences in various
personnel actions as they affected white and black personnel. Thus,
while the training programme still dealt largely with attitudes and
minority history and culture, the concept of institutional discrimination had become a prominent element of EO training.

By the end of the seventies, the equal opportunity research programme which the Army Research Institute had been conducting
continuously in parallel with the EO training programme was
virtually terminated. In the next section the findings from some of the
research studies are summarised.

The continuing evolution of the Army EO training in the late
seventies is described in the Third Annual Assessment of the Army
Equal Opportunity Program prepared by the office of Equal Opportunity Programs, covering the year 1978 (Department of the Army,
1979). The chapter on Education and Training focuses primarily on
the shift in the roles of the Equal Opportunity Specialists emphasised
by the revised regulations (AR 600–21). Before that shift, the role of

the EO specialist was primarily that of a trainer and the training they received at DRRI focused on preparing specialists to carry out that role. The regulation places the responsibility for training squarely on the chain-of-command and re-configures the role of the EO specialist into a staff role providing assistance to commanders when asked. The training provided at DRRI was also revised to reflect this shift. In addition, efforts were made through Executive Seminars to educate senior commanders regarding this shift and to demonstrate to senior leadership that EO is tied directly to unit readiness and can be measured by such things as military justice, discharges, and troop productivity. It may be significant and further evidence of what appeared from many sources to be a decline in the priority of EO training programmes that the Fourth Annual Assessment, covering the year 1979, contained no chapter on EO training and education. (Department of the Army, 1980)

RACIAL CLIMATE AND ORGANISATIONAL CHANGE IN THE ARMY 1972–78

This review was intended to be a roughly chronological outline of the development and nature of the Army's EO education and training programme as it evolved over the past decade. The natural question that occurs is what impact did this massive training programme have? That question, of course, cannot be definitively answered. Although one can document the fact that change has occurred, there is no way to attribute the change directly to the training because one cannot separate the effects of training from the effects of all the other events which were occurring simultaneously. However, one can characterise some of the major trends in racial climate, attitudes and perceptions, and objective differences in what happened to whites and blacks during this time period, all of which have been documented by research studies.

Obviously, a mere change in policy had not changed the underlying sources of racial tension and conflict. In response to the massive outbreak of racial conflict occurring in 1969–70, the Army's race relations/equal opportunity education and training programmes began in earnest. The assumption was that training would heighten awareness of cultural differences and promote improved communications between persons of different races – and racial harmony in Army units would thereby be achieved. Race relations training became mandatory throughout the Army. The hope was that if racial harmony in units could be created, the racial conflict would cease. It did cease beginning about 1972. Open violent racial conflicts became rare. The number of racial incidents reported continued to drop. Racial attitudes and racial climate as measured by surveys continued to improve at least between 1972 and 1976–7 at which time they appeared to level off. Blacks continued to report that the racial situation in the Army was improving even though there was still a long way to go. Objective measures of the disproportions in person-nel actions which adversely affected blacks generally showed a conti-nuing decrease although many of these also showed a tendency to level out by 1976–7. Blacks continued to see widespread discrimina-tion while whites perceived little. The frequency of positive interra-cial interactions increased but remained quite low. The frequency of openly hostile types of behaviour reported by all groups also remained low. On the other hand, however, there was a continuing increase in the number of whites who perceived 'reverse discrimi-nation'.

While minorities generally acknowledged progress in equal opportunity across the board, they remained acutely sensitive to the continued existence of what they perceived as discriminatory treatment which worked to their disadvantage. Whites, on the other hand, for the most part, did not perceive such discrimination and tended to believe that Army personnel procedures and decisions were colour blind. There was evidence in support of two opposite trends occurring within the white population. In 1972, the prepon-derance of whites saw themselves largely uninvolved and unconcer-ned with racial and equal opportunity issues. By the mid seventies, this uninvolved group had essentially split into two nearly equal-sized groups, both of which were no longer uninvolved. One group consis-ted of whites who had become aware of racial discrimination in Army functioning and wished to see it changed. The other group consisted of whites who perceived 'reverse discrimination' and felt angry at and resentful toward equal opportunity programmes. The primary source of racial tensions could once be seen as being the frustration and bitterness of minorities. A second primary source came into being and that was the anger of a growing number of whites who perceived that they were being victimised by 'reverse discrimination'. Interracial tensions were clearly now being fuelled from two sides. (Nordlie, 1973; Brown, Nordlie, and Thomas, 1977)

An important background fact is, of course, the increase in the minority representation in the Army during the 1970s. Blacks became represented in the Army by three times their proportion in the civilian population, and there were also significant increases in Hispanics and women. By the end of 1979, the enlisted Army was only fifty-four per cent white male. (Department of the Army, 1980)

OVERVIEW OF RESEARCH ON RACE RELATIONS TRAINING EFFECTIVENESS

Although many of the surveys conducted prior to 1976 (Nordlie, 1973; Brown, Nordlie, Thomas, 1977; Hiett, McBride, and Fiman, 1974) provided data on perceptions of and attitudes toward unit EO training programmes, it was not until 1976 that the Army Research Institute sponsored a major two-year Army-wide study of EO training. This study resulted in seven separate reports covering unit training in the U.S., Korea, the U.S. Army in Europe, some experimental EO training, EO training in Army schools, and the training of Army personnel at DRRI. The following comments on unit training research results are taken primarily from these reports. (Hiett and Nordlie, 1976; Edmonds and Nordlie, 1977; Gilbert and Nordlie, 1978; Hiett, 1977; Edmonds and Nordlie, 1977(b); Fiman, 1977; and Nordlie, 1978)

Two major problems with EO unit training were documented in the study. First, not more than half of the training required by the regulations was actually being given. Second, where it was being given, the training was frequently of low quality and often related to race relations or equal opportunity in name only – the subject matter being far removed or only tangentially related. (Nordlie, 1978)

A key problem for EO unit training resulted from the policy change which placed the responsibility for conducting the training on the chain of command instead of on trained EO specialists. This change placed the responsibility for EO training in the hands of those who had had the least preparation for it, and removed it from the hands of those who had had the most preparation – DRRI graduates. There was much evidence that unit training, as carried out by company commanders, was a low priority matter and largely a paper programme. Another critical issue was that EO unit training was reaching the level of E5s[2] and below but definitely not reaching the higher enlisted levels as policy and doctrine had intended and required. It appears that E6s and above tended successfully to evade EO training. Thus leaders, who by virtue of their role in the organisation had the most power to effect change, were the least likely to participate in unit training.

In one part of the study, experimental EO unit training was established on three installations to test the effects of a number of specific variables on training effectiveness. (Hiett, 1977) The experiment was not entirely successful, primarily because of uncertainty about how much experimental training actually took place. But this was important in itself because it suggested that, if under ideal conditions, where everyone involved had been briefed and checked out, where lesson plans were provided, and where the company commanders involved knew their units were in the experiment and were going to be tested – if under these presumably ideal conditions, the training still did not occur as required, then there must be something wrong with the basic concept on which unit EO training was built.

Part of the study looked at questionnaire data on attitudes towards, and perceptions of, the Army's Racial Awareness Program. (Hiett and Nordlie, 1978) About half of the whites and slightly fewer blacks believed that the Army was firmly committed to the principle of equal opportunity. Less than half of all personnel in the Army believed that Army leadership enforced EO regulations. While whites perceived somewhat more command support for EO programs than did blacks, there was considerable variation in perceived command support at different installations. About a third of both blacks and whites believed the EO programmes were 'just for show' and about a third believed they were seriously intended. Blacks were more likely than whites to feel that the training was effective in reducing racial tensions. Between 1972 and 1976, an increasing percentage of both whites and blacks saw race relations training as effective in reducing racial tensions; simultaneously an increasing percentage of both whites and blacks saw the training as not effective at all. By 1976, both whites and blacks were fairly polarised on this issue. The 'no opinion' group had virtually disappeared by 1976.

Whites were evenly split on whether race relations seminars should be mandatory whereas blacks favoured mandatory seminars by a margin of five to one. On the average, blacks saw the training as more useful than whites although whites appeared to be fairly evenly divided on questions of usefulness. A great deal of confusion existed with respect to the objectives of EO training. Despite widespread dissatisfaction with the current EO training programme, only a few personnel felt that there was an absence of a *need* for some type of EO programme. All groups of personnel expressed a decided preference for some new approach to EO training. Commanders wanted more responsibility for the programme while EO personnel feared this would lead to destruction of the programme. The personnel most prepared to conduct EO training – DRRI graduates – were doing very little of the actual training, whereas personnel with the least preparation – chain of command personnel – were doing most of the training. And finally, the EO training programme had a basically negative image throughout all levels of the Army with changes being urged from all sides. Overall, there was high consensus that a definite need existed for an EO training programme. There are some indications that the Racial Awareness Program was achieving some of its objectives, but there was a great deal of dissatisfaction with it. Blacks generally favoured the programme, whereas whites were fairly evenly divided. However, substantial proportions of *all* racial groups saw the programme in a negative manner. The overall image of the programme tended to be fairly negative but with the consistent difference between whites and blacks which has been repeatedly noted.

Interviews to explore the negative character of many of the questionnaire responses were conducted with commanders, EO specialists, and selected senior and junior level enlisted personnel. There was almost universal confusion about the objectives of the programme which was reflected in the variety of ways the programme was implemented at different locations. Commanders tended to express the view that the programme was not a commanders' programme, but that it should be. They frequently expressed resentment toward the EO organisational structure which they saw as 'stove-piped' around the normal chain of command. EO specialists, on the other hand, tended to fear that a commanders' programme would result in no programme at all. This conflict was endemic and resulted in many commanders claiming the programme was being rammed down their throats and many EO specialists complaining about lack of command support.

A common complaint expressed by many commanders and some unit enlisted personnel (mostly white NCOs) was that the programme created problems where none existed before or amplified problems which were minor. This type of complaint was most frequently accompanied by expressions of resistance to any type of race-relations or anti-discrimination effort.

The respondents interviewed frequently expressed the view that the focus of the programme was too narrow. In particular, many people felt that the programme was too black oriented and overemphasised 'white guilt'. Many felt that the programme should be broadened to encompass more general 'human relations' topics rather than just 'race relations' although a few felt that this change would dilute efforts to change race-specific behaviours. Another suggested shift in focus was toward solving problems which come up in daily life in the unit. This desire for a contemporary, unit specific programme may have been a reaction to the tendency to focus on minority history and culture without relating them to current problems existing in Army units.

One part of the 1976–8 study of EO training in the Army previously mentioned, focused on required individual EO training given in Army schools. (Edmonds and Nordlie, 1977(b)) The approach of this study involved: interviewing staff and faculty at two selected training centres, four service schools, and three senior service colleges; reviewing lesson plans and associated documents of the training given at the various schools; and a questionnaire survey of students currently enrolled in the training regarding their attitudes toward and perceptions of EO training.

A number of highlights from the findings of this part of the study can be cited. On the whole, EO instruction appeared to be considered a low priority subject matter and was only reluctantly incorporated into course curricula. The *Uniform Service School Standards for Race Relations/Equal Opportunity Instruction* had been implemented in only five out of sixteen courses reviewed, although the *Standards* had been issued nine months previously. The EO courses in schools were generally not taught by EO qualified instructors, and EO training was still largely oriented toward creating awareness. There had been little progress in tailoring training courses to the specific job needs of trainees, and students were seldom tested on or held accountable for knowing EO information. Staff and faculty of schools tended to view EO training as an unwanted orphan – a low priority, directionless programme. There was an overall lack of common understanding of the race problem, although EO training was generally perceived to be important and required but not in the form in which it existed.

EO training was far more favourably received by students at entry-level schools than it was at other schools, but overall the general image of EO training in the schools was negative. There was an increasing demand by school faculty and staffs to eliminate EO instruction given as a block and to incorporate its content into other blocks of instruction. There was a general consensus among faculty and staff interviewed that *race relations* is a poor label for the training and it should be called something like *human relations.* There was little or no use of highly confrontive type training approaches which had been associated with some EO training in the past.

Although Army policy called for EO training in Army schools as well as in all units, there appeared to have been far more emphasis on unit training than on individual training in the schools. With so little individual EO training occurring in the schools, the entire burden of EO training was, by default, laid on unit training, a task for which unit training alone was not equal. Unit training is an appropriate locus for only some parts of the total EO training task. An effective EO training programme would require a more balanced division of labour between school and unit training.

Another part of the 1976–8 study of Army EO training looked at the training received by Army EO specialists at DRRI (Fiman, 1978). Since the publication of the DRRI study in 1978, DRRI has been reorganised into the Equal Opportunity Management Institute (EOMI) and its curriculum revamped. Most of the changes instituted were consistent with the recommendations of the study. Two points may be worth mentioning. First, almost without exception, DRRI graduates reported that the school experience had a powerful, important, and personally meaningful impact on them. The overwhelming consensus on this point would appear to make the DRRI experience unique among military training experiences in general. Whatever other criticisms graduates voiced, almost all emphasised a profound personal growth experience which they identified as important in their lives. It would appear unquestionable that DRRI graduates are far more aware of, and sensitive to, the nuances and insidious characteristics of discrimination at work in an organisation than are those who have not been exposed to DRRI training.

A second important point was the misalignment between training content and the jobs actually being performed by EO specialists in the field, at least in the Army. When the Army shifted from using EO specialists primarily as trainers to using them in primarily staff roles, DRRI training continued to be oriented to training trainers and not staff specialists. This meant that while DRRI training appeared to have a deep personal impact on individuals, it did not provide them with the skills required to do their jobs. In the revamping of the curricula, this conflict between the Department of Defense specifications of DRRI's mission and the Army's specifications of its utilisation of DRRI graduates apparently has been largely eliminated.

OBSERVATIONS ON THE ARMY'S RACE-RELATIONS TRAINING EXPERIENCE

A few observations on this review of Army EO training and research can be made. First, equal opportunity training is required at all levels of schools in the Army and until recently, it was required in all units. In other words, EO training was conceived as a universal educational experience required of all Army personnel and not just a specific educational experience for some subgroups.

Second, there has been no underlying theoretical model which unifies and makes coherent the many diverse elements of the programme. There is no thread of continuity throughout the various EO training experiences to which Army personnel are exposed. Each training experience tends to be either repetitious of others or not clearly related to others.

Third, there appears to have been an unquestioned acceptance of some assumptions about suitable methods for EO training – small group guided discussions – and that a failure in communications was one of the root causes of racial tension. It appears to have been further assumed that racial harmony was a major objective of unit race relations training, but racial harmony is never clearly defined.

Fourth, policy statements have begun to include goal statements concerning the elimination of discrimination which tended to have been absent from earlier goal statements. Still, the policy statements tend to exhibit an almost schizophrenic character with respect to whether policy is oriented toward creating awareness or toward the elimination of discrimination. Within the same policy statement, one can find substantial evidence in support of either interpretation.

Fifth, the original policy on race relations/equal opportunity training and all subsequent modifications do not appear to have been based on any hard evidence that the training content and methods required could or would achieve the intended objectives. The Army Equal Opportunity Program, initiated as a 'special' programme, was launched in the midst of violent racial strife and evolved, by 1980, into a normal routine staff function. The changes in the Army programme over this period can be characterised as being: from emphasis on black–white relations to emphasis on equal opportunity, other racial and ethnic minorities and women; from creating racial awareness to creating management skills designed to produce equal opportunity; from a high priority to a low priority programme; from improving interracial communication to eliminating discrimination; from a vocabulary of race relations to a vocabulary of equal opportunity; from mandatory to non-mandatory; from race relations specialist to human resources management; from confrontation to mechanics; and from intensive research and development to none.

Sixth, in surveys taken during the period 1972–7, Army personnel consistently evaluated whatever EO training they were receiving fairly negatively. However, at the same time, when asked if there was a need for EO training, there was a consistent, high consensus among whites and minorities that there was such a need. In other words, while troops did not like whatever EO training they were receiving, they still believed the need for training that addressed EO problems was high.

Seventh, as objective equality of opportunity for minorities increased, the resistance to EO programmes by whites also increased. For the most part, existing EO curricula did not effectively address the issues of 'reverse racism' and 'white backlash'.

Eighth, the earliest EO training programmes were almost exclusively oriented to black–white issues. Current programmes feature other minorities and the issues of sexism as well.

Ninth, the Army EO programme suffers from low credibility among minorities because they tend to believe that whites in the

Army really do not want minorities to be accorded equal treatment. Many whites tend to think the programme is merely for show or it is to benefit minorities at the expense of whites. The result is that most Army personnel believe the EO programme is cosmetic and does not reflect true Army policy. Such a perception does not enhance the likelihood of EO courses material being believed or learned. One conclusion from the 1976–8 EO training evaluation study was that the Army should consider what steps need to be taken to increase the credibility of the EO education and training programme. (Nordlie, 1978) Some of the factors that contribute to the low credibility of the programme can be noted; the 'special' character of the programme which was perceived as being handled differently from other more 'normal' programmes. Troops, in general, perceived a lack of support for the EO programme on the part of the chain-of-command. Commanders tended to believe that the only aspect of EO that concerned them was 'keeping the lid on' – avoiding racial incidents. Training was frequently scheduled which did not actually take place and reported attendance figures were often inflated. Some EO specialists were of low status, sometimes low competence, and inspired little respect as good soldiers. There was widespread misunderstanding of the objectives and purposes of the programme. There was also widespread misinformation with respect to the actual occurrence of discrimination. Another factor was the pervasive belief that EO concerns were not really related to the ability of a unit to perform its primary mission. The relatively low attendance of EO training by chain-of-command personnel provided negative evidence with respect to the credibility of the programme.

Finally, there is the issue of the programme failing to prepare chain-of-command personnel to effectively carry out the EO responsibilities which they have been assigned. Army policy places the responsibility for all components of the EO programme squarely and unequivocally on the chain-of-command. It further specifies that, in addition to entry-level training and unit training, individual education for Army leaders, managers, and supervisors will be institutionalised throughout the Army school system at all levels. Most of the problems, and inadequacies of the EO education and training stem directly from the fact that chain-of-command personnel have not been adequately prepared to carry out the responsibilies with which they have been charged. With respect to their views of the EO programme, one study (Nordlie, 1978) characterised Army leaders, especially at the company commander level, as being: 1. uncertain of its objectives; 2. distrustful of its intent; 3. unconvinced of its importance; 4. untrained with respect to its content, and 5. uncomfortable with the subject matter. To the extent this characterisation is accurate, it should help account for why EO training may be less than fully effective in most instances, and, indeed in some instances counterproductive.

CONCLUSIONS

First and foremost, the Army was clearly a pioneer in a massive organisational change implemented primarily through education and training. That there has been change in direction is undeniable, although the basic problem has not been eliminated. The results have been mixed but probably positive on balance. One has the impression that the resistance to EO programmes has been increasing while the priority of the programme to Army leadership appears to have been decreasing. This may simply be related to the fact that interracial violence and confrontation have been largely eliminated and to many leaders this signals the fact that the problem has been solved.

A low priority programme normally means that there is no one at the top pushing it – it is policy, but it has no advocate. Without advocates, the programme loses the constant competition with other programmes for personnel, resources and time. None the less, the Army's EO training and education programme has played a contributing role in improving race relations and creating greater equality of opportunity in the Army. In its magnitude and its intent, it has been a landmark programme with few precedents or guidelines. Since the late seventies, however, the programme gives evidence of drifting, stagnating and becoming less relevant to the problems it was intended to address. Compared to its earlier vigour, it appears impoverished and undernourished.

It is of interest to note that the justification for Army EO programmes could have included a moral basis or the simple fact that the law had changed and it was necessary to conform with the law. But for the most part, these justifications are seldom found. Initially, one heard primarily of the need to reduce racial tensions in order to stop racial violence. Later, the programmes tended to be justified in terms of their contribution to the mission-readiness of units. If racial tensions were fed by the lack of equal opportunity, then equality of opportunity must be created in order to increase the ability of units to perform.

One final point should be made. As part of its total EO effort, the Army has, until recently, undertaken research for the purpose of studying how the programme was working and how it could be made more effective. If it is possible to be critical of the Army's programme, it is only because the Army studied itself and obtained data which is largely lacking for most other organisations. If we are able to conclude, as we have concluded, that there are major problems with the training programme, it is only because the Army has had the fortitude to examine its own programmes and the courage to make the results public. This contrasts sharply with the more frequently encountered approach of papering over deficiencies in such programmes, publicising how much effort goes into the programme, and steadfastly proclaiming that the programme is achieving what it was intended to achieve although offering no hard evidence in support of the claim.

NOTES

1 The name of the EO training programme has changed several times. At various times, it has been called Race Relations (RR); Equal Opportunity and Treatment (EOT); Race Relations/Equal Opportunity (RR/EO) and Equal Opportunity (EO). To avoid confusion, the current name, EO, will be used throughout even when referring to earlier programmes.

2 The enlisted ranks of the U.S. Army are categorised from E–1, a newly recruited private, to E–9, the highest level non-commissioned officer.

REFERENCES

– Brown, Dale K., Peter G. Nordlie and James A. Thomas. (1977), *Changes in Black and White Perceptions of the Army's Race Relations Equal Opportunity Program (1972–1974).* ARI Technical Report TR–77–B3. U.S. Army Research Institute, Alexandria, Va.
– Edmonds, William S., and Peter G. Nordlie. (1977a), *Analysis of Race Relations/Equal Opportunity Training in Korea.* U.S. Army Research Institute, Alexandria, Va.
– Edmonds, William S., and Peter G. Nordlie. (1977b), *Analysis of Individual Race Relations and Equal Opportunity Training in Army Schools.* U.S. Army Research Institute, Alexandria, Va.
– Fiman, Byron. (1978), *Analysis of the Training of Army Personnel at the Defense Race Relations Institute.* ARI Technical Report TR–78–B14. U.S. Army Research Institute, Alexandria, Va.
– Gilbert, Marcia A., and Peter G. Nordlie. (1978), *An Analysis of Race Relations/Equal Opportunity Training in USAREUR.* ARI Technical Report TR–78–B14. U.S. Army Research Institute, Alexandria, Va.
– Hiett, Robert. (1977), *Analysis of Experimental Race Relations/Equal Opportunity Training.* U.S. Army Research Institute, Alexandria, Va.
– Hiett, Robert, Robin McBride, and Byron Fiman. (1974), *Measuring the Impact of Race Relations Programs in the Military.* U.S. Army Research Institute, Alexandria, Va.
– Hiett, Robert, and Peter G. Nordlie. (1976), *An Analysis of the Unit Race Relations Training Program in the U.S. Army.* ARI Technical Report TR–78–B9. U.S. Army Research Institute
– Human Sciences Research, Inc. (1979), *Equal Opportunity in the Army—A Handbook for Leaders.* McLean, Va. p. 51. Prepared for the U.S. Army Research Institute, Alexandria, Virginia. This is a revision and update of an earlier handbook of the same name publised in 1972 and distributed Army-wide as DA PAM 600–16
– Nordlie, Peter G. (1973), *Black and White Perceptions of Army's Equal Opportunity and Treatment Programs.* Prepared for the U.S. Army Research Institute, Alexandria, Va.
– Nordlie, Peter G. (1978), *Analysis and Assessment of the Army Race Relations Training Programme: Summary of Conclusions and Recommendations.* U.S. Army Research Institute, Alexandria, Va.
– Stillman, Richard J., II. (1968), *Integration of the Negro in the U.S. Armed Forces.* New York, Praeger
– U.S. Department of the Army (1964), AR 600–21, *Personnel—General, Equal Opportunity and Military Personnel.* Headquarters, Department of the Army, The Pentagon, Washington, D.C.

– U.S. Department of the Army (1974), AR 600–42, *Personnel—General, Race Relations Education for the Army*
– U.S. Department of the Army (1979), *Third Annual Assessment of the Army's Equal Opportunity Program*. The Pentagon, Washington, D.C.
– U.S. Department of the Army (1980), *Fourth Annual Assessment of the Army's Equal Opportunity Program*. The Pentagon, Washington, D.C.
– U.S. Department of Defense (1963), Directive 5]20.35. Subject: *Equal Opportunity in the Armed Forces* Washington, D.C.
– U.S. Department of Defense (1971), *Defense Race Relations Institute Commanders' Notebook*. Annex IV, Defense Race Relations Institute, Patrick Air Force Base, Florida

6

The Defense
Equal Opportunity
Management Institute

Towards the end of the Vietnam War, riots were prevalent on Military installations in the United States and overseas. General Abrams, who commanded the troops in Vietnam at the time, said that poor race relations were a major problem plaguing combat effectiveness. It was at this point that the Pentagon began to consider this a serious problem.

There were many ways suggested to solve this problem, from 'shoot the rioters' to 'permissive understanding' of the problems faced by minorities in the military. The decision was to have compulsory race relations training to improve understanding between the rioting troops.

The compulsory training programme was one of the single most ambitious education programmes of its type ever attempted by any institution in the United States. The responsibility for the development of this massive programme was given to the Defense Race Relations Institute (DRRI), later to be named the Defense Equal Opportunity Management Institute (EOMI). This paper will present an in-depth analysis of this programme and its impact on intergroup relations in the military. (Abbreviations used here interchangeably.)

The Defense Equal Opportunity Management Institute (EOMI) was established by the Department of Defense under directive 1322.11, issued in June 1971. It also established the Race Relations Education Board to provide policy guidance for the education programme and the Institute. Its chairman is the Assistant Secretary of Defense (Manpower and Reserve Affairs) and others include the counterpart Assistant Secretaries of each of the services, the Deputy Chiefs of Staff for Personnel, and the Deputy Assistant Secretaries for Equal Opportunity, Education, and Reserve Affairs. The EOMI opened in September 1971, when about three-fourths of its projected staff arrived at the site selected for it, Patrick Air Force Base in Florida.

The mission of this programme is: to conduct training for Department of Defense personnel designated as instructors in race relations; develop doctrine and curricula in education for race, relations; conduct research; perform evaluation of programme effectiveness; disseminate educational guidelines and materials for utilisation throughout the Armed Forces; and to conduct training for Army and Navy personnel designated as equal opportunity/human resources management specialists. (This mission statement was established by the Race Relations Education Board in 1976.)

The goal of this programme is to achieve behaviour change through education. EOMI continues today as an established programme of the Department of Defense. The training period has been extended from six weeks to sixteen weeks in duration. The primary focus of the present study will concentrate on its evolution from 1971 to 1975, although some discussion will be devoted to the present organisation. The 'behaviour' refers to all forms of action carried out by a EOMI graduate in intergroup situations. This includes a range of actions from the overt musculoskeletal to the subtle expression of emotion or subjective feeling.

The concept of basing efforts to increase racial harmony on an education programme was adopted by the Inter-Service Task Force on Education in Race Relations, which made the original recommendation for a race relations education programme. In its report, issued 31 July 1970, the task force said: 'As pointed out in Secretary of Defense, Melvin R. Laird's memorandum of 28 January 1970, one cannot help but be impressed by the fact that every thoughtful study of race relations in our society, including the report of the special sub-committee of the House Armed Services Committee convened to probe disturbances on military bases, stresses accelerated education in race relations and improved communications as the key to solving this problem.' (Laird, 1970)

The DRRI focus on behaviour change is especially suited to this setting because of the unique character of the military. The military is a controlled society, where it is possible to require certain forms of behaviour from personnel. The Race Relations Education Program rests on the assumption that if someone can learn to recognise when specific behaviour rouses antagonism in others, behaviour can be modified and conflict-provoking situations avoided. The objective is to convert conflict to dialogue and dialogue to problem solving.

The educational method employed in this training programme is small group discussion seminars. EOMI students are being trained to conduct a continuing programme of such seminars at their home installations.

The origin and development of the Race Relations Education Program in the military represents the most massive effort to change attitudes and behaviour that has ever been undertaken in an institutionalised setting. The creation of educational and training programmes, the development of race relations/equal opportunity (RR/EO) staffs, the formulation of new policy, all required a large allocation of resources and a tremendous investment of time and energy. This programme began out of an urgent need to reduce and eliminate race rioting in the military and, consequently, was initiated quickly. There was little precedent in military or civilian sectors for the development of training models and policy guidelines. The bulk of these policies and procedures and training techniques, including the content materials, was developed by a small group of professional and military personnel who were chosen because of their previous experience and expertise in intergroup relations training. This small group of highly dedicated individuals, representing all racial groups in the military, worked long hours to develop a training programme in a very short period of time.

EOMI was designed to reach six primary objectives, giving students:

1 A knowledge of minority group history and the contributions of minority groups to the development of the US and the Armed Forces.
2 A knowledge of selected psychological, social, and cultural factors relating to race relations to increase their understanding of the social and behavioural dynamics related to intergroup tensions and conflict.
3 Racial and ethnic group experiences in various communities to increase their understanding of minority group culture and lifestyle.
4 The opportunity to develop teaching techniques and group skills which will prepare them to lead discussions.
5 The opportunity to become aware of current DOD, service, and command equal opportunity of treatment policies and directives, and their relationship to the need for maintaining good order and discipline.
6 The capability and judgment to work with their commanding officers in determining the specific needs for a race relations group discussion programme and how best to employ the DRRI resources within that command.

The directive also required that all military personnel must receive training in race relations. In addition, this directive established the Race Relations Education Board (RREB) to provide policy guidance for the Race Relations Education Program (RREP) and DRRI.

The RREB is an advisory board to the Secretary of Defense and operates under the policy guidance and control of its chairman, the Assistant Secretary of Defense and Manpower and Reserve Affairs. Other members include the counterpart Assistant Secretaries for each of the services, the Deputy Chiefs of Staff for Personnel, and the Deputy Assistant Secretaries for Equal Opportunity, Education, and Reserve Affairs.

EOMI began in 1971 as a seven-week training programme. The student's day was mostly spent in one way or another related to the training mission, whether this meant individual group discussions, periods of independent reading, field experiences, lectures, using audiovisual equipment, or developing instructional techniques. Even eating lunch might be arranged so that informal communication could be somewhat structured. As a result of increasing demands for improved instructional techniques and service-specific administrative requirements, each of the services developed an additional training programme that was required of all EOMI graduates after they completed the first phase. The service-specific instructions were referred to as Phase II of the course of instruction. With the development of Phase II, the first phase, which was originally seven weeks, was reduced to five weeks. Phase II was then extended to varying lengths according to service needs. In most cases, the Phase II instruction exceeded four to five weeks, depending on the particular class. This paper will not discuss this service-specific phase of instruction.

THE CURRICULUM

The educational approach adopted was to seek behavioural change through education. Efforts were not directed toward specific attitude change although explorations were made to determine whether changes in behaviour eventually affect attitudes.

As was mentioned earlier, the focus of the training is on behaviour change through the recognition by the individual of the effect of his behaviour upon others. Through feedback, one can learn to modify one's behaviour and transform conflict into dialogue.

The educational method used to do this is small group discussion seminars. The students at the DRRI are being trained to conduct a continuing programme of such seminars on their home installations. Heterogeneous groups of about twenty are also used as a major teaching mechanism at the Institute. This is augmented with lecture sessions, audiovisual materials, guest speakers, and a laboratory week-end field trip in the Miami inner city.

The Institute assigns a faculty advisor to every section to act as liaison between the seminar sessions and the Institute and as a faculty counsellor to individual students.

Members of the sections range from mid rank to senior officers; have education levels from high school to doctorate degrees; are nineteen to forty-plus in age; and are of all races and ethnic backgrounds. This heterogeneous mix fosters growth, understanding, and awareness through association and interaction. Student interaction with faculty, both structured and informal, also contributes to this growth because faculty also represents a broad spectrum of ethnic and racial groups as well as ranks within the military. Faculty are assigned from each branch of the services.

The instructional programme covers four functional areas:

1 *Minority studies* provide students with the history of various minority groups and their current attitudes and thinking. This section also covers minority group contributions to the development of the nation and to the Armed Forces.

2 *Behavioural sciences* provide students with knowledge of selected psychological, social, cultural factors related to race relations to increase their understanding of social and behavioural dynamics related to intergroup tensions and conflicts. It also encompasses full discussions of individual racism and institutional racism.

3 *Educational techniques* provides knowledge of intergroup relations, group processes and problems, interaction, group leadership, interracial communication, the listening process, guided group discussion techniques, lesson planning, role planning, and the opportunity to develop skills in leading discussion groups.

4 *Community laboratory experience* provides racial and ethnic group experiences in various minority communities to increase student understanding of minority group cultures and lifestyles. It provides direct observation of examples of materials covered in the classroom. All students spend from Friday evening until Sunday evening in the Miami area, where they are exposed to such situations as ghetto housing projects, migrant camps, Cuban and Puerto Rican neighbourhoods, rap sessions with prisoners who are former service personnel, and Indian settlements. This part of the programme was terminated in 1974.

Change was a constant companion for faculty and staff at the Defense Race Relations Institute. Following the pilot programme, thirteen classes were held between June 1971 and April 1974. During this period, there were 2,682 persons in training. With little more than the general order to train race relations or human relations instructors, the faculty and staff found it necessary, based on evaluation data during the first couple of years to make frequent changes in the curriculum and its structure to adapt to requirements of students who would go back to their installations as instructors. In addition, there were occasional letters from field commanders indicating various places they thought needed changing. For example, some field commanders felt that the pilot programme and a few of the early classes produced students who were overly 'militant' and were not following the chain of command in solving problems of race relations at installation levels. There was also the feeling that the instructors at DRRI were too black/white oriented and it did not deal with problems of other minorities and females. Such adjustments were made in the curriculum. Minority studies, for example, was expanded to include most of the minorities represented in the military. Additionally, a curriculum was developed after considerable discussion that focused upon women's problems, particularly sexism in the military. The final week included material devoting full attention to 're-entry', i.e., the existing chain-of-command, and how to use it effectively.

EVALUATION OF TRAINING

The various evaluation instruments and methods employed, including 'The Pre- and Post-Test Measures of Student Change', 'Commander Evaluations', 'Student Critiques of DRRI Training', 'Graduates' Assessment of DRRI', 'Instructor Perception of DRRI Program', and factors used to evaluate student performance while attending DRRI (i.e., peer ratings, academic tests, faculty evaluations of students), were analysed in three different evaluation research reports and two field evaluation reports by the DRRI evaluation research staff. (Hope, 1979) An independent research firm, Human Sciences Research, Inc. (HSR), found the conclusions of these DRRI reports 'consistent with findings and this (HSR) report'. (HSR, 1977)

The data indicate a rather profound and consistent impact on students. The training is highly endorsed by all involved, with few exceptions. It is seen by most personnel as a very important experience leading to changes in racial and sexual awareness and profound changes in feelings about one's self. Especially in contrast to other training programmes attended by military personnel, the Phase I training appears to be a highly unique and a personally meaningful experience.

The greatest difficulty experienced by DRRI is its inability to cope with new changes in policy and regulations as established by the respective services. DRRI has continued, since its inception, to study and improve its ability to produce race relations according to its original mission which has not been redefined by the Race Relations Education Board. Thus, according to regulations, DRRI cannot change its method of instruction and objectives (HSR, 1977). Nevertheless, the policies and regulations of the services, including the definition of the roles of the DRRI graduates, have changed considerably. For example, the original Army-wide Race Relations and

Equal Opportunities Training Program (RAP No. 1) was a mandatory eighteen-hour course, generally taught by EOMI graduates.

An independent assessment was made of the effect of race relations training on DRRI graduates after they returned to their respective installations. This graduate follow-up survey yielded results quite consistent with feedback from students immediately upon graduation before they returned to the field.

Graduates report very high levels of satisfaction from their DRRI training in preparing them to accomplish race relations instructional tasks in Phase I, but seem less satisfied with their training to accomplish EO (Equal Opportunity) tasks and administrative and supervisory tasks in Phase II. The ratings in Phase I are substantially higher than those of Phase II.

Fiman conducted personal interviews with EOMI graduates in the field and found:

Most graduates at all posts felt that DRRI training was necessary for them to be in the RR/EO field. Eighty-nine percent felt that DRRI-trained instructors would be more effective than a non-DRRI-trained person as an instructor. However, for RR/EO staff work, only 59 percent felt that a DRRI graduate would be more effective. With respect to the phases at DRRI, 99 percent felt that Phase I had been satisfactory or very satisfactory in preparing them for their jobs. They felt the experience in Miami, the emphasis on learning about one's self, and the quality of instructors were the highlights of Phase I. On the other hand, Phase II was seen as satisfactory by only 64 percent of the graduates. (HSR, 1977)

Among the evaluation measures used to assess the impact of human relations training, there were a variety of questionnaires administered to graduates and their commanders throughout the world. Commanders were asked a variety of questions attempting to gain their assessment of how effective the human relations programme was at their own installation. Commanders were asked to judge the impact of human relations training on their personnel and the extent to which intergroup relations were positively or negatively affected by these various programmes. In all surveys conducted, the overwhelming majority of the commanders thought the training programme had a positive effect on intergroup relations.

A more recent study conducted in 1980 (Adleman, *et al.*) focused on the functional relationship between the Equal Opportunity jobs to be performed and training. No personal impact data was gathered comparable to Hope (1979) or Fiman (HSR, 1977 or 1978). During the study by Adleman, *et al.* the EOMI training programme had at the time nine blocks of instruction: 1. socialisation and orientation, 2. human behaviour and organisational development, 3. aspects of discrimination, 4. equal opportunity skills, 5. instructional skills, 6.

cross-cultural knowledge, 7. homogeneous group consultation, 8. service specific, and 9. practicum. EOMI graduates view this curriculum as relevant training for twelve of the eighteen major duties performed by the Equal Opportunity personnel:

1 Formulate and/or revise affirmative action plan (AAP)
2 Collect data, monitor progress, prepare reports required by the AAP.
3 Staff assistant visits.
4 Develop/revise EO training materials.
5 Instruct/facilitate in equal opportunity training.
6 Brief/meet with commanders on EO/AA/HRM matters.
7 Counsel/process discrimination complaints.
8 Provide equal employment opportunity (EEO) services to civilian personnel.
9 Public/community relations work.
10 Perform duties in related human resources areas (e.g., organisation effectiveness/development).
11 Establish or develop EO/AA policies, directives, guidelines, regulations (at all levels).
12 Prepare budget and submit financial reports for EO/AA and related human-resource areas.

Adleman *et al.* found little or no relevant training to be provided for the other six major EO duties:

1 Participate in human relations, base or unit councils.
2 Assist the inspector general (IG) in performing EO/AA inspections.
3 Perform duties that have no connection with EO/AA or related human resource areas.
4 Plan, staff, and assign the workload for EO/AA functions among personnel supervised.
5 Train personnel supervised in EO/AA skill or knowledge areas.
6 Evaluate performance and write fitness reports (job evaluations) for EO/AA personnel supervised.

In a recent review and assessment of EOMI, the following evaluation was summarised: 'Whether or not DRRI/EOMI has had an impact on the various branches of the military is difficult to assess. As a major supplier of EO/RR trainers and/or trainers of trainers, there is little doubt that DRRI/EOMI through its graduates has had a very substantial impact on the process of race relations training in the military.' (Day, 1983, p. 265).

INTERGROUP INTERACTION

Intergroup interaction was a significant part of the training methodology. It was such an important aspect of desired behavioural change that considerable time and effort has gone into researching appropriate intergroup interaction for students. (Amir, 1976)

Intergroup interaction is studied under the rubric of 'contact' between minority and majority groups. The derivation and intensity of these studies has varied considerably.

Amir summarises these abundant studies with the following conclusions regarding favourable conditions that reduce prejudice:

(a) equal status contact between members of the various groups; (b) positive perceptions of the other group as a result of the contact (even under unequal status conditions); (c) contact between members of a majority group and higher status members of a minority group; (d) contact situations requiring intergroup cooperation; (e) contact situations involving interdependent activities, superordinate goals, or separate aims that can be achieved only by intergroup cooperation; (f) contact of an intimate rather than a casual nature; (g) an 'authority' and/or social climate being in favor of and promoting the intergroup contact; and (h) contact that is pleasant or rewarding.

(Amir, 1976, p. 245)

In an attempt to explain the relative success of this programme, it might be instructive to compare these conclusions with the findings of EOMI instructional methods and research.

Equal status contact

Small groups at EOMI are intentionally heterogeneous. Free interaction occurs regardless of rank, race, education and sex. Most volunteered to attend EOMI, but, once in the programme, intergroup discussion is required and there is considerable career and peer pressure on students to remain in the programme. A few students did 'self-eliminate' with the advice of faculty and staff, but this never exceeded two or three per cent of the class.

Positive perception of other groups

Students did develop positive perceptions of other group cultures and 'life-styles'. Empirical data show significant and positive changes in these perceptions during the training period. Many also entered this programme with greater appreciation of other groups than the general military population. Selectivity is a factor in these positive perceptions, in addition to training. Unfortunately, given the range of minorities represented, tests to measure changes in perception do not include data on such groups as 1. Samoans, 2. Appalachian whites, 3. Filipinos, and 4. members of different Indian tribes. Minority studies curriculum does include lectures and discussions of these groups.

Majority and high status minority contact

Interaction between individuals from majority and minority groups is guaranteed by the small-group facilitator who is a member of the faculty. High status minority interaction is a regular occurrence. There is considerable time and effort by the services given to assure the presence of high ranking minority enlisted and officers. In the first two years, one-half of the students sent to the Institute were black and other minorities, representing all ranks of the officers and enlisted corps.

Contact situation requiring cooperation

Cooperation is emphasised between students. This is apparent in the small group which generates activities encouraging cooperation. Each group ranges in size between ten and twenty members and is encouraged to develop its own identity. They often meet after regular hours to continue a discussion started during regular hours. Each group is urged to support its members when one or more are experiencing problems such as in academic assignments or in personal adjustment to new experiences. Each member evaluates the others of his group on their participation and support.

Contact situation requiring superordinate goals

Students attending EOMI are well briefed on the goals and objectives of the Institute. They are told of the experimental nature of the programme and that they would be under very close scrutiny from the Pentagon. They come to feel the meeting of these goals is greatly dependent on them and how well they functioned at their respective installations. Most of the students come to understand the goals and identified with the ideals set forth by EOMI. The success of the programme in improving intergroup relations becomes a strong superordinate goal. This plays an important role in motivating students to cooperate even under occasionally difficult situations.

Intimate rather than casual contact

Students cannot bring their families with them to the Institute. Students live together in dormitories. They generally eat and socialise together. Every effort is made to keep them together as a group, during and after classes. Several evenings a week there are planned guest lectures, movies, or discussions. The somewhat isolated location of Patrick Air Force Base and limited recreation place made for greater emphasis on informality and intimacy among students.

An 'authority' or climate favouring intergroup contact

The Human Goals Program authorised by the Secretary of Defense to protect the rights of all minorities and women in the military has a ubiquitous influence on the social climate. After this was established in the early 1970s, it became much easier to explain the goals of EOMI and have them accepted by those in and outside the Institute. The strong authoritarian system of the military has also helped to promulgate the curriculum and have it legitimised even though it cut across the status quo of the military bureaucracy. This authority structure also encouraged some reluctant students to accept the importance of changing racial attitudes, beliefs and behaviour.

Pleasant or rewarding contact

The EOMI is unquestionably a rewarding experience, according to students' evaluations. At the end of every class, students answer a very detailed questionnaire. The vast majority, ninety per cent and over, have been very favourable. This is documented in the DRRI research reports I, II and III.

CONCLUSION

These conditions hypothesised by Amir, as necessary for better intergroup understanding, appear to be present in the EOMI experiment. Even the issue of equal status contact is present in this military setting though with some reservations. Differential ranks are retained in the small group discussions but are minimised by the presence of a trained facilitator who permits free flowing communication between persons of different ranks. The facilitator, in a sense, 'out ranks' all class participants by virtue of his or her authority as teacher, with powers to affect the careers of students.

Further research is needed to analyse each of Amir's items in greater depth using experimental models under more controlled conditions. Perhaps the most difficult task of any researcher studying EOMI, is having to account for ubiquitous change. Before one experimental condition was tested, others were introduced and very often the original condition eliminated before test results were complete. Nevertheless, the longevity of the programme and the above reviewed research findings suggest a positive evaluation profile, meeting stated goals and objectives with unusual success and effectiveness.

REFERENCES
- Adleman, J., Larkin, T. F., Carleton, D., Olmpia, P. (1980), Functional Assessment of Military Equal Opportunity Staffs: Field Research and Job Analysis, I of Final Report to the Deputy Assistant Secretary of Defense (Equal Opportunity), Logical Technical Services Corporation, Vienna, VA
- Amir, Y. (1976), The Role of Intergroup Contact in Change of Prejudice and Ethnic Relations.' In Phyllis A. Katz (ed.), *Towards the Elimination of Racism*, New York,

Pergamon, pp. 245–308
– Day, H. R. (1983), 'Race Relations Training in the U.S. Military.' In Dan Landis and Richard W. Brislin (eds.) *Handbook of Intercultural Training,* II, New York, Pergamon
– Fiman, B. G. (1978), *An Analysis of the Training of Army Personnel at the Defense Race Relations Institute,* McLean, VA, Human Sciences Research, Inc., April
– Hope, R. O. (1979), *Racial Strife in the U.S. Military; Toward the Elimination of Discrimination,* New York. Praeger
– Human Sciences Research, Inc. (1977), 'An Analysis of the Training of Army Personnel at the Defense Race Relations Institute.' McLean, VA, Human Sciences Research, Inc., April
– Laird, M. R. (1970), memorandum 29 January. Also see Theus Committee Report, Inter-Service Task Force on Race Relations, Department of Defense, DOD Education Program in Race Relations, OSAD/M&RA, 13 July 1970

The implementation of an equal opportunity programme within an organisation

INTRODUCTION

This chapter describes a two-year organisational development programme in which a major agency of the U.S. government utilised a variety of means to improve the effectiveness of its equal employment opportunity (EEO)[1] commitment. The organisational structure and objectives of the agency concerned – the Health Services Mental Health Administration (HSMHA), an arm of the Department of Health, Education and Welfare (DHEW) as it then was – will be briefly described. Five factors will be presented and identified as significant in the development and implementation of the initiative. The latter consisted of three distinct phases and involved the participation of over three thousand employees, including both high level managers as well as supervisory staff. In all, there were forty-seven residential, in-depth, race training seminars and 'workshops'. The elements of each phase will be described in sufficient detail to enable the reader to develop appropriate replications.

Phase one consisted of a residential conference for the top management of the agency. Phase two consisted of two distinct components, namely, seminars for staff with special responsibilities *vis-à-vis* EEO and the publication and implementation of a stronger agency policy. Phase three was initiated by the issuing of a joint memorandum by the director of EEO and the personnel director. This memorandum required all managers and supervisors to participate 'in intensive training and working conferences designed to develop the racial and cultural awareness and skills necessary in applying EEO policies, goals and practices in their own immediate circumstances'. The specific goals for the training which were set out in the memorandum will be described, as will the basic elements of the 'workshops'.

Phases two and three of the exercise were assessed by a consultant who was employed for this purpose. Key elements of his report will be described especially the positive and negative extremes. In writing this chapter, an earlier paper (Shapiro, 1976) will be significantly drawn upon.

THE BACKGROUND

The HSMHA was a major component of the Public Health Service (PHS) which was in turn an arm of DHEW[2]. HSMHA existed from 1968 to 1973, when it was reorganised. During the period of this exercise, HSMHA had approximately 24,000 employees responsible for planning, supporting and administering health and mental health services directly and indirectly throughout the country. There were eleven major divisions with personnel based in ten regional offices, in various institutions (e.g. hospitals, community agencies and Indian reservations), and in two central administrative offices, in Maryland and Georgia. Its annual budget was $1 billion.

The factors which seemed to speed the implementation of the change programme were as follows:

1   A memo from the U.S. President, dated 8 August 1969, to heads of all federal departments and agencies contained two items in particular which became the central elements in the HSMHA initiative.

He said 'assuring equal employment opportunity ... is the responsibility of the organisation's head. It must have his continuing high priority attention and that of all agency executives.'

Secondly, 'Every possible step must be taken by agency heads to make sure that each manager and supervisor in the Government understands and implements the objective of EEO for all Americans. Our supervisors' performance must in every way support equality of opportunity for all employees.'

2   A training programme for EEO counsellors which was run in the spring of 1969 resulted in a recommendation that management in the HSMHA become involved more actively in EEO implementation.

3   The top officials of the National Institutes of Health (NIH) attended a two-day conference in July 1969. This conference, which was attended by the author and the official in charge of EEO in HSMHA, provided a model for subsequent agency activity.

4   The strong personal commitment to equity of the administrator of HSMHA and his willingness to innovate was an important factor.

5   The skills and effective advocacy of the black HSMHA EEO director and his willingness to utilise the technical assistance of a consultant in organisational development and race training was crucial.

THE PROGRAMME

As already indicated, this involved an estimated 4,000 agency staff, comprised a total of forty-seven residential conferences and 'workshops' and consisted of three distinct phases.

Phase one

Eighty-six staff attended a two-day conference in February 1970. Participants included: all major divisional directors, regional health directors, hospital directors, and directors of Health Areas in the Indian reservations. One third of the participants were ethnic minority persons. These latter were employees but not part of management. The planning process for this conference involved the EEO office of HSMHA, facilitators from within, as well as from NIH, and one outside consultant. A working group, chaired by the deputy administrator, but with the full support of the administrator, established the following training goals.

1 To establish that there is a problem, if indeed there is, of equal employment opportunity in HSMHA.
2 To establish a management climate in which changes in policies, roles and practices are positively encouraged.
3 To identify specific goals and allocate and assign responsibility for their implementation together with specific target dates.

The conference design included the following elements:

1 Plenary sessions in which key members of top management, both of HSMHA and DHEW, stressed the high priority which needed to be given to EEO issues.
2 A plenary presentation of the state of EEO within the organisation as shown by statistical analysis of all aspects of its work.
3 'Working groups' in which the problems of achieving EEO were analysed and specific actions identified. Crucial factors in the effectiveness of these groups were the presence of at least one-third minority participants, who could discuss the issues from personal experience of working in HSMHA, and trained group facilitators. Both were necessary to ensure that any denials of responsibility or of the need for remedial action could be tested and worked through.
4 A concluding statement from the Administrator of the agency, in which he outlined a series of action steps. This statement of intent resulted jointly from the recommendations of the conference working groups and the earlier planning sessions described above. This statement was issued as an official policy memorandum on the day after the conference, 4 February 1970. It spelled out specific steps to be taken to ensure equal employment opportunity and dates by which they were to be accomplished. These steps included the setting up of a formal EEO action structure, including permanent staff, EEO councils and a system of management accountability for achieving EEO targets and meeting deadlines. This structure was a significant factor in the success of the change programme.

Two other outcomes of the conference had a profound impact on subsequent developments. First, *HSMHA World*, a monthly magazine distributed to all employees, devoted the entire March 1970 issue to describing the conference and presenting the administrator's statement. In this way, the entire agency was given accurate information concerning a new high-priority campaign, was apprised of top management's expectations concerning these issues and the legitimisation of the programme was advanced at all levels. Second, in June 1970, a procedure was established requiring the EEO officer in a department or division to review all requests for personnel actions, with justifications being required where a minority person was not selected. This officer had to initial all personnel decisions and this gave him/her a degree of authority and negotiating power in personnel deployment for the first time in the agency's history.

Phase two

In July 1970, a series of three race-training seminars for the specialist staff (i.e. EEO and personnel employees) was held. In addition to their training goals they were required to provide specific policy and procedural recommendations for consideration by the top management of the agency. Nearly 400 employees attended these sessions, whose goals were:

1 To develop and increase the commitment of EEO and personnel staffs to an assertive EEO Programme;
2 To develop good rapport between the office of EEO and office of Personnel;
3 To increase the skills of the Deputy EEO officers and counsellors;
4 To develop cohesion within the entire HSMHA EEO structure; and
5 To identify EEO and personnel policy and procedural issues requiring follow-up action at HSMHA and programme levels.

Stated another way the goals were to reduce conflict and develop a team relationship between and within the EEO and personnel staffs; as well as to engender ownership of an assertive programme by both structures. These objectives grew out of an historical context in which both groups were frequently seen by each other as antagonists rather than collaborators in the best interests of the agency and its employees. Also, since most of the EEO staff served EEO only part time and had no clear understanding of either its advocacy role or specific duties, these seminars were seen as crucial to a serious change programme.

The seminars were staffed by a contractor, Curber Associates, who provided a team of trained group facilitators. The planning was developed by the contractor with the top staff of both offices. Interviews were held with some of the participants to develop duties. (The author was co-cordinator of seminars with the President, Curber Associates.)

The first seminar included a small group from the headquarters of each office and served as an opportunity to test the methodology and develop resource persons who were to assist in the next two sessions.

Small group and plenary sessions were used to examine the issues of racism and to apply knowledge learned to define the problem within the agency, and also to examine the implications for each participant and his/her organisation with emphasis upon delineation of their respective roles. A series of specific policy and procedural requirements were identified which were outside the role and authority of the participants. These were seen as necessary to the implementation of the EEO programme at all agency levels.

In the second seminar the black participants spontaneously left a plenary session and caucused for several hours. During this period they worked on issues of identity and barriers to the implementation of the EEO programme. The white participants were asked to examine the implications of the caucus and to identify the EEO problems from their perspective. This process was viewed as very useful to the success of the seminar and was planned for in the subsequent seminar and nearly all later training events. The success of this technique, however, depends upon processing the feelings which emerge and a careful examination of the products of the different groups to facilitate understanding of the underlying factors when differential perceptions are identified.

Policy outcomes of the seminars

In the autumn of 1970, a new Administrator, Vernon E. Wilson, M.D., was appointed to the agency. The directors of EEO and personnel prioritised the recommendations which had emerged from the seminars and wrote an action memorandum for the attention of the new chief. After detailed discussion in three top management meetings, it was revised to take account of the comments of the management group and issued as agency policy on 4 November 1970 in the following form:

Subject: Equal Employment Opportunity

To: Program Directors and Regional Health Directors

1 The attainment of equal employment opportunity within HSMHA is a matter of highest priority for me personally, and for all of us in HSMHA. Our mission is to improve the physical and mental health of all the American people. We can carry out this mission successfully only if our staff is representative of the population we seek to serve, and only when all our staff members are able to use their skills and fulfil their potential to the utmost.

2 I consider it one of my fundamental responsibilities to make the policy of equal employment opportunity a reality throughout HSMHA.

3 In February at Airlie House, the top management of HSMHA recognised

and declared the need for changes in our policies and practices. HSMHA's Equal Employment Opportunity and Personnel staffs recently met in a series of three conferences. They, too, stressed the urgency for changing our policies and practices.

4 In response to this urgency and their recommendations, I request the following:

a. A major management goal of HSMHA, as a minimum, shall be increased employment of minority employees in all programs and levels of responsibility representative of the populati. n of the geographical region or area that the activity serves and is to be achieved by January 1, 1974. Program and Regional Health Directors shall within sixty (60) days develop specific annual goals by grade and occupational series. Regional Health Directors shall develop such goals for all HSMHA staff assigned to the regional office.

(1) The Director of Personnel and EEO Officer, HSMHA, shall within thirty (30) days provide Program and Regional Health Directors with an analysis of annual turnover rates by grade and occupational series as well as an estimate of availability of minority candidates for positions throughout HSMHA. The EEO Officer, HSMHA, and Director of Personnel, in conjunction with the Assistant Administrator for Resource Development, shall review all goals and provide assistance in developing alternatives where a specific occupational series appears to present exceptional difficulties.

(2) These goals and affirmative action plans shall be incorporated into the operational goals and work plans at all organizational levels. The Assistant Administrator for Management will ensure that the Office of Administrator shall in all current and future personnel actions, provide a model for the realisation of the goals. I expect that Program Directors and Regional Health Directors will also provide models for their programs.

b. That the Director of Personnel and the EEO Officer, HSMHA, shall consider alternative mechanisms to recognize outstanding EEO activities.

c. All headquarters, regional and field program managers and supervisors shall participate in intensive training and working conferences designed to develop the racial and cultural awareness and skills necessary in applying EEO policies, goals and practices to their own immediate circumstances. All designated staff will have participated in such training programs by the end of this fiscal year. A plan for this training should be submitted to me from each Program and Regional Health Director no later than December 7, 1970. These plans may include co-operative efforts between programs whenever feasible. The EEO Officer, HSMHA, and Director of Personnel will provide guidelines and consultation in developing and implementing the plans.

d. All present HSMHA employees, with priority attention to minority employees, in dead-end and underutilized positions shall be identified and provided with a planned program of training and counselling to provide opportunities for upgrading or new careers. This activity shall be related to a systematic program of job redesign and development of new career lattices and ladders. An evaluation will be undertaken of the formal and informal barriers operating to exclude or retard minority employment. The Director of Personnel and EEO Officer, HSMHA, will assist Program Directors in implementing these activities during this fiscal year.

e. Specialised recruitment efforts will be undertaken for entry positions.

The Director, Office of Personnel, with consultation from Program and Regional Health Directors, will identify entry positions; and recruiting teams representing the Office of Personnel, EEO staff and, when appropriate, Program staff, will be provided with selection authority to recruit minority personnel for these positions.

f. HSMHA programs will give priority to lower grade employees' participation in the Parklawn Education Centre and other training opportunities. The Director, Office of Personnel, and the EEO Officer, HSMHA, will communicate this priority emphasis to the administrators of the Parklawn Education Center, ensuring that courses relevant to the career needs of lower grade employees are offered.

g. The Deputy EEO Officer, as the staff member with a major role in implementing the EEO Affirmative Action Program, should be considered as part of the management staff of each program and should report to the Director and participate in all regular program staff meetings and in any staff meeting where EEO is an important issue. Headquarters DEEO Officers shall serve full-time except in those programs where an assessment of needs made by the Program Director with the assistance of the EEO Officer, HSMHA, determines otherwise.

h. In order to obviate any actual or potential conflicts of interest, no executive or administrative officer or personnel staff member may serve as Deputy EEO Officer, Associate Deputy, or Counsellor.

i. Program Directors and Regional Health Directors and the Assistant Administrator for Information will work with program information officers to create EEO information campaigns in each HSMHA constituency. Space in existing publications will be allocated on a continuing basis.

j. Program and Regional Health Directors and administrative staff identified herein shall report to me regularly concerning the status of their Affirmative Action Program. This information will be made available to all HSMHA personnel through such publications as *HSMHA World.* The Office of EEO, HSMHA, shall prepare an appropriate reporting mechanism which will be initiated no later than December 7, 1970, to provide me with a continuing evaluation of all Affirmative Action Programs. This will involve periodic audits of programs and field installations.

Phase three

A key aspect of the recommendations in the above memorandum was the requirement 4(2).c that 'All headquarters, regional and field programme managers and supervisors shall participate in intensive training and working conferences designed to develop the racial and cultural awareness and skills necessary in applying EEO policies, goals and practices to their own immediate circumstances.' Accordingly, a second memo was distributed by the directors of EEO and personnel which contained the guidelines for implementing this requirement. It reads, as follows:

Equal Employment Opportunity Training
The primary objective of the EEO training and communication process is to aid in the implementation of the EEO organisational goals, work plans and

affirmative action programs. This will require pre-training analysis of the program or office in order to determine the best method to identify organizational and attitudinal barriers and resources related to accomplishing the specific goals of the EEO program.

The training process should be designed, within the above framework, to bring about greater understanding of and support for the EEO program among all the program or offices employees, with initial emphasis upon managerial and supervisory personnel.

The training should focus upon an organizational and individual commitment to EEO and the creation of a workable environment of mutual acceptance and trust between majority and minority group employees. An expected outcome of the process will be the formation of cohesive and productive teams and support structures which will facilitate the accomplishment of the specific tasks required to meet the EEO goals.

Experience in developing EEO training of this nature indicates the following elements are critical:

1 The participants in training conferences should come from the same and related organizational units and should include:
   (a) All managers, supervisors (unit chiefs and above) and related professional staff.
   (b) Minority employees and community contacts.
   (c) All EEO staff – deputies, counsellors and advisory council members.
   (d) Selected personnel staff.

2 The training should occur within a residential setting in a program of at least three (3) days duration.

3 Training should be focused extensively upon small group activity (effective group size is a maximum of twelve (12) persons) in 'here and now' groups concerned with identification of problem issues, and in backhome organizational team groups, which develop strategy, plans and programs, with transfer of learnings between these groups.

4 Training staff, group facilitators, should be skilled in group process, race-training and organizational development skills.

5 The small groups should each contain a minimum of three minority and other persons who are able to communicate equal employment opportunity advocacy and personal discriminatory and racist experiences.

6 Cognitive information should be presented, describing discrimination within the program and the concept of institutional racism.

Description of the conferences

More than 3,000 HSMHA employees participated in the training conferences designed according to the above guidelines. In all, nine different training contractors were used at a cost in excess of six hundred thousand dollars.

Most conferences began with a general session during which the top management official made opening remarks relating to the purpose of the conference and his expectations.

When these opening remarks contained a firm statement of commitment to EEO, a guarantee from reprisal and a request for openness and honesty, the conferences usually became productive quickly. When these elements were not strongly stated in the opening remarks, the conferences did not become productive until someone (facilitator, participant or resource person) confronted management on the issue of commitment and/or fear of reprisal.

After brief opening remarks, the top manager usually turned the conference over to the contractor and maintained a low profile until he was called on for closing remarks at the end of the conference. Some programme directors became fully involved in the conference process while others remained rather aloof.

The second step usually was that the president of the contracting firm or his dean gave an overview of the conference, shared the preconference data with the participants, and introduced the facilitators and resource people.

The third step usually was that the issues the conference was to deal with were identified. This was done in various ways, some more creative than others. The participants observed and listened to the EEO Council which sat as a panel. Sometimes they sat in a 'fishbowl'. A resource person sometimes would make an historical statement on Equal Employment Opportunity, or on occasion, the participants were broken up into predetermined small groups and given the task of surfacing the issues.

When the issues surfaced in the large group or general session, the small groups were given the task of reacting. When the issues surfaced in the small groups, the task was to reconvene and share the issues in the large group.

After the issues around equal employment opportunity had surfaced (and they were usually mostly organisational or management issues) the small groups would express on print-outs what they thought should be done about resolving them. By obtaining group consensus on what should be done about the issues and facing up to a certain degree to how they wanted the changes to be effected (planning), a kind of commitment was forced upon managers. It can be noted here that most of the demands and recommendations that came from participants were for things which had already been promised by the system and to which they were already entitled, such as upward mobility, fair treatment, etc.

Thus, the focus of the conferences usually turned on bad management practices. A cleavage between racial groups which was not often processed was the desire of whites to make the present system honest while minorities wanted to leave the system the way it was but to give them equal advantages using the 'dishonest' practices that had 'always been used for whites' – 'pre-select me', 'give me preferential treatment', etc.

Finally, by means of reporting back from the various concerns groups, participants were able to note the similarities and differences between them. Then, by the use of 'back home' work groups, they were able to develop strategies and action plans that the group agreed could be implemented on their return. These plans were also reported back to the plenary session of the conference and the Dean handed over the conference to the programme director who made a tentative assessment of the conference and usually reiterated his commitment to EEO principles in stronger language than when he had opened the proceedings.

Participant evaluation and consultant assessment

Unfortunately, there was no planned formal evaluation of the overall effort or of many of the specific training conferences. However, where pre- and post-conference questionnaires were administered, data indicated a high positive response with small percentages of negative response. For example, the response to a questionnaire administered at the three July 1970 seminars was:

Statement: I feel this conference will be (was) beneficial to me personally and/or to the agency.

	Excellent	Good	Average	Poor	Not Sure
Pre-conference response	9.6%	40.9%	33.2%	10.8%	5.3%
Post-conference response	29.5%	40.9%	14.8%	7.4%	7.1%

A review of the phase two and three programme by an outside consultant in May/June 1972 produced this assessment:

'Generally, training efforts in racial/cultural awareness were appropriate and successful. Training in the skills necessary for applying management tools to the implementation of EEO policies, goals and practices was sometimes inappropriate and unsuccessful. For example, some of the packets of conference materials for participants did not contain the HSMHA guidelines for Affirmative Action Plans. Some of the contractors and their facilitators did not possess in-depth knowledge about or experience with the official policies and procedures pertaining to EEO or the workings of the Federal bureaucracy. Racial/cultural training was what most of the facilitators were experienced in.

Planning of the conference (except in some regions) followed the guidelines established. The guidelines were good with the one exception, that they did not provide for an evaluation protocol and assessment criterion. Criteria for the selection of facilitators by contractors was appropriate but was sometimes not applied by the contractors . . .

Applications of conference guidelines were sometimes not properly monitored by the EEO Office due to lack of staff and inability to participate in preplanning.

Use of assessment instruments to attempt the measurement of change in attitude, in organizational structure and in behaviour was minimal.

Follow-up activities to most of the conferences were generally characterised by poor communications between top management officials and contractors. In most follow-up activities, although good rapport was usually established between the consulting firms and task forces and committees that emerged during the conferences, little formal training took place.

Despite the shortcomings enumerated in this report, good judgment, candour, honest opinion, apparent quantifiable minority progress and the participant feedback suggests that the EEO Conference Program must be assessed overall as appropriate, effective, and responsible in terms of facilitating institutional change, correcting injustices and implementing Federal EEO polices. The total cost in the EEO Conference Program seems small in terms of an experimental program in human relationships and social engineering which was attended by over 3,000 HSMHA employees but which touched each of HSMHA's 24,000 employees in some way.

The question remains, 'What did HSMHA get for its money?'

1 HSMHA probably has the highest level of general awareness on EEO matters to be found anywhere in the Federal Government outside the Equal Employment Opportunity Commission.

2 The HSMHA organization became convinced of the commitment of its Administrator to EEO principles and most of its Program Directors and Regional Health Directors followed or modelled his example.

3 The HSMHA EEO Office was strengthened and made highly visible.

4 There was a tremendous sharing among HSMHA employees of personnel information to which they have been entitled, but which they never before got or understood.

5 Some individual HSMHA employees had their EEO problems resolved on the spot or soon after their conferences took place, and a sense of the need for fair play surfaced.

6 Communications within HSMHA were opened up. Some administrators and supervisors remarked openly that they were "seeing" their organizations for the first time.

7 The requirement that supervisors be evaluated on their EEO performance was implemented as well as other mandates that had been neglected.

8 Steps were initiated to strengthen and validate the EEO monitoring system.

9 Organizational sub groups (formal and informal) representing blacks, whites, Chicanos and women, were established and continue to function.

10 Some EEO Councils were reorganized and strengthened.

11 Some managers recognised the implications of the concept of institutional

racism for their programs and have begun to look at EEO among grantees and in other administrative areas.

12 The Administrator's August 25 EEO memo, which developed from the conferences, set the example, model and tone for other HSMHA leaders in dealing with EEO problems.

13 Distribution and upgrading of minority employees throughout HSMHA was expedited as a result of the conferences.

14 Some issues around sexism surfaced.'

Minority employee statistics

The most significant criteria for evaluating this organisational change effort are those which relate to employment patterns of minorities within the agency. The significant question is whether the programme resulted in marked change in the minority employment profile of the agency. An analysis which was carried out in January 1972 showed the following changes in the profile over the two year period July 1969 to July 1971.

1 The number of black employees in grades five to eight increased from 1,222 to 1,977; in grades nine to eleven, they increased from 252 to 310; and in grades twelve to fifteen, they increased from 96 to 158.

2 The number of women in grades five to eight increased fom 4745 to 5373; in grades nine to eleven from 1,432 to 1,730; and in grades twelve to fifteen from 567 to 705.

3 The number of Hispanic employees increased from 36 to 51 in grades twelve to fifteen, but decreased in grades five to eight from 108 to 99, and in grades nine to eleven from 73 to 67.

4 The number of American Indians in grades five to eight increased from 501 to 625; in grades nine to eleven, they increased from 110 to 158; and in grades twelve to fifteen, they increased from 29 to 45.

5 The number of Asians[3] in grades five to eight decreased from 68 to 63; in grades nine to eleven, increased from 10 to 29; and in grades twelve to fifteen, from 22 to 38.

While these figures do not prove, in the strict scientific sense, that the intervention programme alone brought about these changes, it is quite clearly a major factor in the change. It must also be borne in mind that over the period under examination the HSMHA lost 280 employees from its general staff.

CONCLUSION

In 1976, when this author first reported on the impact of this programme, I pointed out that a reorganisation within DHEW in

1973 eliminated HSMHA as a single agency. There was evidence, at that time, that some of the former organisational components of HSMHA had maintained the momentum generated by the EEO intervention. However, other indicators showed that additional intervention would be required if the same organisational energy level were to be maintained in the new structures.

In the thoroughness of the intervention, the commitment of the top management, the extensiveness of the training programme, the effectiveness of the organisational re-structuring, and the genuineness of the management monitoring of progress subsequent to introduction of the policy statements, this effort remains, nevertheless, a model for organisational change both for equal employment and other kinds of affirmative action.

NOTES

1 *Equal Employment Opportunity.* Title VII of the Civil Rights Act of 1964 prohibits discrimination in employment because of race, colour, religion, sex or national origin. The act prohibits employers from refusing to hire, or from discharging an individual because of the person's race, colour, religion, sex or national origin. Similarly, employees or applicants may not be treated differently (e.g. receive lesser compensation) because of the individual's identity. The law also applies to employment agencies and labour unions.

The Equal Employment Opportunity Commission (EEOC) established by the Act, is empowered to administer the law by investigating complaints of discrimination, conciliating the complaints, obtaining agreements and when unable to resolve a complaint, referring it to the U.S. Attorney General for civil action in the appropriate U.S. District Court.

2 *Department of Health, Education and Welfare.* During the period described in this chapter, HSMHA was located within the U.S. Department of Health Education and Welfare. This cabinet level department was responsible for the administration of a vast array of programmes supported by the federal government, including: health services, research and training; elementary, secondary and higher education; social security; vocational rehabilitation and welfare – cash assistance and social services.

Late in 1979 and early in 1980 the department was divided into two cabinet level departments: Department of Health and Human Services and Department of Education. The programmes were divided according to functional area.

3 Asian.

The following definitions are taken from Title VI and apply only to the award of federal contracts to minority businesses.

1. 'Asian-Pacific Americans', which includes persons whose origins are from Japan, China, Taiwan, Korea, Vietnam, Laos, Cambodia, the Philippines, Samoa, Guam, the U.S. Trust Territories of the Pacific, and the Northern Marianas; and
2. 'Asian-Indian Americans', which includes persons whose origins are from India, Pakistan, and Bangladesh.

REFERENCE

– Shapiro, R. M. (1976), 'Implementation of an EEO program Through Race Training Organisational Development Interventions', *Journal of Inter-Group Relations,* 5(2): 30–43

Race training in the United States: an overview

In addition to having better than average group process and intervention skills, one who would undertake to engage in race training should become thoroughly familiar with the background and history of the racial situation being addressed, and the issues, cultural practices and mores of the various groups at odds with one another.

Race training in the United States occurred under different circumstances during four major periods in the evolution of American democracy as we know it today.

During the colonial period the attitudes, feelings and behaviours of the English colonists towards the American Indians were affected and formed in their daily dealings by the almost daily violations of their own conceptions of English Common Law and Christian morality. Public feelings of racial superiority on the part of the whites were constantly formed and reinforced by strings of military and commercial successes in driving the Indians from the land, and justified by labelling and subordinating them as unintelligent heathens and savages while ignoring the unique qualities of Indian cultures. Through thousands of daily acts of superiority that excluded, subordinated and denigrated the Indians, the white public was trained, with few exceptions, to feel physically and morally superior to the Indians. This was true even though the Indian sealed his own fate by almost completely ignoring the superiority of English arms and resisting adaptations to the English cultures. In the event, generations of English colonists were trained to exclude and subordinate the American Indians in schools, churches, town meetings, legislative assemblies, commercial transactions, newspaper stories and fireside conversations.

As slavery took hold in the colonies, white attitudes, feelings and practices of superiority encompassed the African blacks who could be readily labelled and judged inferior by the colour of their skin and their condition of servitude. Thus, generations of white colonists grew up indoctrinated with feelings of superiority on the basis of race. Proof of their superiority was readily apparent in the quality of their lives and opportunities as compared with the lives and opportunities of Indians and blacks. After escaping the tyrannies of Old Europe, the colonists imposed new tyrannies on peoples materially weaker than themselves.

But also after escaping the tyrannies of Europe, the colonists were seeking a fairer society than they had experienced in Europe. Their search found expression in the Declaration of Independence which proclaimed that all men were created equal and had unalienable rights to life, liberty and the pursuit of happiness. The Declaration gave expression to and initiated the dream of an American democracy. Public attitudes on racial superiority were challenged by race and religious training which insisted that exclusion and subordination of peoples on the basis of colour did not fit in with Christianity or the dream of a democratic society. Thus began an intensification of race training that prepared whites to accept Indians and blacks as equals while encouraging Indians and blacks to enter the mainstream Anglo-Saxon culture. This training was carried out in a relatively small number of churches, newspapers, periodicals, lectures, demonstrations and debates among religious and abolitionist groups, and individuals. Most Americans chose to ignore the implications for a democratic society, of exclusion and subordination based on race, and continued to develop three societies: one red, one black, and one white and in power.

With the emancipation of the blacks during and after the Civil War, the federal government undertood through the Freedmen's Bureau and other measures such as voter protection, to train blacks for entry into mainstream U.S.A. At the same time, the same government opened up the West to settlement by whites. The government's efforts on behalf of blacks was strongly resisted, however, and was short lived. By 1890, the Indians were resettled on reservations and blacks were on the verge of being eliminated from participation in the mainstream of American life. By 1910, they were a totally segregated society. Nevertheless, the seeds of race training to have blacks accepted as first class citizens had been sown. Indians were, for the most part, out of public sight and out of the public's mind. The Supreme Court, in the *Plessey v. Ferguson* decision of 1897, legalised first class citizenship for whites and second class citizenship for blacks. Race training institutionalised intimidation of blacks, mainly through lynchings, as the law of the land, and the separateness of the races grew deeper.

From 1919 to 1968, American society was rent by racial strife which imperilled the democratic principles upon which America was founded, and threatened the Constitution itself. Educated and trained by public debate, television coverage of racial injustice and increased awareness of the dichotomy between what America promised and what it practiced with regard to the unalienable rights and equality of man, large numbers of whites joined blacks in a grass roots effort to secure first class citizenship for all citizens of the United States. The effort was spearheaded by the Supreme Court decision in *Brown v. Board of Education* (1954) which overturned *Plessey* by declaring segregated schools unconstitutional. For the first time since 1866, the federal government had entered race training with the objective of teaching whites to accept blacks as equals. It was ten years later that the Congress of the United States passed the Civil Rights Act of 1964, and training of whites to accept blacks, and other oppressed groups including white women, as equals began in earnest.

The Civil Rights Act of 1964 did the following:

1 Prohibited exclusion on the basis of race, colour, religion or national origin from hotels, restaurants, gasoline stations and places of amusement.

2 Prohibited exclusion and subordination in the workplace on the basis of race, colour, religion, sex and national origin by employers, unions and employment agencies.

3 Provided for the protection of minority group members in using public facilities, attending public schools, registering to vote, and enjoying participation in and the benefits of programmes receiving federal financial assistance.

Enactment of this law, and others soon to follow, opened up a floodgate of federal dollars to support race training. Psychologists, psychiatrists, training officers, teachers, ministers and lay people rushed to develop or join developing training programmes that addressed federal requirements of non-discrimination and equal treatment for all United States citizens.

The tactics and activities of the church and civil rights leaders and student protesters were observed, analysed, classified and reduced to principles of group dynamics that could fit into any situation. Dozens of texts, handbooks, workbooks and exercise books were published advocating use of the principles of group dynamics in race, human relations, human interaction, group, interpersonal, organisational development, sensitivity, awareness and other kinds of training. And community participation in certain public programmes was even required by laws.

Training programmes developed by Jewish, Catholic and Protestant religious and lay groups were organised in response to the Kerner Commission Report of 1968 describing America as two separate societies, one white and one black. This is an oversimplification, but soon there were thousands of individual trainers, who operated outside of any formal organisational network, to supplement the work of civil rights groups and religious organisations.

The race training objectives of the church-related groups were normally to make whites aware of the plight of blacks in the United States; to sensitise them to their own racism; and to change their attitudes, feelings and behaviour towards blacks. Confrontation in sensitivity training was encouraged. It was viewed as a constructive tool for 'telling it like it is and getting everything on the table, clearing the air'. After the air was cleared, trainers facilitated change by assisting participants in bringing objectivity, and thus closure, to the issues raised.

Although a few federal agencies experimented with awareness and sensitivity training, it was not long before they focused their objectives on awareness of the requirements of law (Titles under the Civil Rights Act of 1964, and other later laws). Even with this modification of training objectives, a tremendous resistance to anti-racism training developed among whites. Race training in terms of changing attitudes and feeling gave way to changing behaviour only. The laws required it.

By 1970, it was generally recognised among practitioners of training whites to accept minorities as equals that there were six steps to be followed in developing and presenting training programmes that contained elements of race:

1 Diagnosis or needs assessment

Diagnosis was an element of organisational development activity that was incorporated into the preparatory stage of race training. What it meant essentially was that a consultant would gather data and information on the racial and sex composition of the workforce to be trained, and a statistical profile to be used in making the trainees aware of the federal government's requirement for proportional representation in the workforce of an organisation, and its legal responsibilities in terms of achieving proportional race and sex representation.

Attitudinal information was usually gained by administering an attitudinal survey or through seeking out and gaining opinions from informally identified 'leaders' of subgroups that were dubbed pro/con integrationists, radical/conservative activists, racists/anti-racists, etc.

The acts of gathering data and information generally had an important secondary effect on the organisation and its population. They served to inform the organisation of impending changes and prevent the violent resistance to change that had occurred in the past.

2 Planning

Participation in planning by members of a community, as a requirement of regulations in many federally funded programmes, was an adaptation of the methods of participation used so successfully by religious and community groups, civil rights organisations and student activists, during the fifties and early sixties. Social scientists at that time were intrigued and somewhat awed by the dedication, commitment and successes of seemingly unorganised groups of amateurs who, through a loosely organised process, became committed to actions led by leaders who emerged from the pack, so to speak. So, care was taken to include members of all available races and both sexes on the planning, evaluation and other committees that participated in race training activities, whether they were knowledgeable about training or not. Full participation was not only encouraged, it was required. And despite the lack of expertise available in most cases, good things happened: minorities and white women, unsophisticated in the language and concepts of psychology and professional training, demonstrated their ability to cut through the technical details, and demand and get practical training experiences with practical results. It must be remembered, however, that the post World War II period was one in which the concept of democratic participation pervaded every facet of American life: government, business, unions, voting, even the military. People in all kinds of institutions were developing a sense of power through participation.

3 Course development

Several basic race training models were developed along experiential lines during the late sixties and early seventies. These were usually developed by experts with input from one or more of the various interracial committees, councils or special concerns groups: management, white employees, black employees, Hispanic employees, etc. Consideration of the input was usually required by the contract, and members of the planning committees sometimes exercised de facto veto powers over the advice of the experts by the sheer weight of their emotions, but more often because of the practical questions they raised and their determination to be heard and understood. It was a trying time, but a time of great expectations, great stress, and great learning on all sides. Within all the models, confrontation and problem solving exercises were standard. All models relied heavily on the black experience for their core, and case studies and role plays were usually designed to show black characters in the best possible light. This meant, of course, that whites were shown in a less positive light.

By the time the neophytes and professionals had agreed upon race training objectives, modules, strategies and tactics, the goals of the training were often mixed. The goals, which were always stated in the contract, were usually modified to meet criteria for other aspects of the racial situation which had little to do directly with race relations. For example, the goal of most training contracts, stated in different ways, was to assist managment in implementing an Equal Employment Opportunity Program, or a Voting Rights Program, or a Title VI Program requiring non-discrimination in programmes receiving federal financial assistance; or a housing or school desegregation programme requiring non-discrimination in housing and proportional representation. The non-discrimination requirement always imposed on the planners and curriculum developers a different subject matter and approach than was necessary to provide meaningful experiences in how different races could grow together. Nevertheless, race was always a dominant, if not the main concern.

Another example was the requirement, established by the Federal Civil Service, that a person, applying for positions in the new civil rights occupational series, and responsible for implementing civil rights regulations, be familiar with the Civil Rights Movement in the United States. This requirement ensured that some civil rights history be fitted into the curriculum. Because high level white managers had little or no experience supervising Negroes, instruction on how to supervise minorities became a part of the curriculum in a few instances. So, race training as such was diversified from its very beginning by other important considerations.

When the Nixon Administration began to court the Hispanic vote in 1972, Hispanic concerns and influences became a large part of the training curriculum. When sexual harassment became a major issue in 1981, sexual harassment was added to the curriculum; so that today, race training has been edged out of the civil rights training experience at the federal level, but state, county and city governments are beginning to require the kinds of race training that the federal government used extensively from about 1968 to 1980. Since 1980, the focus of civil rights training in the federal government has been on civil rights management of age, handicap and sexual harassment issues: how to recognise and prevent civil rights problems from developing, how to respond to civil rights complaints, how to prevent sexual harassment.

4 Presentation

No element of race training caused more problems, or created more resistance, than that of presenting the subject matter in the manner prescribed and using the tactics agreed upon in the planning. It was in the presentation phase that advocacy first became a major issue. Some trainers became emotionally involved in the issues and lost their objectivity. Some ignored the agreed upon curriculum and lectured from their hearts, often ignoring or misstating facts.

One of the rules of race training required that the training team be interracial and that the team demonstrate through its composition and behaviour, interracial cooperation. As a result, issues of competence arose among team members that led to charges of racism and sexism among the trainers and consultants themselves. Such bickering was usually kept hidden from participants, however.

Another rule required that the leader of a group should emerge as part of the dynamics of the group rather than be appointed by management. One of the results was that participants were some-times manipulated into group roles that they were unprepared to perform competently. Another was that trainers had to become adept at facilitating movement in the groups without appearing to be manipulative.

Another rule required that all discussion should be open and honest, but some consultants were unprepared to intervene properly when highly emotional personal situations arose among participants, and they took sides; they were enticed into personal confrontation, thus destroying their credibility as objective outsiders.

There was sometimes a great deal of manipulation of white guilt on white trainers and participants by black trainers, and accusations of unfairness and subjectivity by participants against white and black trainers.

Despite these deviations from accepted training principles, good things happened, and competent trainers were able to turn even negative experiences, such as those described above, into positive learning experiences. However, the deviations from accepted training principles contained in recognised and highly regarded training manuals, and the embarrassment they caused, were used to justify the slackening off in race training and the demands for less sensitivity training. Whites were tired of being confronted with their wrongs.

5 Evaluation

There have been diverse methods for evaluating race training in the United States since 1964. Perhaps, the most important method was to measure changes in the race and sex composition of a workforce or housing area or school district after training. However, this was found not a reliable indicator of the effectiveness of the training because the establishment of programme goals by heads of agencies, under pressures from federal executives and the threat of court actions, definitely had greater impact in effecting change than training did. It was soon realised by practitioners that one of the key indicators of effective training was whether the participants found the trainers credible – were they believable? Did they substantiate their remarks? Did they display good interpersonal and intervention skills? Or were they threatening and abusive? The accepted criterion for effective evaluation became, 'he was fair, or she helped us see both sides of the issues'.

By the late seventies, most attempts at sophisticated evaluation devices were abandoned, and client agencies were using simple Likert Scales to measure, basically, attitudes of the participants towards the training and trainers. The key issue in evaluation was balance – as in the question: Did the trainers give a balanced presentation? Whether or not it was true, the general impression throughout the federal agencies was that training content reflected the black experience too heavily, and the white experience inaccurately.

6 Feedback and follow-up

In the late sixties and early seventies, practitioners of race training were expected to assist heads of agencies in developing strategies to determine how civil rights training programmes were implemented, whether race relations were better or worse as a result of the training, what follow-up activities should occur as a result of the training, how feedback was to be obtained and used, and even in planning recruitment efforts.

By the late seventies, there were few, if any, requirements for follow-up or feedback. The race training programmes were institutionalised in many cases. Many of the more effective consultants on race and civil rights had been hired on a permanent basis by their clients, or had gone on to other endeavours. A huge backlash against race training had developed, and the national interest had turned from race to sex, age and handicap as the primary issues in civil rights. A few blacks had begun to speak out against school busing, affirmative action and welfare.

With the election of Ronald Reagan as President in 1980, the mood of the country shifted dramatically away from race training and civil rights. The overriding concerns in the country were unemployment among white blue-collar workers and high interest rates; by 1985, the budget deficit was the number one concern of the nation. Requests for race training were down, and most of those were from state and local governments. The same methodologies, techniques and strategies that were used to develop and implement race training in federal programmes were being sought for use again, at state and local levels. The focus at these levels was still on employment, sexual harassment awareness and prevention, and age, and anti-affirmative action training had begun to take hold.

Most, if not all, of the race training done in the United States from 1969 to 1984 shared the following characteristics: 1. it was required and paid for under one of the numerous Civil Rights and Equal Opportunity Acts passed since 1964; 2. it was usually labelled human relations, human interaction, cross cultural, group relations, inter or intra personal relations, or more often, equal employment opportunity training; 3. the objectives of the training were always stated as something other than race training; and 4. the goal of helping whites to accept members of other races as equals was seldom stated. Rather, the goals and objectives were usually stated as, to 'assure harmony in the workplace' or 'understand equal employment opportunity policies and principles' or learn or become aware of 'the background and history of equal employment opportunity'.

The point was that, historically, resistance to the integration of American blacks, other minority groups and white women into the mainstream of American life had been so massive that a backdoor approach to integration had to be developed, and its main vehicles, other than law and advertising, were the kinds of training described above. Usually, the intent of the training, whether stated or not, was to encourage white males to share power with women and other minorities in the institutions that define mainstream America.

Basically, race training in the United States dealt with the requirements of law and affirmative action.[1] The cognitive knowledge, strategies and interpersonal skills necessary to maintain harmony and productivity in the workplace and community were the substantive core of race training. Nevertheless, resistance to 'race training' manifested itself in resistance to affirmative action, and was supported by the policies of the Reagan administration.

There were basically two reasons for the resistance to race training: principles of equal treatment, and advancement on the basis of ability, knowledge and skills, under fair and open competition, heralded the beginning of the end of our white-male-dominated society; and the added competition for power, jobs, education and housing (together with our uncertain economic situation) threatened the self interests of the white male middle class in terms of job security, housing, retirement benefits and safety. Or so it seemed to them. Other reasons for resistance to race training, such as racism, maintaining psychological crutches, lack of funds, and just plain old racism were exaggerated in most of the country. Suffice it to say that competition among individuals in the United States for jobs, goods and services is exceptionally keen regardless of race, and the added competition of millions of white women and minorities, coupled with the present realignments in our industrial/technological base created unusual frustrations and fears and competition.

In this situation, resistance to race training hardened even more, and approaches were required that would make the training more palatable to the clients who were always white, and the participants, who were mostly white.

Today, partly as a result of twenty years of training whites to accept minorities as equals, anti-racism principles have been embedded in the American mind through law and hundreds of religious sermons, training sessions, court decisions, news articles, movie and television dramas, commercial ads, inter-racial commissions, neighbourhood councils, and civil rights studies. Race relations in the United States are now quiescent in most cities and communities. There has been evidence of some heightening of racial and anti-Semitic tension in local political jurisdictions due largely to the tightening economic situation which has caused layoffs from work, evictions from homes and apartments, and the need for retraining of older employees.

Users of race training in the employment area are now local fire, police, recreation and housing departments, which are less sophisticated and pay less money for services than do federal and state agencies. Federal and state governments are still users of race training in the services and benefits areas and still provide contracted employment for many of the older trainers who started out in 1964.

Lawyers have entered the civil rights arena in record numbers, and now conduct a great deal of the training for the large corporations, much of it devoted to how to avoid discrimination complaints. An emerging issue in race training involves the degree to which training by lawyers can remain results-oriented and objective.

In today's racial climate, the focus of civil rights training has turned from race to sex (particularly sexual harassment which is illegal in the workplace), age, handicap and the participation and benefits requirements of Title VI of the Civil Rights Act of 1964, as amended. The training models developed to combat racism have been converted to deal with issues of sexism and the denial of benefits and services. Title VI of the Civil Rights Act of 1964 requires that the benefits and services of programmes receiving federal financial assistance be equitably distributed among programme recipients without regard for race. Presented below is a set of objectives developed for race training which was widely used by the author in all areas of civil rights under contracts with various federal and state agencies:

Objective 1: Provide information on the history of racism in the United States (employment, housing, benefits, services, voting, public accommodations, etc.).

Objective 2: Describe the basic categories of racial acts that are illegal or undesirable, and define the policies and programmes of the government that address the illegal or undesirable activities.

Objective 3: Describe and clarify the concepts of individual, institutional and structural discrimination based on race, that spawn the illegal and undesirable activities.

Objective 4: Define the functions and responsibilities of the participants in the training with regard to each illegal or undesirable racial activity identified.

Objective 5: Identify, describe and clarify the official procedures to be followed in implementing federal and state policies related to race discrimination.

Objective 6: Illustrate and provide experience in the results of illegal and undesirable racial activities through case studies, role plays and feedback.

Objective 1, providing historical information on racism, for example, is met by using empirical, factual materials from academically impeccable sources rather than personal and anecdotal materials that are used in sensitivity training and tend to arouse emotions or go against government policy. The trainer should be familiar enough with the subject matter to be able to define the legal and social concepts used, and to cite authoritative sources when data and information are discussed that go against government policies. He/she should be able to cite other sources, equally authoritative, with opposing points of view, and let participants decide issues among themselves. An example of this situation would be to cite the findings on race of Sir Cyril Burt, W. B. Shockley and A. R. Jensen, as opposed to the findings of the National Science Academy and such scholars as Louis H. Pollack or Jerry Hirsch who have published extensively on the other side of the matter.

A strong trainer might even take an advocacy position, and supplement the historical information with data from statistical charts of the organisation being trained, confirm the results of the activities being described, and challenge the participants to share their experiences with racism or other kinds of discrimination. But it is enough to set the record right substantively with regard to the historical information leading to the problems addressed in the training.

Objective 2, describing the basic categories of activities in, for example, race relations as opposed to political participation, was met by using newspaper clippings, both pro and con, from respected newspapers, government issuances on applicable policies, and feedback from participants about their experiences and feelings with regard to the matters being addressed. Caution is needed in the latter activity, as only a strong trainer will be able to process the negative experiences and feelings of some participants in a way that provides new insights and perspectives to persons who have not shared such experiences. The subject matter should be organised and presented in categories for purposes of definition and clarity to facilitate quicker and easier understanding. For example, illustrations of personal/institutional, intentional/unintentional and structural as opposed to mindless racism, and its results in terms of not fitting in with American ideals of democracy, fair play and the law, are used rather than introducing participants to a litany of black achievements or a run through of black history.

Objective 3, describing and clarifying the concepts of individual, institutional and structural discrimination based on race, is best done by participants themselves in small heterogeneous groups. The trainer should not attempt to manipulate the composition of the groups, but should state up front why he/she is designing the make-up of the groups, and for what purpose. For example, 'We should like for each group of eight people to have at least one black and one woman in it so that we get at least some idea of what it's like to be black or female in today's world. The purpose of the group is to list on newsprint the experiences they've had, or know about, that violate the policies we've been discussing.'

The groups are given a specific task and amount of time to complete the task, rather than permitting them to vie for leadership and power. The lists are then displayed, reviewed and discussed by the large group in general session. The trainer then facilitates the discussion while making appropriate connections between the activities listed, and the requirements of policy and law; and clarifies misunderstanding by focusing on accepted definitions of terms rather than group process. In this situation, the trainer has become more didactic than facilitative, and must have absolute mastery of his/her subject matter.

Objective 4, define the functions and responsibilities of the participants with regard to illegal or undesirable racial activity, was met by identifying the general and specific responsibilities of the occupational groups being trained (for example, police chief, assistant chiefs, precinct captains, lieutenants, sergeants and patrolmen) and developing role plays and case studies that showed the positive effects at each level of responsibility when law and policy were followed, and the negative effects when they were not followed. It was discovered early on that when simulations of racist activities consistently showed whites as racists, white participants tuned out and trainers were left talking to themselves. Whites, like any other group, needed a positive view of themselves rather than the constant reminders of their culpability in racism that characterised the training of the late sixties and early seventies.

Objective 5, identifying and describing official procedures and policies, was met by conducting reading exercises in triads in which the roles of reader, listener and observer were rotated among the participants as they read aloud from official policy statements and regulations. After a short stint of reading, the reader and listener would discuss the meaning and intent of the literature read; and the observer would give feedback on the attitudes and feelings of the reader and listener toward the literature as it was expressed in non-verbal communications. It was found that this type of exercise led invariably to consensus understanding, definition and group understanding and acceptance of policies that were threatening to the participants as individuals. More importantly, by arranging groups of peers (two managers, middle managers, supervisors, employees) and having each group report-out in a general assembly, the trainer placed responsibility for getting the message across upon top management and ensured that the message would be heard and repeated down through the lower echelons of the organisation.

Objective 6, illustrating and providing experience in undesirable race relations, was met through simulations of localised on-the-job or in-the-school racial experiences which, though unlawful or undesirable, could be resolved through application of the principles and procedures provided during the training. For example, two or more groups of five or six participants would be given a simulation of a racial incident and asked to determine the best way of alleviating it using Kurt Lewin's[2] force field analysis theory. By brainstorming how and by whom the situation should be handled, and examining the consequences of each recommended action in dealing with the simulation, the groups arrived at consensus decisions that were in line with stated policy and the law.

Training whites to accept other races as equals under law in the United States was a gigantic undertaking shared in by thousands upon thousands of individuals, and hundreds of groups, organisations and lawmakers. There was no way of knowing, and there is now no need to know, which training methodology was most effective in bringing the United States closer to its democratic ideals of due process, equal treatment and unalienable rights. However, it was certainly recognized that the essential element in race relations was behaviour, and behaviours were changed by law and public policy. Thus, training that combined knowledge of public policy and law with the technical skills and abilities of trainers to recognise, control and facilitate change on the basis of respect for individuals was critical. Today, in a national climate different from the turbulent sixties, a successful trainer must be better prepared to deal with cognitive substance than with emotion. He/she must master the available knowledge on all aspects of race relations: practical and theoretical knowledge of race in economics, philosophy, housing, employment, crime, sports, etc. He/she must be sensitive and understanding of the diverse interests of participants both as individuals and as members of ethnic or religious groups. He/she must be as objective and honest in all relationships with clients and trainees as is humanly possible. And he/she must have extraordinary intervention skills and presence of mind. In short, he/she must come prepared to deal with the expected and unexpected.

Remarkable progress in race relations has been achieved in the United States since 1964; and without question, race training played a major role in it. But whether race training played a larger role than the churches and synagogues, television, law, or law enforcement is not known. Nor need it be. It is sufficient to know that each methodology was essential to the progress made in achieving the American Dream.

NOTES

1 Voluntary or court ordered plans to increase the representation of minorities and/or women in a particular institutional setting.

2 A method of analysis that examined all the forces that maintained a situation in status quo whether positive or negative, and developed a plan of action to use each force, whether helping or hindering, to change the situation rather than try to resolve it.

REFERENCES

– Eysenck, H. J. (1978), 'Racism Refuted'. *Nature*
– Hirsch, Jerry (1981), 'To Unfrock the Charlatans.' *Sage Race Relations Abstract*, 6, (21) May
– Kamin, Leon J. (1980), 'Jensen's Last Stand. A Review of Arthur Jensen Bias in Mental Testing.' *Psychology Today*, February 1980
– Lewin, Kurt (1978), *Resolving Social Conflicts*, Internaional Scholarly Book Service, Beaverton, Or
– Myrdal, Gunnar (1944), *The American Dilemma: The Negro Problem and Modern Democracy*, Vol. 1, Pantheon Books, New York, NY
– U.S. Commission on Civil Rights (1970), 'Racism in America and How to Combat It.' Clearinghouse Publication, Urban Series No. 1, January
– Wade, Nicholas (1982), 'The Shadow Over Race and I.Q.', The Editorial Notebook, *New York Times*, September 10.

ANGELA M. RODRIGUEZ 9

Institutional racism in the organisational setting: an action-research approach

INTRODUCTION

This chapter has as its focus the retrospective review and analysis of an intervention approach that was implemented to promote the reduction of institutional racism in an organisational setting. The effort in question was initiated in 1980, as part of a three-year federally funded project. Its major goal was to increase the understanding of and to actually reduce the barriers to full participation by black and Hispanic employees in their work setting.

The project was conducted at a major hospital in Dade County, Florida, that is described in a subsequent section of this chapter. Highlighted in this chapter are: 1. the definition of institutional racism which provided the conceptual framework for the project; 2. a description of the intervention approach and measures that were implemented to execute the project's major goal and 3. an analysis of the project's findings and intervention outcomes.

DEFINITION OF INSTITUTIONAL RACISM

Before a particular intervention approach is applied to a problem it is important to establish its conceptual definition. The literature on race relations and racism is rich with documentation of different theoretical and conceptual approaches to the study of this subject. These different approaches, of course, have dictated contrasting definitions of racism. The intervention design selected for execution of the project described in this chapter was based on one of the three socio-structural theoretical approaches known as the *normal institutional practices approach*.

This increasingly popular approach to the analysis of race relations and racism proposes that society now operates in ways that feed upon the historic injustice done to minority groups so as to reinforce and maintain their lower status and lesser rewards. Proponents of this approach argue that this is so embracing an operating principle that it no longer requires conscious or even overtly racist acts to sustain it.

Thus racism is explained in terms of the normal operations of our institutions that are laid on top of patterns of historic injustice and exploitation. In his classic treatise on the subject, Myrdal (1962) describes this as the vicious cycle of discrimination and injustice. According to Myrdal the cycle can be made negative by breaking it anywhere; segregated and unequal schooling may lead to poor job preparation, thus poor jobs and on goes the cycle. Once the negative cycle is established, social policies of apparently equal treatment or meritorious reward will continue to result in inequity.

Prior to initiating this project it was believed that while this particular hospital enjoyed a long history of employing minorities particularly blacks, the majority of them were systematically relegated and locked into conducting the most menial and underpaid of the hospital's occupations, i.e., housekeeping, maintenance, laundry and food services. This of course was occurring in spite of the fact that the hospital had developed an affirmative action policy and procedures statement that guided the operations of its affirmative action office. Hence from the project's inception, it was possible to corroborate the theoretical precepts of other proponents of the normal institutional practices approach who see evidence of racism in outcomes, as well as in processes or mechanisms and for whom the direct commitment to altering outcome is more important than ensuring non-discriminatory mechanisms that may not alter patterns set by historical injustice (Coleman, 1968; Gilbert and Eaton, 1970).

Some scholars identify the roots of normal institutional practices in our cultural values as well as in economic stratification systems. Mercer (1971), for example, provides documentation of the flow of unjust institutional practices based on culturally biased standards of behaviour and educational performance. The consequences of this suggest that public knowledge and acceptance of images and reports of minority inferiority may set into place new institutional cycles (Daniels and Kitano, 1970).

Another way in which these mechanisms of institutional practice can be established is through the dynamics of what is known as the self-fulfilling prophecy (Rosenthal and Jacobsen, 1968). In the case of the hospital this was perhaps best illustrated by the fact that while it had an organisational unit responsible for overall career development and training of hospital staff, the percentage of minority employees who participated in its programmes and activities was very small. Unfortunately, it was precisely this group of hospital employees who needed these personnel services most in order to be able to move out of their 'dead-end', 'bottom of the rung' job categories and positions.

When questionned as to why they felt this was occurring, supervisors and managers frequently attributed the reasons solely to lack of career aspirations, motivation and capability on the part of these individuals. These same black and Hispanic employees, on the other hand, expressed a desire and willingness to seek additional training and education in order to be able to progress within the hospital structure. However, they also indicated that the organisation did not really support their efforts in this regard, thus they refrained from undertaking them. These perceptions were later validated by the identification of actual barriers which, when combined with the negative expectations of management, were found to inhibit black and Hispanic employees from the process of self-improvement.

As first stated by Chesler (1976), the primary maintenance of racist practices has three loci: first, in the majority individuals' attitudes and expectations; second, in the interactional, cultural or economic setting that permits transmission and legitimation of these expectations in an authority relationship; and third, in the minority group's adoption of those expectations as conditioners or generators of their own performance.

More specifically the normal institutional practices definition labels as institutionally racist those acts or institutional procedures that help create or perpetuate sets of advantages or privileges for the majority group and exclusions or deprivations for minority groups. Many authors (Carmichael and Hamilton, 1967; Knowles and Prewitt, 1969; Chesler, 1976; and Brown, White and Jordan, 1979) postulate that this usually requires an ideology of explicit or implicit superiority or advantage of one racial group over another, plus the institutional power to implement that ideology in social operations.

Knowles and Prewitt (1969), stress the importance of studying institutions and organisations, as well as their functions in society, as a pre-requisite to any serious and comprehensive understanding of institutional racism. Institutions are fairly stable social agreements and practices through which collective actions are taken (Knowles and Prewitt, 1969; Terry, 1970). Medical institutions, for instance, marshal talents and resources of society so that health care can be provided. Medical institutions include hospitals, research labs, and clinics, as well as organisations of medical people such as doctors and nurses. The health of all of us is affected by general medical policies and by established practices and ethics.

Institutions have great power to reward and penalise. Institutions reward by providing career opportunities for some people and fore-closing them for others. They reward as well by the way social goods and services are distributed; by deciding who receives training and skills, medical care, formal education, political influence, moral support and self-respect, productive employment, fair treatment by the law, decent housing, self-confidence, and the promise of a secure future for self and children (Terry, 1970).

The normal institutional practices approach permits us to assess organisational or institutional practices and outcomes without necessarily connecting to the minds and hearts of individual majority group members. It is, therefore, fundamentally social and institutional in nature and not psychological.

INTERVENTION APPROACH

The project's major intevention approach consisted of an action oriented research study, which was divided into three major phases of activity. These consisted of: 1. an assessment and joining phase in which the staff became familiar with the hospital and its functioning, particularly in reference to its treatment of minority employees and during which project staff established close working relationships with hospital personnel; 2. a diagnostic/restructuring phase in which project staff, together with top hospital administrative personnel, developed, planned and began the implementation of structural recommendations that would reduce the organisation's barriers to minorities, improve organisational efficiency, and increase the organisation's sensitivity to employees in general, as well as minorities in particular; and 3. a post assessment and withdrawal phase in which project staff evaluated their efforts at the hospital, and withdrew in a manner designed to allow that organisation to continue and refine the changes that had already begun.

As noted earlier, the distribution of power and rewards across different ethnic racial groups is one of the major factors or variables that defines the degree and extent to which institutional racism exists in an organisation. It is for this reason that the distribution of power and rewards across ethnic/racial groups was selected as the central focus of the study at the hospital.

A total of six indicators or dimensions of the distribution of power and rewards consisting of black and Hispanic employee representation; compensation; recruitment and selection; training, career development and promotion; affirmative action policies and procedures; and inter-ethnic friction, were identified in the study. As part of the project's assessment phase, staff developed a comprehensive set of quantitative and qualitative measures to obtain specific data regarding each of these indicators or dimensions.

However, before proceeding to describe these measures in greater detail it is important to highlight some of the major lessons learned from this initial phase of the project's activity. Early in the project's inception, it was determined that while there is an adequate body of literature from which to extract a conceptual definition and theoretical framework for an organisational study of institutional racism, there are few if any examples of actual indicators and/or measures that could be readily applied in this case. Such measures were identified and defined through a series of preliminary hospital observations, initial interviews with hospital personnel and elaborate conceptual discussions on the topic with experts in this area.

The need to define and establish these indicators through a process of observations and interviews with hospital personnel, advantageously provided a non-threatening context in which to successfully inform, engage and obtain support of the project's overall purpose and goal. More importantly, this process facilitated the emergence and formulation of indicators that were genuinely relevant and applicable to this particular organisation and study.

MEASURES AND INSTRUMENTS

Quantitative data for the project was collected from a variety of sources including: 1. hospital affirmative action reports, 2. minutes of the hospital's policy-making meetings (i.e., the governing board personnel committee). 3. a discrimination questionnaire developed by project staff, and 4. an employee satisfaction questionnaire. In addition to this quantifiable data, more qualitative, but no less important information was gathered from: 1. hospital policy and procedural manuals, formal interviews with top level administrators, and personnel throughout the organisation; and 2. field observations.

The administration of these different procedures provided 1. an opportunity to understand the hospital in depth; 2. an empirical basis for recommendations; 3. feedback to monitor progress on an ongoing basis; 4. a general evaluation of project effectiveness and 5. a basis for generalising toward increased conceptual understanding of institutional racism and race relations in the work setting.

Personnel information such as current position, tenure, turnover, pay, vacation and sick time were collected from computerised hospital records and analysed by the eight Equal Employment Opportunity Commission job codes (administrative/official, professional, technical, protective services, para-professional, office clerical, skilled crafts, and service/maintenance) and by the three major ethnic/racial groups represented at the organisation (white Anglo, black, and Hispanic). These data were gathered as a baseline and assessment tool for the year prior to the study and then for post-assessment purposes for the year after the project recommendations were approved by the hospital's administration, (Szapocznik, Foote, Rodriguez, and Blaney, 1984).

Quite different information was gathered from a pair of questionnaires, the Job Description Index (Smith, Kendall and Hulin, 1969), and the Discrimination Questionnaire (Rodriguez, 1981), the latter developed for use in this study. The Job Description Index (JDI) is a standard job satisfaction questionnaire consisting of seventy-two items answered yes, no, or not sure. These items are organised into five subscales in addition to a total score. Smith, Kendall and Hulin (1969) in their very complete documentation of the JDI report that its internal consistency averages .79. The subscales of the JDI were related to the characteristics of compensation; training, career development and promotion; and inter-ethnic friction. The Discrimination Questionnaire (DQ) assesses employee perceptions of discrimination. It consists of thirty-seven items which are answered on a five point agreement scale. These items were developed on the basis of focal group meetings and selected through factor analytic techniques. Scoring yields two scales, Affirmative Action Ineffectiveness and Power and Promotional Discrimination, in addition to a total score. The alpha reliability for the total score, Power and Promotional Discrimination and Affirmative Action Ineffectiveness scale were .90, .86 and .86 respectively while two month test-retest correlations were .84, .75 and .85 respectively (see Rodriguez, 1981, for details of the Discrimination Questionnaire's development and validation). The Discrimination Questionnaire also includes demographic and job description items.

A final source of data was the minutes of the hospital's policy-making meetings. The minutes of the hospital's governing board meetings were analysed for content related to affirmative action and minority issues. For the assessment year, content analysis was conducted on all the minutes of all meetings of the full governing board and its personnel and finance committees. According to Szapocznik, Foote, Rodriguez and Blaney (1984), content analysis allowed quantitative assessment of the type and depth of involvement in affirmative action and minority issues at the highest level of the hospital's formal hierarchy. Forms were developed and used for this purpose. The inter-rater reliability regarding who was present and what affirmative action issues were on the agenda was one hundred per cent and regarding who spoke about what issues was eighty per cent. Regarding the type of overall response to an issue inter-rater rank order was .69. (Szapocznik, Foote, Rodriguez and Blaney, 1984.)

The underlying purpose for observing and conducting a content analysis of the governing board's meetings consisted of 1. accessing the upper levels of the hospital power hierarchy and 2. acquiring a sense of the climate, direction and processes regarding organisational goals and transactions, but especially the incidence of discriminatory behaviour. As such it not only enabled project staff to more effectively conduct their diagnosis and intervention efforts, but also to develop alliances between themselves and both hospital administrators and governing board members, as well as between the latter two groups.

In addition to the quantifiable data just described, qualitative, but systematic observations were conducted in the process of assessing the incidence and extent of institutional racism in the hospital. These included project staff's formal and informal interviews and field observations. Also, policy and procedural manuals were carefully examined, as were written affirmative action plans and equal employment opportunity (EEO) reports. The manuals were especially useful in providing formal documentation as to the manner in which the hospital was 'supposed' to function regarding issues related to affirmative action, discrimination, etc. While the manuals specified the limits and boundaries, it was necessary to corroborate these through field observations and interviews in order to determine the adequacy of the organisation's actual functioning in this regard (Szapocznik, Foote, Rodriguez and Blaney, 1984).

Project staff learned several important lessons from the process of developing and administering measures for this study. The first was that conducting personal interviews with organisational staff is a very effective, but sensitive approach to data collection, both from a research and human relations perspective. It required that the interviewers not only have a comprehensive knowledge of the organisational and research issues at hand; but also be thoroughly familiar with the concept of institutional racism; understand its manifestations; and possess the necessary interpersonal and clinical skills to successfully execute the interviews.

An equally important finding in reference to conducting the interviews was that these must follow a structured format of questioning, that is applied consistently in all cases. Otherwise, the data that is generated by them will lack reliability and validity. The interviews, as well as the content analysis of the organisational minutes, were significantly useful as they provided an opportunity to identify and track organisational processes that, otherwise, would not have been apparent through administration of the questionnaires and analysis of the hospital's personnel data. This study, therefore, clearly establishes the need for an organisational assessment approach comprised of various measures and instruments that complement each other and provide a comprehensive evaluation of the problem under study.

ASSESSMENT FINDINGS AND INTERVENTION OUTCOMES

The project's assessment phase produced a number of significantly useful findings in relation to each of the following six indicators of distribution of power and rewards: black and Hispanic employee representation; compensation; recruitment and selection; training, career development and promotion; affirmative action policies and procedures; and interethnic friction. These findings and their diagnostic implications for the organisation are analysed below.

Black and Hispanic employee representation

As previously noted, the distribution of power across ethnic racial groups is a critical factor in determining the degree and extent to which institutional racism exists in an organisation. Minority representation at middle and executive management levels within the organisation can be an indicator of the distribution of power in an organisation. The personnel data and, to a lesser extent, the two questionnaires used in the study provided information pertaining to relative representation.

An analysis of the number of employees by ethnicity and/or race and job category indicated that minorities, especially blacks, were over-represented in the lowest job categories, and under-represented in higher ones. The top two categories (administrators and professionals) contained large numbers of employees with many different job titles which required analysis to determine if any discriminatory patterns existed.

Blacks and Hispanics were identified as relatively under-represented in the total professional and administrative categories with the few blacks and/or Hispanics who had entered these categories rarely promoted to the upper echelons. These data clearly demonstrated that, for top administrative jobs, the hospital's policy of promotion from within simply was not functioning well for minorities. All of the blacks in these positions and half of the Hispanics, had been hired from outside of the hospital during the previous year. The majority of the white Anglos, on the other hand, had been promoted from within, having previously held lower level jobs at the hospital (Szapocznik, Foote, Rodriguez and Blaney, 1984).

The skill level required in their jobs, as reported by questionnaire respondents, was considered to be another manifestation of representation and, therefore, of power. Non-minority respondents more frequently reported higher level skills than did minorities. More interestingly, when coupled with educational level (used as a statistical control), this relationship became non-significant.

It is also noteworthy that the hospital did not record employee training and education levels in its personnel data, a factor that made inclusion of these items in the Discrimination Questionnaire's Demographic Section very beneficial. This led to two very crucial diagnostic conclusions. The first was that extremely overt discrimination – such as administrative jobs requiring advanced degrees for minorities, but only a High School Diploma for whites – probably was *not* occurring. This finding regarding education obtained prior to employment with the hospital – an indicator of institutional racism that is beyond the control of an organisation, but which none the less impacts it – is a good example of the historical processes which underlie institutional racism, and how it can exist even without conscious or deliberate discriminatory behaviour in an organisation. A second and especially important diagnostic conclusion was that education and training played an important role in the promotion process and might greatly increase black and Hispanic representation in upper level job categories. However, the hospital lacked any training programmes required to operationalise this concept.

Compensation

Compensation is one of the major rewards which an individual receives for working in an organisation. Its distribution among different ethnic racial groups in an organisation, therefore, can be an indicator of institutional racism. In the case of the hospital, the analysis of the personnel and questionnaire data clearly demonstrated that black and Hispanic employees had a lower mean pay than whites, even with both job category and tenure statistically controlled. When examined by job categories, lower pay for blacks existed in the administrative, clerical and service/maintenance categories (Szapocznik, Foote, Rodriguez and Blaney, 1984). As was also the case for black and Hispanic employee representation, these differences in reported salary level generally disappeared when education was also considered.

However, blacks in the professional category were paid more than non-minority professionals. This finding suggested that, even though blacks held proportionately fewer professional positions, the ones they did hold were responsible and important ones, requiring considerable expertise. These findings substantiate the significant role which education and training can play in facilitating minority access to positions of power and better remuneration.

Training, career development and promotion

Although somewhat less tangible than compensation, training, career development and promotion are systemic processes that serve as organisational benefits which may result in the acquisition of power and rewards. As already mentioned in the discussions of black and Hispanic employee representation and compensation, the obvious over-representation of blacks and Hispanics in lower level positions and under-representation in upper ones can be attributed substantially to educational differences (Szapocznik, Foote, Rodriguez and Blaney, 1984).

This finding then suggests that the promotion of training and educational opportunities for these groups could become an effective mechanism for eradicating this imbalance. The need for a comprehensive and accessible career development and training programme for hospital employees repeatedly manifested itself throughout the project's duration and became one of the four major areas of recommended action for the hospital. The manifestation of this need was especially crucial in relation to the hospital's promotional practices.

In contrast with white Anglos who had been promoted from within into these positions, blacks and Hispanics in the highest paid administrative job categories were hired from outside the hospital. This dichotomy is a particularly interesting one in light of the fact that a significant number of the hospital officials interviewed indicated that the hospital's philosophy was one of promoting from within. It is also worth noting that individuals promoted from within may have more informal power (due to established friendships and knowledge of organisational functioning) than those hired from outside. While minority hiring from the outside is certainly necessary, it may have the effect of not providing minorities with the same kind of long-standing power base that non-minorities enjoy within the organisation (Szapocznik, Foote, Rodriguez and Blaney, 1984).

Project staff also observed that many hospital employees, particularly minorites, remained in relatively low level positions even when apparently clear paths for career development existed. For example, several blacks had held the position of Licensed Practical Nurses for twenty or more years without apparently attempting to become Registered Nurses. On the other hand, some highly specialised technical-professional positions remained vacant for as long as four years.

Even those black and Hispanic employees who knew what education they needed and wanted to obtain encountered difficulties in doing so, in spite of the hospital's reimbursement plan. The key to the problem was that the employee could not receive the reimbursement for tuition until four to nine months after having incurred the expense. The employee was required to pay for the job related coursework and, once having passed the course he/she could apply to the hospital for reimbursement. Many lower level employees (which, of course, included most blacks and Hispanics) simply could not afford to wait so long to receive the reimbursement. They needed the money immediately for food, clothing and shelter for themselves and their families. A related problem was transportation. In general, the educational facilities were not located immediately near where the hospital's black and Hispanic employees either worked or lived, thus making transportation to classes time consuming and costly.

Another finding was that some job categories showed a particularly high level of turnover among new minority employees – for example, about fifty per cent of black professionals left the hospital within six months of employment. One explanation might be that blacks left for better jobs. Another very different explanation for this high turnover, however, could be that the process of organisational entry is not a satisfactory one for these employees. This suggests that hospital employee orientation and initial training could benefit from improvement. Project staff observed that the new employee orientation was concerned largely with hospital history and somewhat with employee benefits, but not at all with facilitating the new employee's integration into the organisational system. Improving orientation and initial training, and especially making them more sensitive to minority concerns, may be useful. In fact, other studies (Gomersall and Myers, 1966) have demonstrated that orientation can significantly reduce turnover among new employees. Reduction of turnover is advantageous to the institution as it results in increased employee efficiency and a decrease in operational costs.

It is apparent, then, that the closely related areas of education, training, career development and promotion were seen as primary modes of limiting minority access to positions of power and influence and as such became central targets for interventions to reduce institutional racism at the hospital.

Affirmative action policy and procedures

Affirmative action policy and procedures are an important indicator of institutional racism. By definition, affirmative action policies and procedures constitute the organisation's formal mechanism for ensuring equal protection of the rights and opportunities of all employees. As such affirmative action policies and procedures serve to prevent and/or provide guidelines for addressing and correcting acts of employee discrimination. The degree to which this definition is successfully operationalised, therefore, serves as an indicator of the incidence of institutional racism in an organisation. There are numerous examples related to affirmative action performance that serve to illustrate this point. For instance, an organisation may have affirmative action policies that promote equity, but that in reality are not interpreted and/or upheld as such by the affirmative action office, or they may be upheld in an arbitrary fashion depending on the case or personnel involvement. On the other hand, the organisation may have adequate policies and well intentioned, capable officers to interpret and execute the affirmative action policies, but may – as in the case of the hospital – not have the required resources to do so consistently and effectively.

In the case of this study affirmative action activities were evaluated through administration of the Discrimination Questionnaire Affirmative Action Ineffectiveness Scale, careful examination of written affirmative action policies, plans and reports and observation of the affirmative action officer at work.

The Affirmative Action Ineffectiveness scale reflected employees' perceptions of the concern, efficiency, power and importance of the affirmative action office and its policies. In order for affirmative action, in fact, to be effective it must be perceived as effective by the people it affects. Otherwise employees will not take advantage of the opportunities it provides nor will supervisors make the special effort needed to carry out affirmative action policies. Analysis of the employees' perceptions in this regard demonstrated that white Anglos tended to score moderately low on this scale, indicating that they believed that affirmative action for minorities was fairly effective. Hispanics and blacks, on the other hand, believed that affirmative action was less effective than their white Anglo counterparts did. However, it should be noted that minority employees whose reported salaries were relatively high (over $20,000) or low (less than $10,000) believed that affirmative action was being carried out in a relatively effective manner. In contrast, those between the $10,000 and $20,000 salary range believed affirmative action to be much less effective. That is, minority employees in mid-level jobs may have greater expectations for attaining organisational power and rewards than do those in lower-level jobs. However, compared to those in upper-level jobs, those at mid-level have not had these expectations met. Thus, they may more readily see the organisational system as being ineffective in helping them to succeed and, as such perceive affirmative action as inadequately fulfilling its mandate.

The reasons for these perceptions, in part, lie in the very conflicting role demands placed upon affirmative action. As an organisational function and structure it is invested with the responsibility to ensure equal treatment of all employees and is generally perceived as a voice of conscience and advocate for minorities and women. However, it is also expected to defend organisational policy, procedures and decisions on a number of fronts, including the courts, governments, employees and the general public. These conflicting demands have been found to significantly contribute to the ineffectiveness of affirmative action structures. This is particularly the case when the affirmative action unit is hierarchically removed from the organisation's executive levels of power and/or receives inadequate resources and supports.

In the case of the hospital, the affirmative action office consisted of only one staff member who reported to the director of personnel, who in turn reported to one of five hospital vice presidents. For an organisation of approximately five thousand employees the hospital's affirmative action office was not only too far removed from the policy formulation and decision making levels, but critically limited by its lack of support and resources. As compared to affirmative action staffing patterns in other agencies the hospital's affirmative action office was seriously under-staffed, with affirmative action responsibilities and duties overly centralised in the person of the one affirmative action officer. This meant that, except for concerns with specific complaints, highest level encouragement and supervision and lower level collaboration in regards to affirmative action issues were largely absent.

Moreover, the fact that the hospital lacked an adequate management information system prevented efficient tracking and reporting of employee needs, educational skills, promotional potential, etc. thus hampering the development of a comprehensive and equitable personnel profile for the hospital. The data compiled for affirmative action purposes, therefore, was not only of limited scope, but also had to be produced manually. This meant that the affirmative action officer was forced to lose precious time and energy in the manual compilation and preparation of statistical reports and complaints, that could otherwise be spent on the development and implementation of more sophisticated and encompassing affirmative action measures, plans and procedures.

Recruitment and selection

Recruitment and selection are critical organisational processes which often play an extremely important role in preventing blacks and Hispanics from entering an organisation. When recruitment and selection practices occur in a manner that is insensitive to the mechanisms and/or process through which minorities are attracted to organisations, then, they are actually indicators of institutional racism.

In the case of the hospital, the field observations and interviews suggested that considerable effort and expertise were already being expended on recruitment and the results seemed very positive. Several strategies were followed by hospital staff in ensuring that a representative number of blacks and Hispanics were recruited and selected. In the case of recruitment this consisted of advertising vacant positions in minority newspapers, publications, and other media, as well as the larger community's media. It also included close communication and collaboration with two hospital councils: a black and Hispanic council. Each of these was largely comprised of minority community residents committed to working with the hospital in order to more effectively bridge the operations of the institution with the total community.

The fact that the majority of the hospital's personnel interviewers were black and Hispanic was an important mechanism which increased possibilities of minority individuals successfully applying and being hired for the available positions. This, together with the hospital's use of personnel selection committees comprised of balanced ethnic-racial employee representation promoted successful minority personnel selection.

As part of the assessment it was possible to determine the *actual* number of people hired in each ethnic and job category. This information did not reveal problems in the actual number of blacks and Hispanics hired by the hospital during the one-year assessment period. In other words, the number of blacks and Hispanics hired constituted percentages that were comparable to those of the community's overall population. Based on this finding project staff decided that the hospital's recruitment and selection practices did not require any special attention.

Unfortunately, a particularly useful measure of non-institutional racist selection–relative hiring rate (percentage of applicants who are hired as compared to all those who apply) by ethnicity and job category – was unavailable. While at the time of executing the study, project staff did not see the need for recommending any changes in recruitment and selection, in retrospect, it is conceivable that conducting an analysis of the hospital's relative hiring rate by ethnicity and job category could have yielded a more accurate, comprehensive perspective in this regard, as well as identifying any necessary intervention.

Interethnic friction

Project staff initially identified the quality of the interaction and relationships among hospital employees of different ethnic racial groups as a key indicator of institutional racism. Although the other indicators previously discussed in this section consist of systemic structures and/or processes, these obviously exist in an ongoing social context that may exacerbate or aid efforts to reduce racism. For this reason, project staff thought that if inter-group relations were found to be ineffective, interethnic friction, in fact could be an important and influential dimension of institutional racism at the hospital.

For instance, white Anglos might feel blacks and Hispanics were receiving too much special treatment; blacks might resent the relative progress made by Hispanics in Miami; and both minorities might resent their continued lower position relative to white Anglos in the hospital and/or other organisations in the community. The fact that planning for the study coincided with the 1980 Miami racial riots, also emphasised the salience of interethnic antagonism as a potentially important dimension of the study.

It was indeed an unexpected surprise, to learn through development and administration of the Discrimination Questionnaire that little of this antagonism existed within the hospital. Items targeting interethnic friction were included in the initial version of the questionnaire that was administered to hospital employees. However, during the questionnaire's refinement, the items which came to form the Power and Promotion Discrimination and Affirmative Action scales proved to be the most reliable (Rodriguez, 1981). Since none of the interethnic friction items were empirically related to these scales, they were not included on the final version of the questionnaire. Further, project staff interviews and field observations revealed virtually no such friction at the hospital. Thus, interethnic friction did not appear to be an indicator of institutional racism requiring attention in this case (Szapocznik, Foote, Rodriguez and Blaney, 1984).

This section of the chapter has presented a detailed discussion of how project staff approached the assessment and diagnosis of institutional racism at the hospital and the findings which the latter yielded. Highlighted in these findings was the critical need for changes in the hospital's execution of its affirmative action policies and procedures and the training, career development and promotion of its employees. The chapter's next and last section describes the recommendations which project staff introduced and promoted in order to produce the necessary changes in these dysfunctional areas.

RECOMMENDATIONS AND ANALYSIS OF THEIR IMPLEMENTATION

Recommendations and their successful implementation represent the crux of the change process in a study of this nature and are the fundamental activity which translates all the foregoing into action-oriented change. Without the development and implementation of appropriate recommendations, that sensitively address assessment findings, the actual assessment and diagnosis are merely academic exercises that do not produce important impactful outcomes. So it is that the development and implementation of recommendations for change become the final measure of the project's impact and success. In the case of this study, the recommendations were directed at promoting better representation of black and Hispanic employees at high level decision-making positions; reducing the barriers to employee training and career development and distributing the responsibility for affirmative action throughout the organisation. They were first presented to the hospital's executive management team and later to its governing board as a recommended action plan which both of these groups approved.

Affirmative action

As was mentioned earlier, the study's assessment phase revealed several major problems related to the hospital's affirmative action programme. In order to address these project staff made three major recommendations. The first of these consisted of establishing a committee of representative hospital employees, i.e., the affirmative action officer, an upper level hospital administrator, the chairman of the hospital's governing board, and a senior hospital employee who provides direct patient care, to design a long term affirmative action plan for the hospital. Less than a year after this recommendation was made the hospital developed and implemented a five-year affirmative action plan that is sufficiently detailed and comprehensive to effectively assure equity in the recruitment, hiring, development and promotion of minority employees.

In recognition of the critical need for augmenting the distribution of affirmative action responsibilities throughout the hospital, project staff recommended that the affirmative action officer schedule annual meetings with divisional supervisors in order to discuss the hospital's affirmative action plan, its operationalisation within the different divisions and units and to provide technical assistance relative to compliance. This recommendation was successfully implemented as one of the procedures for obtaining input for the design of the five-year affirmative action plan and has been repeated since. Another important recommendation related to affirmative action was that the hospital provide the affirmative action office with additional personnel support.

In order to ensure maximum organisational involvement and support for the affirmative action plan, project staff recommended that the extent of cooperation by administrators and supervisors be considered in determining their merit increases and promotions, as well as in their annual job evaluations. Of the three recommendations discussed in this section, the latter was the only one that was being considered by the hospital prior to the project's inception, thus it received considerable immediate support for implementation at the time that project staff presented it.

Training and career development

A major series of recommendations involved staff training and career development. All these recommendations were aimed at reducing existing barriers to hospital employees' opportunities for career development and advancement.

The first recommendation which was successfully implemented involved teaching freshmen and sophomore level college courses on the hospital grounds. Work on this recommendation began early in the project. More than two years later this programme is still working well. Under the sponsorship of a local university, two undergraduate courses are taught on the hospital grounds each semester, with a thirty per cent reduction in tuition costs to hospital employees. Enrolment averages about twenty-five student-employees per course. As explained earlier, the hospital has one hundred per cent tuition reimbursement, payable to the employee upon successful completion of the courses. Another recommendation was to have this money advanced, at least to those employees who are financially disadvantaged, so that courses would be available to all. As a result, arrangements have been made so that the credit union will loan funds for this purpose. Even though employees must still bear the cost of the loan interest, this is an important step forward in facilitating their enrolment in job related training.

Another recommendation involved the development of clearer career paths (that is, creating a logical sequence of jobs for moving up within the hospital's hierarchy) and clearer communication of these career paths. This work is progressing well: some job lines have been realigned; communication of these lines to employees is much improved. In effect, this facilitates minority advancement by making it easier for persons in lower level positions to know what is required for advancement. Also as recommended by project staff new employee orientation has been expanded from three hours to a full day and now includes discussion of training opportunities and other resources for advancement available to employees.

In order to assist and provide effective role models, support and guidance to minority employees seeking career advancement, the development and implementation of a mentor programme was recommended. It is not unusual for non-minority employees, particularly white males, to enjoy the benefits of informal support and guidance in navigating the organisation's intricate processes from another more established member of the organisation. Oftentimes this practice is one of the most effective barriers preventing minority and female employees from obtaining promotion and moving up the career ladder. Prior to the study's inception this practice was a common occurrence at the hospital.

It was, therefore, necessary to recommend the establishment of a formal mentor programme. As part of the programme black and Hispanic 'mentorees' would be deliberately selected by individual top management 'mentors'. Two factors made this process different from what was occurring before the study's inception. First while still informal, the mentor programme consists of a deliberate process. That is, 'mentors' search out promising 'mentorees' with deliberate intent and with affirmative action concerns in mind. Before, selection was made largely with no explicit awareness of it occurring and with no specific interest in facilitating the career advancement of minority employees. As such, unintentional reinforcement of discriminatory practices was more likely to occur, than under the recommended programme. The second factor consists of the fact that the career development and training director keeps informal, but systematic track of who is being mentored and what progress that person is making as part of the overall planning for and implementation of personnel career development measures. Thus, while the recommended mentoring scheme may still be subject to intentional abuse it is more open, removing unconscious, unintentional, but potentially institutionally racist elements and as such its implementation constitutes a major step forward for the hospital.

Employee assistance programme

The data collected from the individual interviews and field observations conducted during the study's assessment phase revealed a significant incidence of employee problems related to marital conflict, familial stress, individual psychological dysfunction and substance abuse, frequently resulting in poorer performance and productivity. This prevented these employees from being recommended for increases in pay or promotions, and often resulted in reprimands, disciplinary actions and dismissal.

More importantly, however, for purposes of this study, a disproportionate number of the hospital employees having these problems were black or Hispanic. This, then, was another factor contributing to the maintenance of minority employees in a position of ineffectiveness and limiting their opportunities for advancement and progress within the organisation. As such it became necessary to recommend that the hospital institute an employee assistance programme, that would assist all employees, but especially minority personnel, overcome their problems and successfully remain and develop in their jobs. This recommendation was implemented and the hospital now has an employee assistance programme that successfully conducts early assessment and intervention with its employees. A full time employee assistance coordinator was hired for this purpose. His responsibility is to: 1. train and collaborate with hospital supervisors and administrators in early detection and referral of employee problems and dysfunction; 2. evaluate and counsel employees; 3. refer employees to appropriate external treatment programmes and facilities and 4. monitor and support employees' treatment progress.

Management information system

As has been stated earlier, the hospital lacked an effective personnel management information system which was especially detrimental to the effective execution of affirmative action and career development functions at the hospital. Thus, project staff recommended the development and implementation of a sophisticated management information system that would increase accessibility of information for accurate forecasting and planning regarding affirmative action. Additionally, this intervention would aid the spread of affirmative action responsibility and involvement by freeing the affirmative action officer from statistical compilation and report preparation, thereby enabling her to spend more time with the governing board members and hospital administrators and supervisors in planning and monitoring affirmative action-oriented strategies.

The hospital has purchased and implemented a personnel management information system and not only uses it for general personnel information, but also for affirmative action, personnel training and career development related tasks.

CONCLUSIONS

The implementation, on the part of the hospital, of all of the recommendations presented by project staff is one important measure of the study's overall success. However, what remains to be seen and is indeed more critical than this immediate positive outcome is the impact which the implementation of these recommendations will actually have over an extended period of time on hospital procedures, practices and personnel. Perhaps one of the most difficult lessons to accept in conducting the study was that the post-assessment phase as designed occurred too soon in time after the presentation and implementation of the recommended action plan. Thus, it was not possible for the impact of the recommended changes to be captured by the measures that were repeated as part of the post-assessment phase. While the minutes of the hospital's governing board, post-assessment interviews and field observations demonstrated that the level of understanding of institutional racism and the commitment to racism-reducing change processes had critically increased at the hospital this was not as strongly corroborated by the personnel and questionnaire data. This, therefore, suggests that in order to sensitively and accurately evaluate the full impact of a study of this nature a sufficiently lengthy period of time must elapse between the change-oriented interventions and the post-assessment. In the most ideal of circumstances this should be expanded to include a follow-up assessment or evaluation at an even later date. Only when these steps are taken can a rigorous appraisal of the efforts to reduce institutional racism be determined.

NOTE

1 Support for this work was provided by the National Institute of Mental Health, Minority Research Center as a research grant entitled 'An Hispanic Approach to Institutional Racism', no. 5 R01 MH 34841-03, Jose Szapocznik, Ph.D., Principal Investigator, Angela M. Rodriguez, L.C.S.W., Ph.D., Co-Principal Investigator. The author acknowledges the contributions of Franklin H. Foote, Ph.D., Delores Hagins and Manuel Nakanishi, Ph.D. in its preparation.

REFERENCES

- Brown, J., White, E. and Jordan, H. (1979), *Institutional racism: Research for change.* Final Report, National Institute of Mental Health, Grant No. 5 R01 MH 2708–03.
- Carmichael, S. and Hamilton, C. V. (1967), *Black power: The politics of liberation in America.* New York, Vintage Books.
- Chesler, M. A. (1976), 'Contemporary social theories of racism.' In P. A. Katz (ed.), *Towards the elimination of racism.* New York, Pergamon Press.
- Coleman, J. (1968), 'The concept of equality of educational opportunity.' *Harvard Educational Review,* 38: 7–23.
- Daniels, R., and Kitano, H. (1970), *American racism: exploration of the nature of prejudice.* Englewood Cliffs, New Jersey, Prentice-Hall.
- Gilbert, N., and Eaton, J. (1970), 'Favouritism as a strategy in race relations.' *Social Problems,* 18: 38–52.
- Gomersall, E. R., and Myers, M. S. (1966), 'Breakthrough in on-the-job training.' *Harvard Business Review,* 44: 62–72.
- Knowles, L. L., and Prewitt, K. (eds.) (1969), *Institutional racism in America.* Englewood Cliffs, New Jersey, Prentice-Hall, Inc.
- Mercer, J. (1971), 'Institutionalized Anglo centrism: Labelling mental retardates in the public schools.' In P. Orleans and W. Ellis (eds.), *Race, change and urban society.* Beverly Hills, Sage.
- Myrdal, G. (1962), assisted by Sterner, R. and Rose, A. M. *An American dilemma: The Negro problem and modern democracy.* New York, Harper and Brothers.
- Rodriguez, A. M. (1981), *The Development of the Institutional Racism Perceptions Scale: An Organisational Study of Black-Americans and Hispanics.* A Dissertation. Cincinnati, Ohio, December, 1981.
- Rosenthal, R., and Jacobson, L. (1968), *Pygmalion in the classroom.* New York, Holt, Rinehart and Winston.
- Smith, P. C., Kendall, L. M. and Hulin, C. L. (1969), *The measurement of satisfaction in work and retirement; a strategy for the study of attitudes.* Chicago, Rand McNally.

– Szapocznik, J., Foote, F. H., Rodriguez, A. M., Blaney, N. T. (1984), *A Strategic Structural Systems Approach to Organizational Change and Institutional Racism*, 3 December, unpublished manuscript.
– Terry, R. W. (1970), *For Whites Only*. Grand Rapids, Michigan, William B. Eerdans Publishing Company.

Race relations interventions within a probation service

INTRODUCTION

During the 1950s and 60s the West Midlands conurbation was one of the biggest attractors of new commonwealth migrants who largely replaced migrants from Northern England, Scotland, Eire and Wales. By 1971 over ten per cent of the total new commonwealth population in Great Britain had settled in the West Midlands.

The reasons for settlement patterns of migrants are now commonly known. In the West Midlands they coincided with areas of old privately rented housing and poor physical and social conditions to which has since been added acute unemployment problems.

The new commonwealth migrants – the black minority groups – had joined other disadvantaged groups and entered into the urban cycle of deprivation which was to be further accentuated for the racial minorities, by cultural deprivation and the effects of prejudice, discrimination and racism.

Changes in the structure, nature and behaviour of the community call for changed responses from the serving agencies, and many initiatives were being taken within West Midlands Probation Service in the 1970s/early 1980s which were both reactive and proactive as trends and impressions identified areas of work which needed attention and greater concentration of resources.

In 1977 following seminars with Chief Probation Officers (C.P.O.s) nationally, the Home Office began moves to influence change in what was then described as 'the cultural dimension of Probation and After-Care Work'. It was suggested that in each area with a significant ethnic minority population, one officer should be appointed to act as a point of reference on race relations matters and advisory notes were offered as to the duties which such a person might undertake.

In 1978 a working party in the West Midlands determined that a centralised and collective approach would be more realistic and advised on the appointment of one full-time officer to address themselves to the expansion of work in this field. This was accepted by management as a possible way forward and in August 1979 an ethnic advisor was appointed to West Midlands Probation Service.

The perceptions of the innovatory moves made from August 1979 to May 1984 are therefore, from my standpoint as a member of that advisory working party and the subsequent holder of the post of ethnic advisor to West Midlands County Probation Service during that period.

ASSESSING THE NEEDS

The broad outline of this new post was to collate, enable, stimulate and initiate a variety of developments from within an advisory role which would take the service forward in the development of practice, policy and training. Management took the view that whatever internal changes might be made the service could not expect to operate effectively without a measure of understanding and response from other agencies, systems, probation services and the local communities. The post therefore included an instruction to become involved extensively, wherever appropriate opportunities for contact could be made, in order to act as a catalyst for widespread change. This offered extensive scope but also dissipated too much of the energy which one individual could project.

The innovatory moves outlined are those which took place as a direct result of the specialist appointment. Four main streams of focus throughout this period which ran parallel with initiatives taking place in the field are dealt with separately in more detail, namely: practice and projects; training; community liaison and policy development.

Research and review

The Home Office has made it clear why up-to-date and accurate statistics concerning the position of racial minorities should be collated (see HMSO, 1975).

The first step was, therefore, to engage in an internal service review. Immediately after appointment the ethnic advisor visited every probation office in the county, special units, hostels, prisons and projects. The aims of this communication exercise were:

1 To introduce the post of ethnic advisor as a county resource;
2 To encourage the free expression of attitudes;
3 To discover the practical needs of officers to enable effective service delivery;
4 To stimulate the exchange of ideas and information, locally and nationally;
5 To evaluate current policy and practice with a view to forward

planning and action.

A diversity of opinion was expressed upon the issues raised in discussion, ranging from a resolve that inaction and containment would eventually allow 'problems to sort themselves out' to radical restructuring of the institutional framework.

A statistical survey was conducted running parallel to the review. The data collected was pertinent to the issues and identified:

1 The ethnic minority groups most in need of the agencies' services;
2 The location of the specified minority groups, relating areas of settlement to client need;
3 The nature of contact with the agency, discovering which services were being utilised;
4 Identification of different 'take up rates' between the majority and minority groups and whether any statistically significant differences were discernible.

Clearly the survey revealed aspects of service provision to black groups which needed more detailed exploration of all the factors involved.

The statistical survey had been supported and assisted by the Home Office Research Department. Using their expertise was an important tactical move which brought positive results. A channel was opened through which the findings could be shared. They were accepted as valid. Data was now available to prove that certain impressions could be substantiated and conclusions could be drawn. Tests were applied to the statistics which determined statistically significant differences in the proportion of Afro-Caribbean and Asian groups represented under different categories of supervision revealing, in real figures, 893 clients of Afro-Caribbean origins, 305 of Asian origins, 150 of mixed racial origins (i.e. thirteen per cent of the total county caseload). Comparative figures showed that the black minority groups were *under*-represented in the probation supervision category and highly *over*-represented in the categories of supervision following custodial sentences.

There were many factors involved, but it was this piece of research which led to subsequent decisions and vindicated the positive action which had been taken in special provision already underway. The age range was also an important factor as the greatest percentage of work with black clients was with young persons (i.e. under twenty-one), in particular those of Afro-Caribbean parentage.

Discussion took place with the Commission for Racial Equality about the possibility of publishing the entire internal review and findings of the statistical survey. They advised strongly in favour.

This was a considerable challenge for probation management at that time as no probation service had ever published on race.

Nevertheless, the decision was made to do so and a precedent was set from the outset of *sharing* information which continued throughout the next five years.

The report was prepared for publication under the title of 'Probation and After-Care in a Multi-Racial Society' and became available to the public in May 1981 (the month following the public disturbances in Brixton) and the evidence it provided was considered by Lord Scarman in compiling 'The Scarman Report'.

The statistical survey plus the impressionistic review jointly gave an over-view of the service's interaction with black clients. The report offered twenty-eight recommendations relating to discriminatory actions or practices; projects; resources; training; recruitment and deployment of staff; interpreters; volunteers; development of an information and consultancy service; research; methods in practice; public liaison and national networking. In February 1980 all recommendations were accepted by management for implementation in the West Midlands Probation Service. The specialist post had been operational for six months. It is my opinion that this piece of work could not have been achieved with such speed without a central approach which enabled all the threads to be drawn together. This first step founded a secure base on which to proceed.

COMMUNICATION INITIATIVES

Whilst the Scarman Report was under preparation, West Midlands Probation Service agreed to host a series of conferences on aspects of race at both a local and national level, to participate in others being organised in different parts of the country by the CRE, and to engage with the media. The chief probation officer (Michael Day OBE), the ethnic advisor and other members of management responded to invitations to speak, to chair meetings and otherwise engage in meetings on racial issues, usually with the brief of relating the social situation to probation and social work. All were to experience highly charged atmospheres, verbal attacks – both public and personal – which were far outweighed by the support and encouragement which probation initiatives engendered. The trigger word was 'racist' or 'racism' which was not yet fully understood by the majority of British people. Some magistracy were particularly offended as use of the word was perceived as challenging to the impartiality of the courts. The subtleties and deviousness of racism were not recognised. Spokesmen at that time became translators of events and were invited to make public statements on television, radio and in the press. It was an acutely sensitive political arena in which to engage and the public responsibility of the position was felt by all concerned.

West Midlands Probation Service then extended invitations to all chief probation officers, and their ethnic liaison officers in England and Wales. Twenty-six Services responded and sixty people attended a conference in Birmingham. The aims being:

1 To inform all probation services of the findings of the West Midlands Probation Service's report prior to publication;
2 To introduce CRE recommendations on national policy on race and probation;
3 To make links with other services for exchange of information and explore possibilities for the development of regional groups and training for ethnic liaison officers on a regional or national basis;
4 To request support for CRE initiatives nationally in organising multi-agency conferences.

Multi-agency conferences followed in the West Midlands hosted by the West Midlands Probation Service and CRE, and the pattern extended to other parts of the country. Various innovatory moves often resulted from these consultations.

Two national conferences for trainers took place in the Midlands with over one hundred trainers from probation/social work services and academic institutions present. The second event was organised totally by black trainers and speakers but no corporate way forward was discovered in training at this point as the diversity of views was too great, yet it was clear that trainers were seeking for answers and assistance in this area of training.

Ethnic liaison officers in probation services came together for a training course organised by West Midlands Probation Service which strengthened the links between them and exposed the numerous difficulties they faced in their respective services but also they were brought to the recognition that much could have been accomplished that had not been attempted.

This was a critical period during which the efforts of West Midlands Probation Service to act as a catalyst for widespread change were challenged from within the service by many who felt that such energy could have been more profitably used internally. The message which the publication of their corporate views in fact produced was that the issues they had raised were of *national* importance and that any and every individual in the service was now being encouraged to consider the full range of their work and personal attitude towards racial matters. Resistance to doing so was evident and statements were frequently heard that 'racism' was a matter to be dealt with by management. However, by taking these initiatives West Midlands Probation Service became a central point through which information flowed in and out and the information service envisaged became a reality.

To stimulate interest further the magazine *Probation and the Community – Ethnic Bulletin* was designed. Every three months the ethnic advisor collated (and wrote) a range of articles: conference and project reports; training news; legislation; new books; news and comments by black writers and many other facets were covered. 750 copies were printed, the frontispiece reading:

This Bulletin has been devised to meet the following aims:

1 To keep staff informed of initiatives in the ethnic minority field and to stimulate interest, thinking and discussion on the cultural dimensions of the work.

2 To offer to ethnic minority groups/individuals, a platform to share their views of the Service and to demonstrate our interest in their welfare.

3 To make links with universities, polytechnics and training organisations to enable them to be aware of Probation initiatives and approach in practice.

4 To make links with PACs nationally and the Home Office for dissemination of information.

5 To communicate with other agencies, institutions, the magistracy and justices' clerks, thus adding to our collective knowledge and understanding of the needs and views of the minority groups in the community.

It was open to contributions from anywhere. A second bonus was that it proved to be an effective public relations tool giving an insight into a statutory agency from a different angle and it was read with interest in the community. This was one of the initiatives which raised interest in recruitment from black applicants. Over half the copies were distributed free of charge – including to all members of the probation service. Subscribers paid £1.50 per year for three copies which found their way into many libraries and public places. The bulletin was a platform for the sharing of news and views which brought rewards in the building of race relations. Other publications on specific aspects of race, culture and probation work followed.

A consultancy service developed which took on an interesting pattern. Initially requests from officers to consult about their casework were minimal. Most contact related to divorce court welfare work with Asian families. The need to understand more of the Asian social system and family dynamics was recognised in work which related directly to family welfare, but in work stemming from the criminal courts the same concern and cultural interest did not appear to be so evident. It was therefore necessary to 'sell' the consultancy service more widely in other ways.

This developed through the community liaison role, discussed later, by linking individuals with a range of expertise and cultural knowledge to either individual officers or teams needing to consider group approaches to their work. In this way the consultancy role was shared and became another facet of building 'race' relations.

The advisory role was different and more difficult. There were numerous occasions on which advice was asked, given and apparently accepted but it was not implemented. The brief did not include monitoring or oversight in the divisions and therefore did not allow for intervention if 'advice' was not carried through into action. Some of the twenty-eight recommendations which had been formally accepted fell through lack of application by those designated to take responsibility.

MEETING SPECIAL NEEDS OF THE BLACK OFFENDER

As we saw earlier, while thirteen per cent of the total county caseload consisted of people of Afro-Caribbean, Asian or mixed racial origins, these racial groups were being processed by the judicial system differently from the white majority. For example, there was a significant tendency for blacks to be given custodial sentences more frequently than their white counter-parts. Consequently, ethnic minorities figured to a disproportionately greater extent than the white majority in the post-custodial supervision provided by the service.

Of the many possible causes for this state of affairs, one was undoubtedly the inability of the service to communicate with the black offender and to understand the social environment from which he or she comes. Equally the inability of the latter to see the value and potential of the probation service for mitigating their problems bespoke a need for the service to sell itself and its services more effectively. A series of initiatives was clearly needed to overcome the barriers and build bridges with this large group of clients.

Intervention therefore followed on the undermentioned lines: focus was placed on reaching black offenders at the earliest possible moment with the objective of deflecting them from a custodial sentence. This meant additional resources were needed. St Basil's Centre, a voluntary project already offering advice, information services and projects for black youth, provided one, later two, black workers who were present every day in the Birmingham City Courts.

Their task was to make the approach to young black people arriving in the Court precincts *before* they reached the sentencing arena to offer information, advice or assistance. They ensured that defendants were aware of their rights, understood the legal aid system and were introduced to the probation service in a constructive way. The workers were able to offer their personal support during their appearance and follow through if further help was appropriate, visiting families or custodial institutions and assisting with problems at a personal or practical level. In this way they were also helping to bridge the communication gap between black youth and white authority and reduce the reluctance to seek help within the system which had such a punitive image.

However, the help from the system had to be available in a far more constructive and readily accessible form. Individually officers had become frustrated by the social and economic situation which had reduced resources in many areas, particularly in employment, and the clause in a probation order requiring 'industriousness' had little relevance as it was no longer enforceable. The strategy which developed to meet this situation was to link these young offenders to resources which would offer the best chance of remaining in the community, preferably before sentencing. To this aim the City and Handsworth Alternatives Scheme (CHAS) developed and the search for resources took on a greater impetus. CHAS was funded by the Home Office and started operation in 1979 as a pilot scheme under the direction of the National Association for the Care and Resettlement of Offenders (NACRO) with all black staff catering for an all-black clientele. The aim was to provide a service to the Birmingham Courts to assist with the treatment of young black offenders in the seventeen to twenty-five age range, by harnessing community resources and facilities to provide a range of credible and more acceptable support services. The provision included advice and practical help with accommodation, employment, education, recreation, and a high level of social support.

The argument for the black staff in a black client setting is a controversial one. This is not general service philosophy, as black officers would be working with a multiracial caseload or even an 'all-white' caseload in the rural areas, however, it was obvious that many young black people found the relationships with the black workers more rewarding, illustrated by a black client who explained, 'I do not have to explain myself to a black person because they already understand where I am coming from' – meaning that in every sense of the words.

Another initiative sprang directly from the work of a black probation officer in the Handsworth Area. The Cultural Centre is a scheme which began in 1978 funded by the Inner City Partnership Programme and which has gone through rapid phases of expansion and development. In 1983 a second set of premises were acquired (i.e. an old cinema building) which is in the process of renovation and conversion into a second Cultural Centre with a focus on entertainment and theatre known as CAVE (Community and Village Entertainment). Whilst these two centres now have a different focus the underlying philosophy is similar.

They offer the community resources and facilities in which to meet and enjoy creative experiences, aided by professionals, in learning, skills training, leisure and recreation. The centre's staff aim to aid the process of self-discovery and enhance creative potential in many ways. Although the emphasis is placed on the arts in the widest sense of the term, groups form in response to community and individual need or interest and are as divergent as weight-training; electronics; gardening; Asian cookery; typing and jewellery making. Artistic talent in music, dance, drama and art have led to opportunities in employment, entrance to higher education courses and the formation of professional groups. CAVE is now promoting a series of workshops, films and performances throughout the city and each three-month package ends with a festival. There is no distinction between 'offenders' and any other participant or performer. This breaks with the old tradition of dealing with 'offenders' as a separate group and also allows the probation service to operate in the community in a positive preventative role.

Appointments of black and Asian MSC workers were made with the special responsibility for development of services for the minority groups, interpreting, family support etc. Funds were acquired for the appointment of an Asian conciliation worker for the domestic courts operating through the community project 'Link House'. Black and Asian volunteers were recruited and enabled to work in groups or creatively as individuals; and the numbers of black and Asian applicants for CQSW Training Courses increased from amongst those who had made constructive links with the probation service.

Task related groups were at work in different parts of the county addressing particular aspects of racial issues related to practice. Such groups have covered social enquiry report monitoring; translation facilities; resource and interest groups; divorce court welfare work with Asians; community support for offenders; mental health and welfare; racial awareness.

In addition a group met regularly, initially in an advisory role (Ethnic Minority Liaison Advisory Group) and later as a steering group, to plan and organise the race forums held every three months approximately.

Developments in practice were therefore continuous, through the stimulation offered in pockets and by groups of committed individuals which very gradually increased in number. Yet it was a constant dilemma to know how changed attitudes and an increased knowledge base could be monitored and the question remained as to whether they were being reflected in practice.

This responsibility was beyond the resources of one centralised post and had to await the time when reflection could be given within teams, by colleagues, and be built into the supervisory role of middle and higher management. It was clear that this would not take place universally until they were themselves convinced of its necessity and relevance, which brings me to the question of staff training and its relation to professional practice.

STAFF TRAINING IN RACE RELATIONS

From 1979 to 1983 West Midlands Probation Service engaged in a series of conferences; seminars; workshops; open forums; community groups; project development; area, team and individual discussions. Focus ranged from specific aspects of racial issues; cultural diversity; communication skills; and the agencies' roles and responsibilities in relation to the black and Asian members of the community. The research which had taken place offered material for contentious debate but clearly highlighted reasons in favour of positive action and it was consistently voiced that one such action should be training and re-appraisal of all staff in the racial dimension of their professional role and personal attitudes. As more staff grew to accept the validity of training in this area there were challenges to the central training department to provide 'it'. But there were no ready-made recipes to offer.

No compact training packages had been discovered which had proved to be effective in probation training because race training cannot be 'packaged' in this way. It is a state of mind which has to be explored. White consciousness must be understood in the context of racism and the power base from which it has stemmed, and much training relies heavily upon the skills and expertise of the trainer and his/her relationship with the participants.

This preliminary phase, therefore, took dogged persistence, drew harsh and negative responses at times but began the clearance of the way forward. By 1984 a sufficiently solid foundation had been built which was judged to be secure enough to build upon it a comprehensive outline of a more structured programme. A group of officers working independently for six months came to the same conclusion as the central training section/ethnic advisor that the service was now ready for the greater impact of racism awareness training, on the lines of the American model pioneered by Judy Katz.

To implement racism awareness training, firstly it is necessary to acknowledge that racism exists, that it is the key factor in race relations and that it is a part of the experience of black people in Britain, including black *staff* as well as clients and the community. This message had been projected to the service through films, literature, role play sessions but the greatest impact had been made by the race forum, an open meeting for all staff every three months which focused sharply on the issues of racism and brought together all individuals who were motivated to explore the issues and influence the development of service policy in this area.

These forums had been attracting between sixty and one hundred members of staff and were becoming a visible indicator of the growing support in the body of the service for a number of innovatory moves, in which training was a key component. Awareness of racism therefore gradually became the core around which was built the components of cultural information and awareness; interpersonal communication skills; race relations legislation; public service delivery; and institutional organisation.

The training process was designed to develop understanding of the reality of racism, how it operates in society and its effects upon individuals, organisations and the community, recognising the power base from which it stems. Participants were encouraged to 'own' the responsibility for personal and institutional change; make commitment to positive action and monitor the process of change. Increased appreciation of cultural diversity, the relevance and sensitivity of practice was a continuous educative component. It was apparent that the management of the service needed to be aware and supportive at every stage of the process if effective change was to be implemented.

The full management team subsequently undertook a programme of racism awareness training in May 1984 which reinforced their collective determination to develop positive policy and a systematic racism awareness training programme for staff. This type of training needs between three and five consecutive days for people to work through the uncomfortable experience of confrontation of white racism.

Race training obviously requires the cooperation of all personnel but without the contributions made by black staff and black trainers it would be far less effective as communication of the direct experience of racism makes a significant impact on a training programme. Most officers with training responsibilities do not have the direct or relevant experience, information or grasp of the complex and emotive issues which need to be explored in race training. They are, therefore, largely dependent upon making contact and building programmes using external resources which undoubtedly includes people who are not trained trainers. In the West Midlands Probation Service emphasis has been placed on the making of such contacts, recognising their value in a consultative advisory capacity, offering support and guidance in development of training skills, and giving proper attention to remuneration for their services.

In this way the West Midlands Probation Service has entered into this experimental phase of training with members of the community with the determination to work together in partnerships for the mutual benefit of the service and the community. Thus the image of the probation service has been enhanced and enriched through training ventures.

In addition, every in-service training course was assessed by the training section for the inclusion of a 'slot' on the racial/cultural aspect of the theme, which has become known as the 'integrated or discreet' approach. Such sessions cannot possibly substitute for a specially designed programme as they are usually limited in time and have a specialised focus. The integrated approach has to be used but regarded as yet another step towards raising interest and awareness of issues which need further exploration. At the same time the training of social work students was being supplemented by training initiatives in the field.

Practitioners in the urban areas were increasingly being requested to offer students an 'ethnic dimension' within fieldwork placements and there was a risk that learning would be taking place at the expense of the black minorities. This situation was recognised as unacceptable and central responsibility was taken to provide opportunities for experiential learning in racial and cultural aspects of their work *without* the necessity to be directly involved in case-work. Programmes were devised which allowed the students to come together in groups and participate in a series of five events all of which brought them into contact with Afro-Caribbean and Asian culture within the community as *participants* not merely observers.

As West Midlands Probation Service caters for an average of one hundred students on placement per annum this was a sizeable undertaking. There were many spin-offs from this 'package' approach. The students found it to be of such benefit that they introduced the idea within their academic institutions, some of which began to build on it by developing their own community experiential events; by enabling students to run seminars inviting their new community links to share in debates or show films; many chose to focus course project papers on a racial or cultural theme; and questions with an ethnic focus began to appear with greater regularity on examination papers.

The ultimate goal is therefore to stimulate individuals towards taking personal responsibility to seek out the many avenues at their disposal through which they can continue to develop their own sensitivity and re-educate themselves for the multiracial and multi-cultural society of the 1980s.

COMMUNITY AND AGENCY LIAISON

There is no commonly agreed understanding of the role of ethnic liaison which can have an internal agency focus, an external community focus, or both. Due to the size of the county, priorities had to be identified which in general terms were to:-

1 Respond to any invitations received by the probation service from ethnic minority groups, thus building a continuity of contact;

2 Discover which groups or projects were prepared to build a relationship which allowed them access to the probation service, thereby enabling creative ideas to form as to how joint initiatives (partnerships) might offer a wider range of constructive alternative assistance for clients from within the community;

3 Initiate contact with any *new* ventures and share this information internally.

There was a fourth priority, which became more apparent as contact increased throughout different areas of the county, which was to improve the poor image of the probation service within the black communities, it having been adversely affected by numerous factors which had not been fully appreciated in the service.

The black members of the community were, in the main, unfamiliar with the functions of the service and had difficulty in understanding the dual role of agent of the court and social worker. Probation had also been bracketed in a close relationship with the police and the prison service both of which held many 'fear-based' images. The concept of professional social work assistance ran contrary to traditional cultural social systems of extended family and community support and was viewed as imposing external control, thus reducing the responsibilities of family elders and exposing families to shame in their own communities. There was therefore resistance to the infiltration of western values into close-knit families and the threat this poses to culturally based beliefs and customs.

The low offence rate amongst the older black and Asian groups meant that there had been little spreading of knowledge of the service within the home through positive contact and the few black and Asian staff within the service were insufficient to reflect an image of a multiracial service. In addition there remained the complex issues relating to language and communication patterns through which many misinterpretations had occurred. The worsening relationship between the young black British-born and the agents of white 'power' lay as a heavy and salutory warning that interventions must take place which had meaning and relevance at all levels within the community if the probation image was to gain in credibility.

Liaison work of this nature is not undertaken most effectively at random. It takes a regular pattern of visits over a length of time to establish trust and develop a potential working relationship. There is a reservoir of goodwill, skills and assistance available in the black and Asian communities and yet there have also been many bad experiences, disappointing and frustrating encounters with statutory agencies. Therefore a period of test, trial and challenge is often a necessary preliminary to the development of fruitful relationships, some of which move into the formation of working partnerships.

The purpose of contact may have a clear focus. West Midlands Probation Service initiated deliberate moves to publicise the service by working jointly on the preparation of pamphlets and literature in mother tongues explaining agency functions and giving information about resources (e.g. 'You, the Courts, and the Probation Service' – in five Asian languages). Meetings were organised to give talks about the local agency and link the community group to their local probation office if appropriate. Consumers' views were monitored in the community to elicit views about the agency and its service provision to the community, their special problems or needs, seeking to gather ideas for ways in which improvements could be made and learning of the effects of racist attacks, National Front activities and legislation upon the local communities.

Some contact was task-centred to raise interest in social work as a career; recruit interpreters, volunteers, advisors; discover people with special or extensive knowledge of aspects of racial issues who might be prepared to contribute to training courses; others with special skills such as arts, crafts or cookery willing to share their skills in residential establishments or probation-based groups. There was a need to enlist assistance with the development of community service work placements, with discovering accommodation for young offenders in difficulties or perhaps prior to their release from custody. There were voluntary agencies or groups to be identified who might be in a position to establish formal links with the service to negotiate ways of taking a measure of responsibility for client care and support. The religious bodies also had become more involved in social welfare and sometimes have their own community social workers or welfare support services attached to day-centres at their places of worship. West Midlands Probation Service was able to offer places on some of their in-service training courses in exchange for reflections on the cultural aspects of the topics covered, on a mutual exchange basis.

The links to be made and information to be exchanged was extensive, and the possibilities for closer working and supportive relationships between voluntary and statutory bodies became apparent.

A seal of approval seems to be offered to voluntary projects which are linked to statutory bodies and the weight which is bestowed on the recommendations given by statutory agencies, as to which voluntary projects should be supported, should not be underestimated. It is essential that support be given by statutory agencies, who have so much to benefit from these innovative partnerships.

In the West Midlands Probation Service the numbers of black and Asian volunteers was increasing steadily and they were, in some areas, choosing to work as support groups and offer links with the local communities for young people in custody.

Community and agency liaison is about bringing people together to learn from and with each other; about building trust, respect and understanding, and about using energy and resources creatively and corporately for the benefit of all.

A CORPORATE RESPONSIBILITY

Since the West Midlands Probation Service Report opened the door for public statement and comment on probation and racial equality, other documents have followed with findings and proposals all on similar lines. In October 1981 at the annual conference of the National Association of Probation Officers (NAPO) a policy document ('The NAPO Report on Racial Issues') was unanimously accepted. The Central Council of Probation Committees published a report 'Probation – A Multi-Racial Approach' in February 1983, which addressed all the issues opened up within the service and gave the much needed stamp of authority to probation intervention in the field of race relations. All probation committees were requested to respond after debate with probation management, as to how the recommendations made were/or might be implemented, enabling a national picture to form for the first time. Common areas of concern were identified which could be taken further at a national level. In June 1984 a national working party recommended a general policy and strategy for race training which also spelled out the implications of the present system, and the blockages within it, for the recruitment, training and appointment of black staff.

An Association of Black Probation Officers also now has a corporate voice through which they are able to make both individual or collective statements and ensure that they are heard in any arena, but particularly those which are debating issues of race, culture and equity.

The Central Council for Education and Training in Social Work's publication 'Teaching Social Work in a Multi-Racial Society' (Oct. 1982) has also brought to the fore issues which draw attention to the joint responsibility of those developing theory and those relating that theory to practice. Perhaps a greater unity than ever before is required to enable teaching of multiracial social work to take place effectively.

It has been, in the main, the services within the urban conurbations which have taken the race issues further forward. They have been deeply influenced by the perceptions of society which their black fellow-citizens have shared with them and have recognised that change is both inevitable and desirable within the white-dominated legal and social systems. The struggle continues within the urban areas to develop the resources, and practical, appropriate and sensitive approaches to change the prevailing social and economic situation.

REFERENCES

– Central Council for Education and Training in Social Work (1983), *Teaching Social Work for a Multi-Racial Society*, London, C.C.E.T.S.W.
– Central Council of Probation Committees (1983), *Probation – A Multi-Racial Approach*, London, C.C.P.C.
– Katz, J. (1982), *White Awareness: Handbook for Anti-Racism Training*, Norman, Oklahoma, University of Oklahoma Press
– National Association of Probation Officers (1981), *The NAPO Report on Racial Issues*. London, N.A.P.O.
– *Report of the Home Office Advisory Committee on Race Relations Research* (1975), London, H.M.S.O.
– Scarman, Lord (1981), *The Brixton Disorders 10–12 April, 1981*. London, H.M.S.O.
– West Midlands Probation and After-Care Service (1981), *Probation and After-Care in a Multi-Racial Society*, Birmingham, W.M.P.A.C.S.
– West Midlands Probation and After-Care Service (1980–84), *Probation and the Community – Ethnic Bulletin*, I–XII. Birmingham, W.M.P.A.C.S.

11

Group process methods of intervention in race relations [1]

The notion that relationships within a group of people or between two groups can be improved by providing an occasion for them to talk to one another has a long history. We have long since learned that such a simple view cannot by itself provide much help in designing specific training experiences. None the less a rather heavily qualified version of it underlies most current forms of training intervention. This chapter will begin by reviewing very briefly what has been learned from the past few decades of work using group training methods and then focus more directly upon the relevance of this to settings in which race is a major issue.

The development of sensitivity training in the United States in the forties actually derived from a series of workshops concerned with the implementation of equal opportunities legislation in the state of Connecticut. However the procedure which became central to sensitivity training and its later and rather more unruly derivative, the encounter movement, was much more general in conception. This was to have members of a group discuss their feelings and perceptions of one another face-to-face. The conditions thought necessary to create such an enterprise included time away from day-to-day commitments, voluntary attendance and participative leaders who allowed groups to make their own decisions about how to approach this task.

The immense popularity of such groups in the sixties and early seventies has now greatly decreased, but they leave us with an extensive legacy of research findings as to their efficacy. A fairly recent review (Smith, 1980) indicates that over 100 relatively well-designed research studies were published. These studies show that sensitivity workshops are able to generate a variety of measurable effects including changes in self-perception, changes in behaviours toward others and performance on certain tasks. Many of the measures used in these studies were collected shortly after workshops had ended. Those studies which also included measures collected some weeks or months later showed a less positive picture.

There were still some effects detected which were not found among controls who did not attend the workshops, but these effects were much less frequent. Thus the overall message of this research is that groups can often create short-term changes, but many of them are not conducted in a manner which ensured the continuance of those changes.

The belief is now widespread that the reason why group effects often fade out is that the groups in which training has occurred are temporary ones specially convened for the purpose. This diagnosis has led many to abandon training experiences based on *ad hoc* groups and turn instead to those groups which have a continuing major importance for those in them. There has been a consequent massive development of interest in group work within work organisations, usually referred to as 'organisation development' and within families, in the guise of family therapy and marital enrichment. Group work within such intact long-lasting groups has a quite different emotional flavour, less heady and exciting and often more tense and difficult, but its protagonists would argue that whatever is achieved is more likely to persist. Some research evaluations have yielded very encouraging results while others indicate that even where one works with intact groups there are many other factors which need to be taken care of if one is to assure a continuing and positive outcome. These include the creation of a clear contract as to the purposes and procedures of an intervention, an agreement among those attending a workshop that the issues that they are addressing are ones which they can usefully address, even in the absence of those not present, and behaviour by the leaders which facilitates the creation of a trusting climate of relationships.

WORK IN MULTIRACIAL SETTINGS

Group work with multiracial populations shows the same range of approaches as those outlined above, although only recently has there been much evidence of a trend away from temporary person-centred group work and towards groups which are based on more long-lasting organisational structures. In this section a number of published descriptions of relevant types of group work will be examined.

Perhaps the clearest instance of a person-centred approach is provided by the work of Carl Rogers. Rogers was himself one of the principal figures in the popularisation of encounter groups in the sixties. His work in this field is not strictly within the area of race relations as usually defined, but it is my view that his work none the less provides pointers as to what will and will not be effective forms of groupwork in the race relations area. In 1973 he led a group in Belfast comprising four Catholics and four Protestants, which met for sixteen hours and was filmed throughout (McGaw *et al.*, 1973). By his own account the group was markedly successful (Rogers, 1978). The early sessions were given over to bitterness and confrontation, but towards the close of the group a reconciliation occurred between the two sides. This reconciliation was sufficiently substantial that the film had to be heavily edited before public showing in Belfast, lest it endanger the lives of group members. The eight group members none the less devoted considerable energy in subsequent months to arranging for the film to be shown in many church halls within both Belfast communities. Rogers does not claim that his single group had any lasting impact on the structure of community relations in Belfast, but mounts a persuasive argument in favour of running thousands of such groups. He is thus firmly of the view that community conflict can be substantially modified by intervention at the personal level.

A slightly larger-scale intervention in the same conflict was attempted by a quite separate team of American group workers a year earlier. Fifty-six Belfast community leaders spent ten days at a workshop in Scotland, where they participated in groups which mixed members of the two communities. The predominant procedure used by the group workers was the relatively unstructured approach originated by the Tavistock Institute, with the addition of role-playing and other exercises toward the end (Doob and Foltz, 1973). This workshop generated a good deal of confusion and disagreement both while it took place and subsequently. Dissatisfied participants wrote to a Belfast paper on their return, which led to a subsequent highly damaging and distorted account of the workshop in a tabloid paper. Some members of the workshop staff also published an account of what they felt to be the damaging effects of the workshop (Boehringer *et al.*, 1974), while others interviewed forty of the fifty-six participants nine months later and concluded that there were lastingly positive effects (Doob and Foltz, 1974).

Comparison of the two Belfast workshops does not make it possible to know whether factors such as small size, participant selection or a happy choice of timing enabled Rogers to achieve a more uniformly positive effect than did the staff of the larger workshop. The alternative possibility is that Rogers' style of working with groups is better suited to situations of highly charged conflict. We need to examine workshops within more typical areas of race relations before any conclusions can be confidently drawn.

Smith and Willson (1975) report a study of two workshops set up to explore the use of group work in the context of race relations. One workshop focused on relations between Asians and whites in Slough, while the other was for white teachers and black parents drawn from several schools in Leeds. Each workshop took place over a weekend. Participants were interviewed by a researcher before and again some time after the workshop. Measures were also obtained from control groups who did not attend the workshops. The Slough workshop was conceived as an opportunity for those present to work on issues relating to race relations, without prescribing precisely how this should occur. There were two white and two Asian leaders, and twelve participants, of whom six were white and six Asian. The workshop time was mostly spent in two separate groups, each of them racially heterogeneous. One group became highly personally involved with one another, while the other spent most of its time discussing specific local instances of racial discrimination. The research team's interviews were completed three months after the workshop, at which time they concluded that this workshop had not achieved any detectable lasting effects.

The workshop at Leeds was markedly different, both in conception and in the fact that it did lead to lasting effects. The three workshop staff, who were all white, were of the opinion that the most effective design would be one which identified in advance a specific problem issue. The issue identified was that of the school performance of West Indian black children. Workshop participants were recruited who were concerned with this issue, namely equal numbers of black parents and of white teachers. The teachers were drawn from several schools with a substantial enrolment of black West Indian children. Twenty-seven participants attended the workshop. The workshop design was influenced by the ideas of those who have used group methods within work organisations. Part of the time was spent in small groups which placed together those of the same race, or those who were concerned with a particular type of school. The remaining sessions were spent all in the same room, often with each group sharing with the others concerns or proposals which had been formulated in the homogeneous groups. Probably the most important session was one in which the teachers and parents presented to one another lists of issues which they wished to explore with the other group. This generated considerable tension, but was accomplished through active encouragement by the leaders of listening to the other group, rather than attempting to contradict or deny what was said. The workshop closed with formulation of various plans for continuing contact and future action in the various schools represented.

The research assessment of this workshop showed that some lasting changes were still evident three months after the workshop. Teachers were found to have become more favourable in their evaluation of the West Indian way of life. They now saw black parents as more concerned about their children than they had previously, and they were more aware of the problems facing black children. The parents for their part were found to have increased their attendance at PTA meetings. They also now saw teachers as *less* concerned about black children, and they approved *less* of the teachers' disciplinary methods. A number of other specific events occurred in the months after the workshop, which most probably derived from it and served to sustain its impact, such as additional meetings for black parents in the schools. The overall impression is that the workshop led to increased engagement in working on the issues by both teachers and parents.

The four workshops so far discussed were all composed of roughly equal numbers of the racial or sectarian groups concerned. Although one might argue that such a balance was an obvious prerequisite for effective intervention in this area, this has often not been the case, and some would argue that it is not even desirable. The remaining sections of this chapter review interventions where blacks are present only as a minority, or are not present at all. Before passing on to such approaches, it is worth considering why there are not more published accounts of projects where participation has been equal. All four of the projects reviewed were seen as pilot projects. None of their proponents were seriously advancing the proposition that interventions on the scale they employed would have a lasting effect on community relations. Each wished to show, or to test out, whether the prospects were good that a larger scale application of such methods could make a significant impact. The evidence of the last of the four projects is markedly more encouraging than the others. It appears that the prospects for a lasting impact are better where a specific issue is identified as a target for change, and where the workshop is designed with that target in mind.

GROUPS WITH A MINORITY OF BLACK MEMBERS

Many training groups contain a minority of one or more black group members. However, even where research studies have been undertaken to assess the outcome of a particular training experience, it is rare for specific attention to be devoted to this particular aspect of group composition. The best known study which bears on the issue is that by Lieberman *et al.* (1973). The overall intent of this study was to make a thorough evaluation of eighteen encounter groups of students at Stanford University. The eighteen groups used widely varying approaches, and four of them were specifically designated as black–white encounters. The groups were conducted in the late sixties, at a time when the case for black separatism was being strongly argued. It was found that in contrast to participants in the all-white groups, members of the black–white encounters showed increased endorsement of black separatism and increased mistrust of the other group. These findings are based on the scores of nineteen whites and seven blacks. No separate means are reported for blacks and whites, so that it is not clear whether these changes were spread evenly between blacks and whites or not. Meetings of the black–white groups were rated by research observers as more angry than the all-white groups. Case study reports of each of the groups make clear that some of them were markedly more successful than others. The most successful of the mixed groups was one containing four blacks and six whites in which the leader (who was black) several times used a 'fishbowl' procedure where members of one subgroup observe the other subgroup talking among themselves. The least successful of the groups started with six whites and three blacks. The leader, who was also black, felt from the start that there were not enough blacks present. He frequently confronted individuals, used few structured exercises and was not seen as supportive.

This study provides some indications that groups with a minority of blacks may create a detectable effect in those who attend. However it is difficult to assess whether the effects created were in some way specific to the place and time of the project, and whether they were found equally among each of the four groups. Other studies of sensitivity training have shown markedly different results. For instance Rubin (1967a,b) studied eleven-day residential groups for professionals in New England. Eight of the fifty participants were black. Significant increases in 'Human Heartedness' were found after training, which were not found among controls. Such an effect is clearly quite different from those found by Lieberman et al. (1973), but there is no way of knowing whether the presence of blacks was required for the accomplishment of the effect, nor of whether the effect occurred equally among blacks and whites. In a somewhat better-controlled study, Hull (1972) showed increases in 'Worldmindedness' among student groups containing a minority of foreign students. Such changes were not found among controls nor among all-American groups.

The weakness of all the studies mentioned in this section is that they fail to report separately the effects of the experience on majority white members and minority blacks. Case study accounts suggest that the dynamic of such groups at least initially is rather often built around black attacks on white racism, and white denial of personal responsibility. This would certainly lead one to expect that each group would be affected in a different manner. One might expect to find increased white acceptance of responsibility for racism, but effects on blacks which would vary depending upon how the whites had responded to the workshop. White acceptance of responsibility would be likely to go with an increased range of behaviours by blacks, asserting their various concerns with increased confidence and clarity. White denial of responsibility on the other hand would go with greater black anger. While such different outcomes have not been systematically documented, a report of a workshop by Freedman (1976) gives some support to this view. Freedman and his colleagues conducted a forty-eight hour workshop for five blacks and eleven whites. He reports that on all of the seven rating scales distributed at the end, whites showed greater change than blacks.

Thinking in recent years about the design of training experiences has moved forward in a manner consistent with this assumption. If the goals of a workshop are primarily the accomplishment of a reduction or at least recognition of white racism, might this not be better accomplished in the absence of blacks? Indeed, is not the presence of a token black minority in a workshop itself an expression of racism, if the only purpose served by that minority is to help the white majority face up to guilt about racism? Conversely, if blacks wish to pursue goals other than helping whites face up to their racism, may they not have a better chance of achieving these other goals in the absence of whites? Such thinking, expounded for instance by Katz (1978), has led to the rapid growth in recent years of anti-racism training for whites, which will be explored in the next section. It thus appears that training workshops with a black minority currently find little favour. If the issue to be addressed by the workshop is an intergroup one, it will usually be more effective to have either equal numbers from both groups or a racially homogeneous group. While such a view is certainly one which may be reasoned out logically, it has to be acknowledged that one of the reasons for the current situation may well be that workshops set up by whites and with a majority membership of whites appear likely to potential black participants to reinforce racism rather than to confront it. Even in the Lieberman *et al.* study fifteen years ago, considerable difficulty was encountered in recruiting blacks. In the projects in this country studied by Smith and Willson (1975), recruitment difficulties were best overcome where it was possible to show that a substantial number of blacks would be coming.

RACISM AWARENESS TRAINING

There has been a marked trend in many areas toward the use of more specifically structured training designs. To some extent, such a trend represents a backlash against over-optimistic and diffuse designs used in the past, but it is also argued by those who favour this development that gradually increasing understanding of an issue has led to more precise specification of how to work on it. Katz's formulation of anti-racism training is influenced by techniques developed by behaviour therapists. Training is divided into six structured stages, each of which comprises a range of exercises. The total package comprises forty-eight exercises, but it is not intended that they all be used within any one programme. Specific choice of elements to be used would depend upon the time available and the type of persons attending a workshop.

In the first stage participants get to know one another, and are introduced to concepts such as prejudice and racism. This is accomplished through discussion based on films or written material, rather than by didactic teaching. Examples of exercises in this stage are discussion of dictionary definitions of prejudice and of racism, briefly sharing a previous personal experience of racism, and the design of an imaginary racist community. The last of these is particularly important. Subgroups of four to six are given an hour to specify in some detail the structure of the community they have invented, and the ways in which it is racist. A further hour is devoted to sharing the various designs, drawing out from the discussion members' definitions of racism, and comparing the designs with institutions in real communities.

Stage two introduces the concept of institutional racism. This is conveyed through a brief lecture, through simulations and through discussions of films, songs and stories. This stage also includes a close analysis of specific institutions with which participants are familiar in terms of how far their various policies and procedures institutionalise racism.

Stage three moves to a more personal level by providing opportunities for sharing of feelings which are likely to have been elicited by the material in the two earlier stages. The workshop leader encourages sharing of members' feelings and particularly of their fears about confronting their own racism. Other possible exercises include guided fantasies and non-verbal encounter exercises, such as that where one member tries to break into a group where others are trying to exclude them. Finally they are asked to record aspects of their own personal prior experiences of race.

Stage four focuses on cultural racism as expressed through language and film. Exercises include looking at the connotations of colours such as black, white, red and yellow, completion of a culturally-biased IQ test and listening to tapes of a debate about the genetic basis of differences in IQ.

Stage five confronts participants with the consequences of their own whiteness. They are asked to list adjectives which best describe themselves, and then adjectives which best describe whites, and to account for why they choose different adjectives. They explore their reactions to the phrase 'White is beautiful'. They are asked to spell out some of their own prejudices and invent arguments to justify them. They discuss a series of racist statements in terms of why each one is racist, and on which of them they have changed their view. Finally they are asked to examine how much consistency there is between their expressed attitudes and their behaviour.

The final stage is devoted to the planning of future actions. The focus is on identifying specific actions that can be taken and the sharing of plans with others. Participants consider what would be lost as well as gained by the taking of their planned actions, and try out some of them through role-played simulations. Finally evaluations of the workshop are completed.

This workshop design has been described in some detail, both because it has been carefully worked out and because variants and segments of it have been quite widely used both in Britain and North America in recent years. It is important to attempt to define what are its essential elements, since as with any other training innovation, there are inevitable pressures to simplify and water down what is proposed and one needs to be sure which elements are essential in a programme and which are not. Two elements appear crucial in the Katz package. Firstly, the fact of racism is confronted head on: one cannot run a programme and call it racism awareness unless it unambiguously asserts the facts of racism in our society. Secondly, Katz lays great stress on the power held by whites to maintain (or to change) the racist structures of society. A lot of the impact her programme achieves is likely to be through its emphasis that though racism may be institutional, *you* the individual member of the workshop do things daily which serve to sustain that structure and *you* can make plans to change this.

Katz and Ivey (1977) report a study of the workshop's effects, based upon two samples of twelve students each. The students participated in the workshops as a course at the University of Massachusetts. They were found to show changes in attitudes not shown by untrained controls. Furthermore these changes were still present one year after training. Trainees were also asked to select a specific behaviour related to racism which they would like to change. The changes which they made subsequently were not only apparent to themselves but also to a 'significant other' who was asked to complete additional ratings. However Katz (1976) notes that although behaviour change was still detectable, some students did not in fact carry through the behavioral change objectives which they had set themselves. This project is so much more clearly described and evaluated than the others upon which this chapter touches that it seems churlish to criticise it. However it should be noted that while it was shown that the attitude change created lasted for a full year, the persistence of the behaviour changes is less clearly reported. Before one could say that the effects of racism awareness training have been thoroughly studied, one would need larger samples and more detailed follow-up measures. For the present the method looks promising, and that has been sufficient encouragement for most practitioners.

It is only recently that such methods have come into use in this country (Peppard, 1980) and published references to their use are few (Shaw, 1981; Satow, 1982; Gurnah, 1984). However, since 1979 a network of racism awareness trainers has developed and now numbers some dozens of practitioners. Many of the race relations units established by local authorities have sponsored racism awareness programmes. A recent joint government and local authority working group (Department of the Environment, 1983) was able to report from a survey that they undertook that racism awareness and similar types of training were being used by half a dozen authorities or more, some of them on a quite substantial scale. The principal group offering such training are the Racism Awareness Programme Unit. A form of racism awareness training has also been in use for police officers and for officers in the immigration and nationality department of the Home Office. However, no published information is available as to how many of these programmes use the full set of activities devised by Katz and how many use abbreviated or simplified approaches. While there are also no published research evaluations of any of these British applications of racism awareness training, informal comment indicates that these programmes are by no means always received as positively as was the case in the original Katz project. Some of the reasons why this might be so are discussed in the next section.

One point of contrast with Katz's original formulation is that British practitioners most often argue that it is useful to include one or more non-whites in a workshop staff, even where the workshop is for whites only. There are in fact rather more black racism awareness trainers in Britain at present than white ones. The practice of having black leaders in white groups is less vulnerable to the criticism of tokenism than is the presence of a minority of blacks as participants, since it is clear that workshop staff, whatever their colour, are there with the prime purpose of helping others learn. The presence of a workshop staff which includes both blacks and whites creates both tensions and opportunities to enhance the workshop's effectiveness.

In general it works best if the workshop staff have already devoted time before the workshop to establishing an effective working collaboration. There have also been a number of racism awareness programmes for blacks only, particularly in the field of community work. Still other leaders have departed further from Katz's reasoning and argue that it is equally fruitful or even more so to run racism awareness groups for blacks and whites jointly.

CHOICES FOR INTERVENTION

It was pointed out earlier that there has been a slow trend away from using group training methods focused solely upon the individual and towards using methods which locate the individual within a context such as organisations and families. In this country, most interventions have focused on individuals, even where a programme is located within a particular organisation. For instance racism awareness programmes within local authorities are directed toward individuals, not toward organisational policies. They are designed to act upon the individual's awareness of racism and the individual's plans for future actions. The furthest move toward a more organisational focus is provided by Bradford, who propose that by 1986 they will debar their officers from serving on job selection panels unless they have participated in racism awareness training. Another recent project has involved racism awareness training for teams of social workers comprising a family placement unit. Here an intact organisational unit is trained in its entirety, thus augmenting the likelihood of change persisting. More thorough-going organisational projects are so far confined to the U.S.A., and are discussed in other chapters of this book. The purpose of this section will be to explore the potential strengths and weaknesses of both an individual and an organisational focus.

It has to be acknowledged right away that the task of conducting training in race relations which creates a lasting effect is fraught with difficulty. It is clear that Britain is a racist society and likely to remain one for some time. All training efforts are vulnerable to the criticism that the effects that they create on this or that aspect of racism are either trivial or likely to be obliterated as soon as they start to threaten any part of the established structure. Such criticisms are frequently and confidently asserted, but they are weak on empirical evidence and confound two vitally different possibilities. The first possibility is that racist social structures are a product of socio-historical factors acting over centuries rather than decades. On this view we can only hope to study and understand racism, not to change it. The second possibility is that although racism may have evolved over long time periods, there are ways of modifying it which have not yet been discovered. The first position is fatalistic, the second perhaps naively optimistic. A range of views exists within the optimistic position and it is these which will be explored.

The most clear statement of the view that the training of individuals can lead to social change is that of Carl Rogers. His work in Belfast has already been considered. The crucial element in his position is that we can only expect to create major effects where individual group experiences are reduplicated thousands of times. Since no attempts have yet been made to create interventions on the scale for which Rogers argues, we can only speculate about the likelihood of their success. Evidence from the field of industrial training suggests that the prospects would not be all that good. For instance, several large North American business organisations, who arranged in the late sixties for virtually all their managers to partici- pate in sensitivity training found that the openness and participative decision-making which characterised their training groups did not necessarily carry over into day-to-day decision-making groups. One might object that in this example not everyone receives training at the same time. When the effects of training faded out this could be because of the influence of others who had yet to attend training or others for whom the effects had already worn off. But it is never likely that a really large-scale intervention can be instantly carried through – there is bound to be delay before everyone has participated. Furthermore, there is the question of voluntarism. Rogers' groups are composed of volunteers, but it is never likely that all members of an institution will wish to volunteer to attend groups.

The case in favour of training individuals has been debated in terms of Rogers' work, since he is the most lucid exponent of that approach. There is no reason to believe that the difficulties which have been discussed would be any less acute in the race relations field. It must therefore be concluded that there is little likelihood that training individuals will by itself lead to changes in institutional behaviour. There are two reasons why it might none the less be worthwhile to run individually-oriented programmes such as racism awareness workshops. The first of these is that such programmes, particularly where they are run within a specific organisation or locality, may enhance the possibility of doing training later which focuses more directly on organisational change. The second reason is that participation in a racism awareness workshop may enhance the quality of life of an individual, without reference to possible social change. Those who seek out such workshops on this basis are likely to be the less overtly prejudiced members of society, but the workshops may well serve to support and sustain them in their other endeavours. Radical groups all too often lose their effectiveness through conflict and splitting over issues of strategy or ideology. The effectiveness of such groups just as much as any other group is dependent on adequate attention being paid to the building of support and cohesion, and individually-oriented training programmes may be one way in which this process can be enhanced.

One view which is opposed to the training of isolated individuals is that which sees racism in terms of power relationships between different groups in society rather than between different individuals. Gurnah (1984) sees racism awareness training as creating conditions for change which are perhaps necessary but certainly not sufficient. He argues that such programmes misdirect energies, which would more effectively be employed in the creation of action groups, either from within the black community or on a mixed basis. Awareness of racism is in his view not the problem, whereas the creation of the political will to act and take initiatives is a higher priority. Gurnah thus sees these two courses of action as alternative to one another, but it is equally possible to argue that investment in either course of action could augment the possible impact of the other. An example has already been cited of the way in which the diffusion of racism awareness workshops has led some practitioners to conduct workshops for intact work teams within organisations.

The danger which Gurnah correctly identifies is that the very rapid rise in the use of racism awareness training in this country will be seen by those in authority as by itself sufficient to change the racist policies of their organisations. When in the course of time continued training input of this type is found not to have achieved any very powerful or visible effects, disillusion may well set in. It will then become increasingly difficult to argue for other forms of intervention and action which would build on the will to act which has been fostered by racism awareness groups.

The creation of effective mixed action groups will often require bringing together samples or representatives of the different groups involved. However it has long been established that contact between different racial groups does not by itself guarantee any change in attitudes or behaviour. Amir (1969) summarised a series of conditions which make more likely a positive outcome of interracial contact. These include shared goals for the meeting, intimate rather than casual contact, activities which are pleasant rather than unpleasant, contact which is approved rather than disapproved by the general climate of opinion and by relevant authorities, and equal status for both groups within a meeting. Even a list such as this makes clear that considerable preparation and negotiation will be necessary before groups can be created with a good prospect of success.

However in applying the list to the design of interracial workshops it is apparent that there are elements which would need adding to the list. A particularly crucial addition would be that some or all of those present have the power to implement changes after the workshop. Some of the potency of Katz's design lies in her insistence that everybody has the power to make some kinds of change, and there is truth in this. But relatively powerless members of society have a circumscribed range of such possible change. The changes sought after a workshop need not necessarily be large-scale ones, but there should be a clear relationship between the issues focused upon and the powers of those present. The Leeds workshop studies by Smith and Willson has already been described. In discussing their findings Shaw (1981) suggests that the crucial element in the success of the project may have been the presence of two school headmasters. The vital point would not be that the headmasters were particularly powerful community leaders, but that they were the key figures for a workshop focusing on educational problems.

A weekend workshop with somewhat similar conception but broader focus is described by Woodall (1976). He recruited a workshop of thirty-six in a major southern U.S. city. Those attending included the mayor, chief of police, newspaper editor, ministers, community action workers, ghetto high-school seniors and black militants. The report says nothing about how such a group was assembled, even though it may well have been the most difficult part of the project. The design of the workshop focused on trust-building during the first day, while the second was devoted to three problem-area groups, which focused upon housing, employment and education. The effects of the workshop were widespread, including the establishment of interracial student advisory committees in the schools, community relations training for the police and the establishment of informal communication channels which proved valuable in coping with a crisis over housing which occurred in the city some months later.

SOME PRINCIPLES OF TRAINING DESIGN

Thus far, this chapter has had more to say about the outcomes of workshops than about the moment-to-moment conduct of them. Some mention has been made of the use of structured exercises, particularly in racism awareness groups, but no amount of exercises can guarantee the success of a workshop unless other crucial elements are also present. The first of these is that everyone shall be clear as to why they are there. Such clarity is not always easily accomplished, but the available means are the provision of written materials describing the aims and procedures of the workshop and the use of interviews or group meetings with prospective participants. The values of workshops include open communication, and the leaders should show in advance that they are able to communicate clearly what the workshop will be like. The clarity of such communication is most strongly at risk when one is recruiting members for a workshop at which it is crucial to have certain key persons there. The temptation is to pass lightly over whatever reservations the key people have, reasoning that the greatest priority is to have them there at all. Such a strategy all too often boomerangs, illustrating how key people are not only key ones in a workshop's success but also in its failure.

A second principle is that the behaviour of workshop leaders provides a model which will strongly affect the outcome of the workshop. If the workshop leaders are a racially-mixed group, the quality of their relationship will inexorably convey itself to the workshop and influence whatever dynamic is uppermost in the workshop as a whole. Leaders who avoid conflict between each other beget workshops which do likewise. Leaders who fail to support one another find their groups lacking in supportiveness.

The leader's judgment as to how to design a workshop, in terms of high or low structure, focus of the sessions and so forth must rest on some implicit or explicit model of the manner by which change is created. In a framework developed more fully elsewhere (Smith, 1980), it is proposed that the leader's task must be to maintain a balance of supportive and confronting forces within the workshop. When conflict or confrontation is high, the provision of support sustains the group's ability to remain engaged rather than to evade issues. Where support and cohesion is high the leader may need to focus upon encouraging more attention on disagreements or differences of perspective, in order to ensure that the differences present in everyday living are not denied while the workshop is in progress. Support and confrontation may be provided either by structured exercises or by more spontaneous personal interactions. They may be required of the leader or they may be provided by members of the workshop. The leader's vital function is to watch over that process and have available a range of ways of modifying what is happening when it departs from that required. Scrutiny of Katz's design for racism awareness training indicates that it stresses the building of support initially and gradually increases the strength and personal relevance of the confrontations to which participants are exposed through the ensuing phases.

A particular danger in interracial groups is that confrontation may be avoided, through denial either by the leaders or by participants that racism poses problems for a particular group or for society more

G

generally. Various group leaders have argued forcibly (e.g. Jones and Harris, 1971) that moments of crisis and confrontation are absolutely crucial to the ultimate success of interracial groups. Where a leader permits such a confrontation not to occur within a group focusing on racial issues, that leader is colluding with the position that there are no racial issues to be confronted in our society. Judging when a group is ready to handle such crises is one of the hardest skills for a group leader to acquire. The precipitation of such crises is made a good deal easier by the presence in a group of both blacks and whites, and this provides a quite strong counterargument to Katz's preference for non-mixed groups. Simple structures may be employed which can quite reliably lead to the confrontation of issues, such as having blacks and whites meet separately for a while, and then meet to share the images or concerns they have explored while apart.

A final quality required of all leaders is that they explore ways of making it easier for workshop participants to implement changes after a workshop is over. This may require the collection of information in advance, the formulation of precise plans while the workshop is still in progress, and the holding of follow-up meetings.

One of the greatest obstacles to the building of cumulative knowledge about group process interventions is that published descriptions of workshops are usually able only to provide detail of who was there, what structures were employed and what follow-up information is available. Conclusions may then be drawn, as they have been in this chapter, as to which structures will or will not lead to certain types of changes. What is lost is the detail of moment to moment behaviour of the leaders, which may in fact colour and overshadow reactions to any particular structure. For all that we know at present, it could turn out to be true that leaders' behaviour while recruiting members is more important than what they do once the workshop is assembled. We need more experience with a larger and more diverse sample of interventions before this and many other points will become clearer. Then will be the time for us all to decide whether to be optimists or pessimists.

NOTE

1 I am grateful to Paul Sommerfeld for his comments on an earlier draft of this chapter.

REFERENCES

- Amir, Y. (1969), 'Contact hypothesis in ethnic relations.' *Psychological Bulletin*, 71: 319–42
- Boehringer, G. H., Zeruolis, U., Bayley, J. and Boehringer, K. (1974), 'Stirling: the destructive application of group techniques to a conflict.' *Journal of Conflict Resolution*, 18: 257–75.
- Department of the Environment, (1983), *Local Authorities and Racial Disadvantage: report of a joint Government Local Authority Working Group*, H.M.S.O., London

- Doob, L. and Foltz, W. J. (1973), 'The Belfast workshop: an application of group techniques to a destructive conflict'. *Journal of Conflict Resolution*, 17: 489–512
- Doob, L. and Foltz, W. J. (1974), 'The impact of a workshop upon grass-roots leaders in Belfast'. *Journal of Conflict Resolution*, 18: 237–56
- Freedman, A. M. (1976), 'Hang-up in black and white: a training laboratory for conflict identification and resolution'. In H. L. Fromkin and J. J. Sherwood (eds.) *Intergroup and Minority Relations: an experiential handbook*. La Jolla, CA., University Associates
- Gurnah, A. (1984), 'The politics of racism awareness training'. *Critical Social Policy*, 10: 6–20
- Hull, W. F. (1972), 'Changes in worldmindedness after a cross-cultural sensitivity group experience'. *Journal of Applied Behavioral Science*, 8: 115–21
- Jones, F. and Harris, M. W. (1971), 'The development of interracial awareness in groups'. In L. Blank, G. B. Gottsegen and M. G. Gottsegen (eds.) *Confrontation: Encounters in Self and Interpersonal Awareness*, New York, MacMillan
- Katz, J. H. (1976), 'A systematic handbook of exercises for the reeducation of white people with respect to racist attitudes and behaviors'. *Dissertation Abstracts International*, 87 (1A), p. 170
- Katz, J. H. (1978), *White Awareness: Handbook for Anti-racism Training*, Norman, Oklahoma, University of Oklahoma Press
- Katz, J. H. and Ivey, A. (1977), 'White awareness: the frontier of racism awareness training'. *Personnel and Guidance Journal*, 55: 485–9
- Lieberman, M. A., Yalom, I. D. and Miles, M. B. (1973), *Encounter Groups: First Facts*, New York, Basic Books
- McGaw, W. H., Rice, C. P. and Rogers, C. (1973), *The Steel Shutter*, (Film), Centre for Studies of the Person, La Jolla, CA
- Peppard, N. (1980), 'Towards effective race relations training'. *New Community*, 8: 99–106
- Rogers, C. R. (1978), *Carl Rogers on Personal Power*. London, Constable
- Rubin, I. M. (1967a), 'Increased self-acceptance: a new means of reducing prejudice'. *Journal of Personality and Social Psychology*, 5: 233–8
- Rubin, I. M. (1967b), 'The reduction of prejudice through laboratory training'. *Journal of Applied Behavioral Science*, 3: 29–50
- Satow, A. (1982), 'Racism awareness training: training to make a difference.' In A. Ohri, B. Manning and P. Curno (eds.) *Community Work and Racism*, London, Routledge, Kegan Paul, pp. 34–42
- Shaw, J. (1981), 'Training methods in race relations within organisations: an analysis and assessment.' *New Community*, 9: 437–46
- Smith, P. B. (1980), *Group Processes and Personal Change*, London, Harper Row
- Smith, P. B. and Willson, M. J. (1975), 'The use of group training methods within multiracial settings'. *New Community*, 4: 1–14
- Woodall, T. E. (1976), 'From crisis to collaboration: thoughts on the use of the laboratory method in resolving black–white issues'. In H. L. Fromkin and J. J. Sherwood (eds.) *Intergroup and Minority Relations: an Experiential Handbook*. La Jolla, CA., University Associates.

12

Race relations training and organisational change

The history of efforts to alter race relations in organisations and communities throughout America is replete with rhetoric and good-will seldom translated into new behavioural patterns and organisational outcomes. The same persons and institutions deriving benefits from the current status of racial privilege and stratification often are involved (more or less consciously) in maintaining this state of affairs. Thus, change is a complex and difficult intellectual and social process. Training programmes designed to alleviate racial discrimination or tensions in the organisational context must understand the full nature of the problem, how serious is it felt to be in the local situation, and what it will take to change the organisation. In this chapter our concern is with the ways in which race relations training can be carried through into the implementation of long-lasting organisational change.

BACKGROUND

Racial minorities in the United States have been constrained severely by law and social custom. Now most forms of legally supported and intentional discrimination have been struck down by the courts, and overt racial discrimination has become less frequent. Individual acts of an insensitive or prejudicial character are still quite common, but that is not the same as programmatic discrimination. In such a changing social context, people of colour have made extraordinary achievements. The growing number of black elected officials, increased entry by minorities into management-level positions in the private and public sectors, and black and Latino participation in athletics and the arts are all evidence of gains, however protracted, that people of colour have achieved despite severe obstacles.

However, the effects of legal and intentionally discriminatory practices remain long after court decisions and social customs signal the reduction of overt discrimination. Racial oppression and privilege have become institutionalised, embedded in the norms (regulations and informal rules) and roles (social practices and their attendant duties and rights) in a variety of social, economic and political organisations (Feagin and Feagin, 1978, p. 12). Racial discrimination need not be intentional to be potent; nor does it have to be legally approved to exist in many subtle and covert ways.

The most advanced analyses of current forms of racial discrimination and oppression draw our attention to the existence of different 'life chances' or outcomes of life in America for people of different races. Regardless of anyone's intention to create such outcomes, the workings of vast and impersonal social forces continue to create and sustain major differences among the races in such critical areas of life as: economic status; education; health care; life expectancy; infant mortality.

Racism has become more subtle, often unintentional, and is supported by the apparently impersonal and 'fair' workings of large institutions. For example, prior to fairly recent changes in admissions' policies by institutions of higher education in the late 1960s, admissions offices regularly determined whether to admit applicants solely on the basis of 'objective' criteria. These criteria included grade point average, class rank, standardised tests and the quality of the high school the applicant attended. Except for those institutions with explicit racial quotas, policies were consciously colour blind. The consequences or outcomes of this policy for blacks and others were disastrous, because prior educational discrimination made it impossible for applicants of colour to compete on an equal basis with their white counterparts. What on the surface appeared to be a fair policy discriminated in effect. The effects were no less harmful because the discrimination was not intentional.

Another example may be provided in the context of industrial employment and advancement. A firm that has few minorities at foreman and executive ranks may wish (or feel the pressure) to advance talented minority workers to these ranks. At the same time, it may feel bound by allegiance to meritorious promotion standards that give precedence to work performance, work history and seniority, and external (educational) credentials. Since fewer minority workers may have these credentials and history, even those with substantially high work performance records may not be considered seriously for promotion. This apparently 'fair' stance appears fair because it refuses to use race as a standard that contravenes other important values such as seniority and credentials. Since there are fewer minority workers with seniority in the organisation, however, this apparently fair policy continues to deprive minority workers of opportunities for mobility and higher levels of organisational responsibility. As Jones notes, 'Institutional racism exists when the norms of an institution are predicated on assumptions of racial equality that are not met in the society. Then application of the institution's policies and procedures produce racist consequences' (Jones, 1972, p. 130). In the context of long-standing norms and practices of racial inequality and exclusion, a 'more fair' policy might self-consciously attend to overcoming historic disadvantages by using racial characteristics of the person and racial balance in the organisation as criteria for individual advancement.

These examples make it clear that how one *defines* or *measures* racism, racial discrimination or fairness is a critical matter. The term 'racism' is defined in a variety of ways, and has been measured primarily by five broad forms of evidence.

1 *Personal attitudes or values,* as evidenced in public opinion polls or survey questionnaires of a broad range of the American public.
2 *Personal acts or behaviours,* as evidenced in individual activity that creates disadvantages or lesser privilege or reward for some people or that leads to them being discriminated against.
3 *Cultural values or norms,* as evidenced in symbol systems (language), value frameworks or fashions more highly cherished by one group than another being accepted as the 'right' and the 'good'. Further, in the ways some social and political roles, expectations and identities are distorted and/or made available only to selected groups.
4 *Institutional procedures,* as evidenced in social mechanisms that provide differential advantage and privilege to people of different races, including locating the means of institutional control predominantly with one group.
5 *Effects or outcomes,* as evidenced in the unequal distribution of economic, political, and social status resources or rewards among varied racial groups.

These alternative but non-exclusive forms of evidence, or definitions, help distinguish between *individual racism* (nos. 1 and 2), and *institutional racism* (nos. 3, 4 and 5). They also distinguish between *cultural or attitudinal racism* (no. 1 and no. 3), and *behavioural racism* (no. 2 and no. 4). Figure 1 illustrates these distinctions.

On the basis of these different definitions, we can measure or assess racism in various ways – by examining individuals' attitudes or opinions, individuals' actions or behaviours, organisational policies, organisational programmes and operations and outcomes or consequences as reflected in various groups' resources and life chances. For instance, the most common understanding and therefore assessment of racism has taken the attitudinal route. Between 1942 and 1984 social scientists conducted many surveys attempting to measure

Figure 1. Definitions/measures of racism

	Attitudinal or Cultural	Behavioural
Individual	Personal Attitudes, Opinions, Values	Personal Acts, Behaviours, Choices or non-choices
Insitutional	Organisational/Societal Norms, Symbols, Fashions, Myths	Organisational/Societal Procedures, Programmes, Mechanisms

the attitudes of whites towards blacks (some looked at black racial attitudes as well). The data show that overall attitudes have changed steadily during that forty-year period (Condran, 1979; Hyman and Sheatsley, 1964; Schuman and Hatchett, 1974; Taylor *et al.,* 1978). Whites seem to be more accepting of blacks as political equals, though the figures vary according to region, respondents' educational level, the issue (e.g., residential vs. intelligence items) and other variables. While it is quite likely that these polls accurately reflect a growing liberalisation in whites' racial attitudes, they also may reflect respondents' hesitance to express their prejudices publicly. However, 'The mere fact that subjects feel that segregationist attitudes are less socially acceptable today indicates a somewhat more favorable racial atmosphere' (Rothbart, 1976, p. 347).

Research on the relationship between attitudes and behaviour has created substantial evidence that changes in behaviour may have more potent and lasting effects than changes in attitudes, *per se.* Kenneth Clark (1953, p. 76) made the argument succinctly before the United States Supreme Court in *Brown* v. *The Board of Education, Topeka, Kansas:*

> . . . *individuals and groups modify their behaviour only to the degree and in the direction demanded by the external situation as it is perceived. While to bring about a specified desired change in behaviour within a given period of time may require a concern with the internal effects of past influences, the habituation of verbalized attitudes, and past patterns of behaviour, these factors do not operate as a permanent block to further changes but rather determine the strength and duration of the external pressures which are required to effect them. When these are determined and applied, appropriate relearning – demanded changes in behavior – occurs and is internalized and reinforced in the same way as the previously learned behavior.*

In the Brown v. *The Board of Education* (II) decision to end segregation in schools with 'all deliberate speed', the justices were less interested in board members' attitudes and those of white parents than with the institutional behaviour they had just mandated. To this day, laws are passed, executive orders are issued and court decisions are rendered in the continuing attempt to end racial discrimination.

Beauchamp (1977) explains clearly why changes in major institutions, rather than solely among individuals, also have become a vital means to end racial discrimination. Such actions are necessary because of the existence of 'discriminatory social attitudes and selection procedures so deeply entrenched in contemporary society that they are almost certainly ineradicable by good faith measures in an acceptable period of time' (1977, p. 85). Unless societal organisations and institutions change we cannot expect to sustain individual changes in either attitudes or behaviours.

ORGANISATIONAL DISCRIMINATION

In the context of the prior discussion of individual and institutional definitions of racism and racial discrimination, we can now identify a working definition of organisational discrimination: it is a set of behaviours or institutional acts that create or perpetuate sets of advantages or privileges for whites and exclusions or deprivations for minority groups. It requires, in addition to a set of *social mechanisms* (institutional practices) and an *ideology* (policies/norms) of explicit or implicit superiority, the *power to implement and maintain* systems of privilege or deprivation (Carmichael and Hamilton, 1967; Knowles and Prewitt, 1969). Institutional practices, and their support in organisational cultures/norms and power loci, are critical to this definition; they also are vital targets or components of any change effort.

In most, if not all organisations, there exists a hierarchy of occupational roles, power and responsibilities. People of colour and women are disproportionately located in lower-level positions, positions characterised by lower salary scales, little decision-making power, limited opportunities for advancement, less autonomy and less access to information. In her study of a large corporation, Kanter was able to categorise jobs according to mobility and found minorities and women over-represented in the dead-end jobs (Kanter, 1977). Others have divided the labour market into segments and have found people of colour located disproportionately in peripheral segments with less access to opportunities for personal advancement and organisational growth (Edwards *et al.*, 1975; Gordon *et al.*, 1982).

Perrow (1970) argues that the location of power in an organisation depends in large part on the dominant technology employed. Depending on the organisation, power may lie in its research and development component, its production department or its marketing sector. Wherever the power lies blacks are not likely to be found. In this context, Bowser (1979) distinguishes between a vice-president for personnel and a vice-president for finance. Even if the two are relatively equal in salary, Bowser writes, 'roles for Blacks and other minorities . . . are parallel roles that most often give nominal status and appropriate incomes but no critical decision-making influence over the fate of the entire organisation' (Bowser, 1979, p. 176).

The same pattern is clear in predominantly white institutions of higher education. University and college presidents and vice-presidents generally are white (and male), with the typical exception of vice-presidents for student services or community relations. In admissions, directors are generally white, though in response to student unrest in the sixties, institutions often appointed directors of minority recruitment and added blacks and Latinos to their staff. But even here there was a racist consequence; minority individuals were assigned limited responsibilities, which in turn limited their prospects for higher-level positions in the field. in maintenance and food services blacks and Latinos rarely supervise, even at institutions where they comprise the majority in these sectors. In university faculties, blacks and Latinos continue to be disproportionately found in the assistant professor and lecturer ranks.

These examples of institutional practices based upon normal operating procedures, reflect long-standing organsational norms and cultures, and are supported by power structures. Indeed, organisational discrimination does not have to be supported by law/statutory authority to be potent; it is usually enough to be supported by informal cultural understandings that are shared widely throughout an organisation. These understandings generally anticipate inadequate performance for minority members, and thus track minorities into less responsible positions. Such practices need not be conscious/intended; they may be an unintentional 'consequence' of our cultural history and standard ways of doing business. Regardless of their historic cause and character, such patterns of organisational discrimination continue to work to the disadvantage of minority employees and, therefore, must be a target of organisational change.

PRINCIPLES OF ORGANISATIONAL CHANGE

The attempt to alter patterns of organisational discrimination, whether by race relations training methods or any other medium, must attend to the body of knowledge available regarding how and why organisations change their policies and practices. Even if the assumptions we make about organisational change prove to be erroneous, paying deliberate attention to them may help uncover sources of later failure and success.

Many organisations have established affirmative action or non-discriminatory policies; many also have created race relations training programmes as an initial step in translating policy into practice; few have designed or followed up such programmes in ways that ensure the changes necessary to actually eradicate or substantially lessen discrimination or racism in the organisation. This pattern draws our attention to the literature on implementing new polices in ongoing programmes of organisational change. Most such theories of implementation were developed in the public policy realm, examining and explaining the relations between legislation or judicial decisions and the behaviours of major public institutions. But they also can be applied to life in major organisations and to organisational changes flowing from newly-made policies.

Studies of the implementation of organisational change focus on four sets of variables relevant for achieving non-discriminatory structures and practices: 1. clear and specific policies; 2. the involvement of legitimate and credible policy-makers; 3. supportive organisational infrastructures; and 4. support for new behaviours from front-line actors (Hargrove, 1976; Pressman and Wildavksy, 1973; Sabatier and Mazmaniam, 1980; van Horn and van Meter, 1977; Williams, 1982).

Clear and specific policy

The first steps in generating a thrust for organisational change occur at the point of policy-making itself. Considerations at this initial stage include the need for policy to be clear and specific. Of course, the very nature of racism and race relations in American society is so clouded that being clear about non-racist or anti-racist goals can be a difficult task. For many Americans, the meaning of racism itself is unclear and conflicting definitions abound. Moreover, the fact that scholars and public officials debate the meaning of these terms may indicate there is more at stake here than an abstract definition. Basic value conflicts underlie some of these distinctions, and whoever controls the language may control the definition of what is and is not a 'social problem'. For example, just what is an affirmative action 'quota', and how does it differ from a programme 'goal'? What is 'intended' versus 'unintended' discrimination? What is 'reverse discrimination'? Can we be 'racist' or perform 'racist acts' if we do not have racist intentions? In the midst of these definitional arguments and confusions, it is difficult to make a clear and specific policy statement. Most organisational leaders retreat to vague and general policy, thereby offending few people, sparking little negative reaction, and generating little organisational direction or support for vigorous anti-racist action.

Aside from confusion or unclarity, many organisational leaders disagree about the appropriate ends or goals of change in race relations in their organisations or units and sub-units. If every distinct level or unit in an organisation has its own production or service goals, and its own leadership and decisional authority, it also has its own goals or standards for minority membership, performance and interaction. The proliferation of accountable sub-units complicates the problem of organisational change precisely because it tends to diffuse authority on subtle yet complex matters such as discrimination and affirmative action. At the same time, innovative developments in any sub-unit are to some extent constrained by what is happening in other units throughout the organisation.

It is not surprising to see different views on racial matters reflected throughout various echelons of organisational policy-making. Some managers feel that anti-racism efforts in the workplace are not an appropriate focus for profit-making enterprises; they feel that their business is to generate a profit and to serve their shareholders (and incidentally consumers). Other managers argue that it is in their organisation's best interests to pursue such policies, both because they promise workplace peace (which hopefully leads to healthy production) and because every organisation has a social responsibility to contribute to a fair and just environment. Conflicts about these issues are part of the broader American value conflict or dilemma regarding collective responsibility for solving racial problems.

It is important that policy statements clearly and specifically discuss ways in which the anti-racism agenda is related to the organisation's 'bottom line' (i.e., its profits or service goals and mission) and to each unit's role in achieving these goals. If this bottom-line perspective is not offered, changes in race relations will not be seen as central to the mission. Of course, most organisations have rather diffuse mission statements for public consumption, but within the executive suite or board room the mission is clearly and specifically defined. It is part of the culture and guides policy-makers' actions, organisational norms and supervisors' behavioural expectations.

Legitimate and credible policy-makers

Research studies indicate that implementation is most likely to occur throughout various levels of an organisation if and when the policy-making units or individual decision-maker is seen as legitimate and credible. In other words, organisational members often assess whether the 'correct' decision-maker is making a particular decision, whether he or she is 'believable' (really means it and intends to be taken seriously) and whether the capacity exists for such changes to be actually accomplished. To the extent that a series of organisational sub-units are involved in these affairs, each division will need to be clear that *their* boss is vigorously in support of new policies and is committed to their implementation. By the same token, informal elites who have been involved in the organisation over a long period of time may occupy quite powerful roles as semi-official 'culture carriers' or 'gatekeepers' to power. While these persons may not be top-rank executives, their forthright support of changes, especially ones so fraught with cultural values, also is critical. When top executives deliberately involve these informal leaders, it announces to the remainder of the organisation that this is a serious and credible agenda.

In some situations organisational elites suggest that a policy not of their own making has been thrust upon them by external authorities, such as the courts, federal contracting or monitoring agencies or local community pressures. Under these circumstances organisational members are likely to feel justified in defying or subtlely sabotaging the policy, primarily because it does not have the complete endorsement of their organisation's elite. In fact, local elites may use this device to 'signal' that resistance to the policy will be tolerated or even encouraged.

Questions about the legitimacy of decision-makers also may develop if the policy on affirmative action or anti-racism activities is announced and promulgated by the organisation's affirmative action officer, and not by the president or chief executive officer. Then the policy is likely to be seen as an artifact of this particular staff member's special interest, and not something done in the name of the entire company by line officers. Moreover, it is known that these special assistants and non-line staff officers typically do not have sufficient power to carry out the major responsibility for establishing or implementing the total organisation's agenda on social justice issues; thus, 'their' policies do not have to be taken seriously.

If official organisational authorities and informal leaders mandate new policy and make their support for new policy clear and unambiguous, it is more likely that the policy will be implemented successfully throughout the organisation. As reported in *Black Enterprise* (Gayle and Gray, 1982, p. 37):

The mandate factor that determines the success of any affirmative action program is the tone set by the chief executive officer and executive committee and the interplay between affirmative action and department heads. (The tying of affirmative action efforts to evaluations and bonuses has added a concrete, often effective and sometimes disputed, tool to the hiring and promotion arsenal.)

A senior executive frequently mentioned in positively shaping a company's commitment to minority advance is Coy Eklund, CEO of the Equitable Life Assurance Society in New York. As he states (Gayle and Gray, p. 39):

> I recommend assessing the actual numbers of people on different organi-sational levels. Then establish goals for the next year that evidence a desire for progress, and put these goals on an equal par with production or research goals. I also recommend rewarding or penalizing management performance; if you don't do that, you have virtually nothing. The company head must provide genuine leadership, because the attitudes of people move with the attitudes of top executives inside the company.

As Eklund suggests, one index of the credibility of senior decision-makers is whether they, too, must pay some sort of price (e.g. penalities for managerial non-performance) or take some new action (e.g. adopt new roles) in pursuit of an anti-discrimination agenda. To the extent that all new behaviour and all adaptations are the responsi-bility of lower level managers or front-line workers, they may be seen as an unfair burden, and resistance may develop. However, if the burden of change is obviously shared throughout the organisation, the decision is more likely to be seen as legitimate by all members.

Supportive organisational infrastructures

Substantial recent research suggests that the structure of the organi-sation, or of operating sub-units, may make it more or less probable that implementation of policy changes actually occurs (Gross *et al.*, 1971; Sabatier and Mazmaniam, 1979; Monti, 1979; van Horn and van Meter, 1977). The core question appears to be whether there is the tangible support and resources to put new policies into practice throughout the organisation.

The kind of supportive infrastructure required for effective implementation differs, of course, as the nature of organisations differ. For instance, an organisation that runs on coercive influence principles is quite different from one relying on voluntary compliance of members (Etzioni, 1961). Implementation of change in the Army or in a tightly controlled bureaucracy is quite different from implementation of change in a school, community organisation or small producer cooperative. The latter are likely to be 'loosely coupled' or diffusely controlled systems, with little clarity about or monitoring of members' behaviour throughout the system, and with little coordination of sub-unit tasks and standards. In these systems much more voluntary support for change is required.

One critical issue affecting change in a complex organisation is the coordination or integration of connecting or overlapping units. Nadler (1981) notes that changing only one sub-unit of an organisation or one element of an infrastructure may reduce its congruence with other components; then, the organisation may try to to limit, encapsulate, or reverse the change. 'It is therefore critical to take a holistic or systematic perspective when thinking about a major organisational change' (Nadler, 1981, p. 197). Given the realistic limits to any sub-unit supervisor's responsibility, this observation stresses the important role of senior organisational officials in influencing the behaviour of all sub-unit managers.

An open and effective communication system also permits dissemination of new cultural values and decisions that support new organisational policies and practices. The revision of an organisation's culture or code of behaviour so that it includes anti-discriminatory statements and proposed actions is essential. Moreover, the development of a plural culture, one that includes and/or reflects minority values and styles is critical. When these new norms are transmitted widely through an effective communication system, there is more likelihood that peer group dynamics may support implementation. Moreover, the delivery of rewards to those organisational units or managers and members who take the lead in supporting implementation of anti- or non-discriminatory programmes is a sure sign of the true intent of authorities to enforce change efforts. Rewards can take the form of increased resources to leading units and incentives for managers meeting programme objectives (e.g. more minority employees in skilled and high level positions or a better sub-unit racial climate). In reverse, sanctions may involve reductions in pay and resources for those units or managers failing to meet these objectives, or failing in good faith to try to meet them.

Without constant social or normative support, new behaviours are unlikely to be attempted; if attempted, they soon will be extinguished. Prior research on affirmative action officers, those organisational members officially entrusted with carrying out policy mandates, indicates the importance of such support for their effective role performance (Chesler and Chertos, 1981). The case is even more critical for people carrying out such objectives in a line unit, without an official portfolio.

In the final analysis, the provision of resources adequate to moving ahead on implementing racial change is the crucial test of organisational commitment to new policies. Resources move the infrastructure and put 'hard' meat on the symbolic bones of rhetoric and policy announcements. Whether resources come in the form of funds for new recruitment and training programmes, new reward systems and incentives or new positions and hires, they all demonstrate the organisation's willingness to 'put its money where its mouth is'. Without such resources, line managers will not be significantly motivated or, if motivated, will not be able to direct change.

New behaviours of front-line actors

Many studies and theories of organisational change and the implementation of new policies omit a concern for the values and behaviours of lower-level or front-line actors. Based upon a primarily 'rational' model of organisations, they assume that when new policy is communicated clearly by credible and legitimate authorities it will be acted upon positively by loyal followers throughout the organisation. Nothing could be further from organisational reality! Front-line actors are key ingredients in any organisational change effort. Thus, the study and manipulation of 'micro-implementation processes' (Berman, 1978) or 'grassroots' change efforts is a critical ingredient in an overall design for change.

A rational and 'top down' model for creating and sustaining organisational change may work well when lower-level actors have little discretion in their behavioural responses to organisational dicta. But in commitment-centred systems, where actors have considerable voluntary control over their role options, commitment must be fought for and won if change is to occur. This requires communication designs and normative renewal efforts that reach throughout the organisation, beyond middle-level managers, to the roots of working people 'on the line'. It requires consideration of the values and skills of line workers or agents and their responses to rewards and sanctions. On these bases, commitment and energy may be mobilised from the 'bottom up' as well as from the 'top down'.

Simplistic notions of change or non-change, of adherence to or resistance to policy, do not effectively capture the options open to front-line personnel, nor the impact of their responses on others. Dolbeare and Hammond (1971) and Rodgers and Bullock (1972) indicate there is a wide variety of responses to authoritative orders, ranging from unquestioning obedience or compliance to firm commitment to programme objectives, to lackadaisical carrying out of unpopular orders, to subtle and even overt forms of resistance and harassment of implementors or of beneficiaries of new policies. Merton (1940) and March and Simon (1958) have summarised these alternatives and Johnson (1967) has created an intriguing set of dichotomies between public behaviour and private views of new policy, as follows: private acceptance and public compliance; private acceptance and public non-compliance; private non-acceptance and public compliance; private non-acceptance and public non-compliance.

These distinctions mirror our prior discussion of the different forms or definitions of racism and racial discrimination. 'Private' refers to internal attributes, such as attitudes and values; the dichotomies indicates that persons privately may be either accepting or non-accepting of anti-discriminatory programmes. 'Public' refers to external behaviours; the dichotomies indicate that persons publicly may either comply or not comply with the behavioural standards of new policies and programme efforts. These different private and public stances may occur in various combinations. For instance, under the threat of punishment or negative sanctions for discriminatory behaviour, an organisational member publicly may comply with new standards while privately rejecting them; or he/she might privately accept them but be unable or unwilling to publicly act in consonance with their implications. This discussion reinforces the view that problems of personal and organisational change in race relations are quite complex, and it is an error to oversimplify the issues and approaches involved. These complex distinctions are particularly important when the attempt is made to monitor or supervise new behaviours throughout the organisation. Then assessment and feedback are essential components of any change effort, and their design requires the specification of outcomes in terms just as specific and sophisticated as the above dichotomies.

A brief summary of principles

Throughout this discussion of key variables, we can see the assumptions of several different theories of change. Some theorists and practitioners of organisational change, with regard to race relations or other matters, advocate educational and enlightenment strategies including information and persuasion. Their key assumption is that the alteration of people's ideas and the generation of a new organisational culture will lead to new behaviours that create a more positive racial climate in the organisation. A second major theoretical and practical perspective emphasises power or coercive pressure as the preferred change mode. They key assumption here is that the alteration of power in the organisation alters the 'rules of the game' and the 'gamemakers', thus sending a message throughout the system that incentives and punitive actions will be applied.

Coercion is a regular part of all organisations' efforts to maintain social control of the workplace in order to produce desired products and services. Persuasion also is part of all organisations' efforts to coordinate and influence the behaviour of its human members. If both elements are not part of an organisational change effort, certain risks occur: 1. coercion without persuasion often builds resistance and eventual sabotage; 2. persuasion without coercion permits a wide range of voluntary acts that may not achieve coherent purposes. Thus, detractors of the enlightenment/educational model of racial change criticise its reliance on voluntary behaviours on an issue regarding which Americans have steadfastly refused to change much of their behaviour. Detractors of the power/pressure model criticise its use of coercion as counterproductive, and as generative of resistance and rebellion by people who will fight back regardless of the content of the change effort. The critical question is not whether to use coercion or persuasion, but what kind of persuasion and what kind of coercion, and how shall they be interwoven in an overall design for change.

In any organisation, various kinds or forms of persuasion may be at work. Some are quite incidental and casual, as in reasoned discussion of organisational preference for certain kinds of behaviour. Others seriously attempt to socialise or mould members' opinions and options, strongly suggesting that various styles of dress or leadership will be looked upon more or less kindly. The existence and support of a peer culture in the workplace helps reinforce some individuals' moral or attitudinal priorities, and constitutes an additional and subtle form of organisational persuasion. Other legitimators of preferred behaviour also may be involved, as in suggestions that certain behaviour is better tuned to the organisation's mission and/or image, community mores, religious values or American standards of fair play and racial tolerance.

In any organisation various forms of power and influence also are at work. Some forms of power are derived from the rule of legitimate authority, and to the extent formal authority takes a clear and unequivocal stance on new race relations this power can be mobilised for change. A second major form of power and influence is embedded in the system of instrumental rewards and punishments an organisation uses to guide and pay off the behaviour of members. Just as all organisations utilise incentive systems to indicate and reward preferred behaviour, they apply negative sanctions (such as failure to gain merit increases, docked time, suspension, firing, etc.) to indicate and 'correct' inappropriate behaviour. To the extent infrastructural modifications can tune rewards and sanctions to more positive racial relations, and punish or not reward discriminatory acts, this form of power may also be helpful to the change effort. A third major source of power for people in organisations is the capacity, in terms of personal skills and organisational resources and opportunities, to actually behave and operate in new ways. To the extent the resources and opportunities for individual and organisational changes are made

H

available, change is more possible.

Since our interest is in the modification of organisational behaviour (e.g. the behaviour of people in their organisational roles and the programmes and operations of organisations themselves), we can avoid the argument about whether one can 'legislate morality' or 'require' new attitudes. The record is clear that organisations can and regularly do legislate or coerce organisational behaviours. Sooner or later that may alter individuals' attitudes and personal moralities, but even if it doesn't, the climate and operations of the workplace may be changed by the new behaviours. While we agree people should not literally be forced to change their ideas, they can be induced to change their behaviour; over time ideological change tends to follow (Festinger, 1957; Bem, 1970).

The choice or mix of appropriate strategies of persuasion and coercion also is influenced by the nature of the organisation in which change is occurring, and the point of entry of the people intent on making change. Access at the top can fruitfully use the power invested in senior executives to conduct educational programmes backed by the persuasive and coercive power of the prevailing culture and power holders. Access at the bottom often involves an educational programme to alter the ideas of the powerful, or to mobilise front-line actors to generate a new form of power, one vested in their numerical advantage and essential role in the production or service process.

In the following section, we describe several different models of the way in which these principles of organisational discrimination and organisational change can be applied to the design of race relations training programmes and implementation efforts.

MODELS OF THE TRANSITION FROM RACE RELATIONS TRAINING TO ORGANISATIONAL CHANGE

The following discussion assumes that an organisation is prepared to participate in a race relations training programme and to implement a long-term programme of change. The announcement of the policy of organisational change, and its realisation in the training event itself, constitute new policy. The critical problem is to identify the pathways whereby sustained and high quality organisational change on an anti-discrimination agenda now can be implemented. In figure 2, we present twelve different models for establishing and enhancing the link between new policy and attendant race relations training events and the implementation of organisational change. These links utilise the four key sets of variables related to implementation discussed in the prior section. We generally assume that each succeeding model builds on the one prior to it: that is, generally model no. 4 incorporates 1, 2 and 3 . . . except where explicitly noted.

Models announcing clear and specific policy: the training programme itself

The policy of organisational change with regard to race relations is announced and identified first through the conduct of training events. Organisational authorities' assumptions and operative decisions regarding the implementation process are signalled by the character of training. In our view, the training agenda cannot be limited to a focus on race relations, *per se*. Although it clearly is important to examine people's beliefs and understandings, to provide cognitive and emotional stimulus and redirection, training to alter racial relations in a complex organisation also must attend to the problem of organisational change. Thus, the outcome of race relations training events should not only include new perspectives and skills with regard to race relations, but new skills, information, feelings and commitments to act on the problems of organisational change.

Model 1. The simplest and most popular model in organisations throughout the country, this programme provides information designed to alter the attitudes of organisational members. Tactics include sponsoring a series of lectures or distributing and discussing written materials. It can also involve sending organisational members off-site to seminars or classes in race relations. It is a pure educational/enlightenment approach.

Model 2. This programme differs from model 1 in its attempt to provide skills and practice in making the behavioural changes that accompany new information and attitudes. Tactics of sponsoring speakers or sending organisational members to special events are the same, and so is the focus on an educational/enlightenment approach.

Model 2a. This programme is a minor modification of model 2 which includes the notion that race relations training is not a one-time event or project, but an ongoing activity and an ongoing process in the lives of the organisation and participants. Thus, a continuing series of seminars or other events might be called for.

Models involving legitimate and credible policy-makers

A continuing priority is to involve organisational authorities who may not be enthusiastic but who have the power to kill or support a programme. One tactic is to exclude them from events but send them positive messages about the programme. Another tactic is to include them in a symbolic manner in events, asking for their endorsement

Figure 2. Components of various models of race relations training relevant for implementation of organisational change

	Model											
	1	2	3	4	5	6	7	8	9	10	11	12
Policy via race relations training programmes												
. . . attitudes	x	x	x	x	x	x	x	x	x	x	x	x
. . . attitudes and skills		x	x	x	x	x	x	x	x	x	x	x
Involve powerful decision makers												
			x	x	x	x			x	x		x	x
Infrastructure change												
. . . resources and rewards				x		x	x	x	x	x	x	x
. . . norms and support				x	x	x	x	x	x	x	x
Front-line												
. . . training								x	x	x	x	x
. . . monitor and supervise									x	x	x	x
Community-based initiatives												
. . . internal caucuses											x	
. . . external pressure												x

via an introductory and closing benediction or perhaps a talk on the reality of organisational life. A third tactic is to include them fully as participants, subject to the same risks and growth opportunities as everyone else. This problem cannot be dealt with fruitfully if it is abstracted from the other assumptions of the training and implementation design. If the overall change strategy requires covert relationships with organisational authority, then it makes sense to exclude them from the programme and to make sure they receive only carefully screened information. If the overall strategy is one of openness, then they can receive full information via participation, access to evaluations or debriefing.

Model 3. This programme moves beyond policy pronouncements and training programmes, *per se,* to lay the groundwork for effective use of legitimate and credible decision-makers. It involves in a meaningful way powerful decision-makers and organisational culture carriers in vocally and publicly supporting the training programme and subsequent changes in hiring and promotion, creating new norms, etc. It still relies primarily on an educational/enlightenment strategy, but by securing the support and thrust of powerful figures, lays the basis for a power/pressure strategy as well.

Models mobilising supportive organisational infrastructures

An important condition for ongoing personal change is institutional and organisational support that reinforces changes initiated in an awareness programme (Buchanan, 1967; Schmuck, 1968) and enforces new behaviours. Positive reinforcement is meaningful, but so is negative reinforcement. As Triandis has argued, we must 'create institutional arrangements in which exploitative behaviours are no longer reinforced' (Triandis, 1972, p. 132).

Model 4. This programme begins to manipulate the organisational infrastructure. New resources are made available in order to implement changes in the racial climate, and rewards and sanctions are tied to these resources. This approach develops a power/pressure strategy, because in addition to utilising the energy and commitment of key decision-makers, and signalling their posture to others, rewards and sanctions are applied as instrumental pressure for new behaviours.

Model 5. This programme also begins to modify the organisational infrastructure, but does so by generating a new normative system and providing social support for the development of new behaviours. However, it is an alternative, and not a complement, to model 4 because it does not also provide resources and manipulate reward systems. This model often is more popular than model 4, because it offers symbolic rewards (support and values) rather than tangible ones (money and other material resources), and thus does not reallocate what many organisational members feel is the scarce 'coin of the realm'. It represents an enlightenment-oriented rather than power-oriented approach, precisely because it does not mobilise the organisation's scarce resources in support of programme implementation.

Model 6. This approach combines models 4 and 5, by adding to the training programme and the vocal commitment of key decision-makers both aspects of the infrastructure – support and normative pressure plus resources and modification of the reward system. It then combines the educational strategy with a power strategy, and has mobilised three of the four major sets of variables outlined previously.

Model 7. This approach includes modification of all elements of the infrastructure, but omits the involvement of key organisational leaders. Perhaps the programme has been engineered without their knowledge, or perhaps these elites have decided not to demonstrate programmatic leadership. Whatever the basis, their non-involvement fails to demonstrate that credible and legitimate authority stands behind the implementation of change; by omission it suggests quite the opposite. How can new norms and resources be provided without commitment from top decision-makers? In some cases, middle-level managers have made the decision to reallocate resources by themselves; in other cases, top-level managers have made the decision but do not wish to 'go public'.

Models focusing on the behaviours of front-line workers

If front-line workers are fully involved in the change effort their own energy is a crucial positive resource. If they are excluded, their ignorance, lack of energy or resentment may stall and sabotage the development of improved race relations.

Model 8. This programme utilises all the prior factors and, in addition, provides training to front-line workers. Sometimes such training is not accompanied by alterations in the infrastructure. In these cases, it cannot be considered a serious effort at racial change, because key supports and resources for front-line change are missing. However, such 'window-dressing' programmes are common and often distract energy from more meaningful programmes.

Model 9. In this programme specific monitoring and supervisory functions have been included. The concern for assessment and feedback is an expression of the organisational superstructure or authority system, and creates the empirical criteria for allocation of positive and negative sanctions.

Model 10. This programme departs from models 8 and 9 in that while training and monitoring of front-line workers are included and infrastructure support provided, it fails to include public and vocal support from top executives. Programmes can be successful under these conditions, but only if other tactics are being utilised to generate and utilise the tacit or covert support of organisational leaders. Otherwise, the 'rug will be pulled out from under' these newly-trained front-line workers when they engage in actual change efforts.

Models utilising alternative sources of persuasion/pressure

We discussed previously the problem of generating energy and commitment for change throughout all levels of the organisation. Some organisations have provided an arena within which racial minorities can develop and exercise power by participation in special training programmes with and for their own group members. While these programmes may overlap in considerable degree with those oriented toward white workers, managers and executives, they also may include special components that deal with minority staff members' concerns about identity, personal and collective survival, and the expression of their own needs and concerns in the organisation.

Active community-based movements for social change also can be a helpful resource in altering and eradicating organisational racism. Just as it is not possible to make and sustain major alterations in individuals' lives without altering the organisations and communities of which they are a part, it is not possible to make and sustain changes in organisational structures and operations without altering the community context in which the organisation operates. Organisational change programmes which ignore this assumption treat the organisation as if it existed in a vacuum, and usually only create minor and temporary changes, ones not related to community resources, power and values. Community-based movements for change can help identity institutional racism as a 'problem' and raise this issue to the level of public awareness where it must be dealt with. In some cases, this has meant drawing public attention to obviously or newly visible conditions or indicators of injustice. In other cases it has involved generating the power that turns a 'condition' into a notable 'problem', typically by creating a turmoil or threat that commands attention (Ross and Staines, 1972). One reaction to this problem of problem-recognition may be for the organisation or community to call for a consultant on race education to help them prepare a change programme. When it appears that a programme of race education might get underway, an active community group may also be helpful in legitimating that programme, or the staff members involved, to local organisations. Community-based social movement groups may also be able to play helpful roles when ongoing monitoring or organisational change efforts become important. Such monitoring could be turned over to stable community groups who have an interest in anti-racism programming, and who may have the time and energy act as watchdogs to the organisation over time.

Model 11. This approach adds to a new factor to the prior models; it calls for special training for dispossessed groups within the organisation, in an attempt to forge them as an interest group that can act to create pressure on the organisation.

Model 12. This approach adds to the others the intervention of local community or external governmental agencies (courts or federal monitoring agencies) as an additional source of power and pressure for change.

SUMMARY

We have tried to identify key considerations which must be addressed in order to significantly reduce discrimination and improve race relations in organisations. To risk restating the obvious, improved race relations do not mean simply increasing interracial civility or even social interaction. It means creating policies and practices that result in more equal *opportunities* and *outcomes* for whites and for people of colour.

Organisational tolerance or maintenance of social, political and economic inequality in job roles, wages and access to power prevents just relationships between whites and blacks and Latinos. Wellman observes correctly that 'the issue that divides black and white people ... are grounded in real and material conditions' (1977, p. 37). Training programmes grounded in educational or attitudinal change approaches alone cannot change these conditions. Organisations must design programmes that lead to the implementation of structural change and that demand new behaviours from organisational members. Unless the real and material life of the organisation changes, we witness only token and truncated responses to the problem.

Training programmes can help create the organisational infrastructure to support creative and far-reaching policy changes. Sometimes, however, pressure needs to be applied, and it may come from the top or the bottom of the system, as well as from external forces. Training programmes can help build a skilled constituency for change, a cadre that knows when and how to apply pressure, educate others, and make the sacrifices often necessary for change to occur. Ultimately, however, significant policy changes must be fashioned, implemented and enforced consistently and evenly. High-level executives must at some point commit themselves in tangible ways to organisational change in the area of race relations. Such changes are clearly compatible with efficiency and high levels of production; indeed, they represent the most efficient and humane use of a full range of human resources. Just as the 'normal' way of doing things often has had racist consequences, the 'new' way of doing things, once institutionalised, should have different and more just consequences.

REFERENCES

- Beauchamp, T. (1977), 'The Justification of Reverse Discrimination.' In Blackstone and Heslep (eds.), *Racial Justice and Preferential Treatment: Women and Racial Minorities in Education and Business*. Athens, Georgia, The University of Georgia Press
- Bem, D. (1970), *Beliefs, Attitudes, and Human Affairs*. Belmont, California, Brooks/ Cole Publishing Company
- Berman, P. (1978), 'The study of macro- and micro-implementation.' *Public Policy*, 26 (2): 157–84
- Bowser, B. (1979), 'An empirical model for measuring racism in large-scale organizations.' In R. Alvarez and K. Lutterman (eds.), *Discrimination in Organisations*. San Francisco, Jossey-Bass

– Buchanan, P. (1967), 'Crucial issues in organizational development.' In G. Watson (ed.) *Change in School Systems.* Washington, National Education Association
– Carmichael, S. and Hamilton, C. (1967), *Black Power: The Politics of Liberation in America.* New York, Vintage Books
– Chesler, M. and Chertos, C. (1981), 'The affirmative action program and the organization: structural conflict and role dilemmas.' In *Consultations on the Affirmative Action Statement of The U.S. Commission on Civil Rights.* Washington, D.C.
– Clark, K. (1953), 'Desegregation: an appraisal of the evidence'. *The Journal of Social Issues,* IX (4): 2–76
– Condran, J. (1979), 'Changes in white attitudes toward blacks: 1963–1977.' *Public Opinion Quarterly* (Winter): 463–76
– Dolbeare, K. and Hammond, P. (1971), *The School Prayer Decisions.* Chicago, University of Chicago Press
– Edwards, R. Reich, M. and Gordon, D. (1975), *Labor Market Segmentation.* Lexington, Massachusetts, Lexington Books
– Etzioni, A. (1961), *A Comparative Analysis of Complex Organisations.* Glencoe, Free Press
– Feagin, J. and Feagin, C. (1978), *Discrimination American Style: Institutional Racism and Sexism.* Englewood Cliffs, New Jersey, Prentice-Hall, Inc.
– Festinger, L. (1957), *A Theory of Cognitive Dissonance.* Stanford, California, Stanford University Press
– Gayle, S. and Gray, L. (1982), 'Ten best places to work.' *Black Enterprise,* February, pp. 37–44
– Gordon, D., Edwards, R. and Reich, M. (1982), *Segmented Work, Divided Workers: The Historical Transformations of Labor in the United States.* New York, Cambridge University Press
– Gross, N., Giacquinta, J. and Bernstein, M. (1971), *Implementing Organizational Innovations.* New York, Basic Books
– Hargrove, E, (1976), 'Implementation'. *Policy Studies Journal,* 5 (1): 9–15.
– Hyman, H. and Sheatsley, P. (1964), 'Attitudes toward desegregation.' *Scientific American,* 211 (1): 16–23
– Johnson, R. (1967), *The Dynamics of Compliance.* Evanston, Northwestern University Press
– Jones, J. (1972), *Prejudice and Racism.* Reading, Massachusetts, Addison-Wesley Publishing Company
– Kanter, R. (1977), *Men and Women of the Corporation.* New York, Basic Books, Inc.
– Knowles, L. and Prewitt, K. (eds.) (1969), *Institutional Racism in America.* Englewood Cliffs, New Jersey, John Wiley and Sons, Inc.
– March, J. and Simon, H. (1958), *Organisations.* New York, Wiley
– Merton, R. (1940), 'Bureaucratic structure and personality.' *Social Forces,* 18: 560–68
– Monti, D. (1979), 'Administrative discrimination in the implementation of desegregation policies.' *Education Evaluation and Policy Analysis,* 1 (4)
– Nadler, D. (1981), 'Managing organizational change: An integrative perspective.' *Journal of Applied Behavioral Science,* 17 (2): 191–211
– Perrow, C. (1970), *Organisational analysis: A sociological view.* Belmont, California, Wadsworth
– Pressman, J. and Wildavsky, A. (1973), *Implementation.* Berkeley, University of California Press
– Rodgers, H. and Bullock, C. (1972), *Law and Social Change: Civil Rights Laws and Their Consequences.* New York, McGraw Hill
– Ross, R. and Staines, G. (1972), 'The politics of analyzing social problems.' *Social Problems,* 20: 18–40
– Rothbart, M. (1976), 'Achieving racial equality: An analysis of resistance to social reform.' In P. Katz (ed.) *Towards the Elimination of Racism.* New York, Pergamon Press
– Sabatier, P. and Mazmaniam, D. (1979), 'The conditions of effective implementation.' *Policy Analysis,* 5: 481–504
– Sabatier, P. and Mazmaniam, D. (1980), 'The implementation of public policy: A framework of analysis.' *Policy Studies Journal,* 8 (2): 538–60
– Schmuck, R. (1968), 'Helping teachers improve classroom group processes.' *Journal of Applied Behavioral Science,* 4 (4): 401–35

- Schuman, H. and Hatchett, S. (1974), *Black Racial Attitudes: Trends and Complexities.* Ann Arbor, Michigan: Institute for Social Research
- Taylor, D., Sheatsley, P. and Greeley, A. (1978), 'Attitudes towards racial integration.' *Scientific American*, 238 (6): 42–9
- Triandis, H. (1972), *Attitudes, Conflict and Social Change.* New York, Academic Press
- van Horn, C. and van Meter, D. (1977), 'The implementation of intergovernmental policy.' *Policy Studies Annual Review*, 1: 97–120
- Wellman, D. (1977), *Portraits of White Racism.* Cambridge, Cambridge University Press
- Williams, W. (ed.) (1982), *Studying Implementation: Methodological and Administrative Issues.* Chatham, Chatham House Publishers

JOHN W. SHAW
PETER G. NORDLIE
RICHARD M. SHAPIRO

13

Concluding remarks

A theme which constantly recurs throughout the book is that of organisations, impelled, perhaps, by a variety of different motives, wishing to change themselves in order to act more equitably towards members of minority racial groups. This desire for change may stem from differing causes. External events such as changes in law have occurred in both Britain and the U.S.A. and have provided leverage for change. Also civil disorders, community criticism, individual complaints, miscarriages of justice and official investigations into the questionable impartiality of public agencies have all added their weight to the motivation for change. Moreover, boycotts and demonstrations have brought home to reluctant authorities the need to examine themselves and to put their own houses in order. In rare instances, the initial impetus change can be traced to the altruism or conscience of top executives. More often, however, it has been the desire to avoid chaos or, as in the case of the military in the U.S.A., to head off the likelihood of impaired 'mission effectiveness' which has galvanised these huge bureaucracies into actions and programmes described in the earlier chapters.

It is the contention of the editors of this volume that regardless of the motivating factors, whether external or internal, the primary character of the change process will be similar in structure and methods. Given the desire for change, whatever its origins, the ways in which organisations can renew themselves have been well-documented in the literature (Jaques, 1952; Whyte and Hamilton, 1964; and Marrow, Bowers and Seashore, 1967) as well as in several chapters in this volume. Peaceful, self-initiated change may not be the chosen route in some cases, however, so that outside forces, whether in the form of legal actions or revolutionary activity, can take over the initiative.

Where the desire for change does exist within an organisation, a certain rationale of method is implied and this is seen to contain certain key features. Firstly, at the outset, the current state of things must be clearly delineated. We need to know, in precise terms, those features of the system in question which impede its achievement of its legally defined goals and statutory responsibilities. Awareness of the current malaise may come from a variety of sources and may accumulate over a considerable period of time. It seems that in the nature of things, a painful period of self-criticism and self-examination is often necessary to overcome organisational inertia and provide sufficient stimulus to initiate change efforts. As already noted, public dissatisfaction with the way an organisation performs its role may express itself in a variety of ways both internally and externally. But in order for that system to be changed, that dissatisfaction must be given a more definite shape by the collection of relevant factual material which shows unmistakeably just how far short of equity and efficiency performance has fallen. The most striking examples of this process are reports of official enquiries such as the Scarman Report on the Brixton disorders, which indicated significant deficiencies in urban policing in London.

Secondly, comes the need to define the specific apparent causes of the system's injustices and its unacceptable practices. These may concern the racial imbalance of its workforce or the discriminatory ways in which clients of minority racial groups are routinely and normally treated. To arrive at an acceptable diagnosis, relevant information needs to be systematically collected and continually updated. One possible method of accurate diagnosis may include the use of a representative internal group and some of our contributors describe how such a group may be utilised. Also relevant to the acquisition of a sound basis for diagnosis formation is the use of external assistance in collecting accurate data about organisational practices and in interpreting already existing statistics. As in all cases where self-examination is called for, there are almost infinite possibilities for rationalisation, denial and projection so far as the significance of the data is concerned. These factors point to the need, which several contributors underline, for collaboration with outside bodies, and the public where appropriate, throughout the process of diagnosing the causes of organisational malaise.

Thirdly, our contributors stress the importance of defining goals in a concrete fashion. What, for example, will need to happen to specific organisational policies, procedures, practices, resources and roles if equal opportunity and fair practice is to replace discrimination and disadvantage. It is important to recognise that some causes are easier to identify and rectify than others. For example, a penal institution may find it relatively easy to widen the range of goods in its shops and to vary its menus to include minority dishes than to overhaul its promotion system so as to implement an equal opportunity policy with respect to its own employees. The setting of targets and the formulation of specific objectives against which subsequent results can be measured is therefore vital to ensure that difficult tasks are not shirked and that the organisational change activities are not reduced to futile exercises in rhetoric.

Changes may need to be made on three different levels. The first of these is personal discrimination against members of minority groups. In such cases an organisation's main concern is to ensure that member behaviour is at all time free of individual racism. To achieve this goal, sanctions against behaviour can be enshrined in a code of behaviour but this will not necessarily solve the problem. There are cases of offensive and provocative behaviour which do not unambiguously break such a code, yet will need to be dealt with if an atmosphere is to be purged of personal racism. We emphasise, therefore, the importance of training in which sensitivity to and awareness of such matters are discussed and their harmful effects exposed. Supervisors especially need training in how to deal with such incidents. Equal opportunity specialists are key people here and need to be able to deal with both the discriminators and the discriminated against sensitively.

The next level of concern relates to practices and rule of the organisation itself which may directly or indirectly discriminate against members of minority groups. In both Britain and the U.S.A., legislation has been enacted to prevent organisations from retaining practices which directly or indirectly discriminate against minority groups and women. Direct discrimination is clearly illegal and seen to be so. Company rules may not appear discriminatory to majority corporate members, but they may indirectly discriminate as, for example, the policy of a store that requires all women assistants to wear skirts, which effectively prevents the employment of Muslim women. Any rule about uniform which prevented a Sikh from wearing his traditional headgear would be equally discriminatory, even if unintentional when first formulated. We recognise that indirect institutional discrimination is among the most difficult of problems to remedy, especially when certain rules are regarded as sacrosant such as the height regulation in certain police forces. Such procedures need to be examined with particular objectivity and in this examination the representative internal groups, containing minority members, have a key part to play.

The third level of concern is with what can be called cultural racism. Some behaviour offensive to minorities may stem neither from personal attitudes nor organisational rules but from the culture or climate of the company. This culture will find expression in the language, jokes and slurs in an organisation. It may be gauged by an outsider more through listening to 'canteen talk' than by reading official reports. Since it is informal and unofficial such culturally determined behaviour cannot be changed by official fiat but by education, training and, especially, leader example.

Fourthly, the best practice for inducing change involves the establishment of a consultation and planning group which will formulate an action-plan as a blueprint for change within an organisation. The composition of this task force is a matter of some significance. It ought not to be solely representative of the powerful majority, but should include minorities, and outside members such as consultants or facilitators. In formulating its plan, such a group needs to recognise that to be effective it should concentrate primarily on those matters which are within the power of the organisation itself to change, while not ignoring relevant external sources of authority which may need to institute concomitant changes. There is always, however, the danger within an organisation that requisite action may not be taken in accordance with the action plan. Therefore, any plan should include provision for dealing with such eventualities through identification and allocation of specific tasks.

Fifthly, experience teaches us to recognise the importance of the way in which an action plan is implemented. The highest echelons of authority and management ought to be enlisted in support of the policy and asked to make their commitment to it absolutely clear. Several contributors emphasise the importance of this factor. The channels of communication within organisations, such as Force Orders, orders of the day, annual reports and presidential directives should be fully used to give legitimacy to the changes required. Job descriptions need to be amended where necessary to take account of new responsibilities recognised by the policy. Many organisations have created new posts with specific responsibility for equal opportunity, positive action and harmonious inter-group relations. In view of the specific pressures faced by incumbents of such posts, thought needs to be given to the provision of emotional and structural support within the system. Procedures have to be established for monitoring compliance with the new policy (we refer to this again below).

Sixthly, training interventions are crucial to a change programme in any system and several contributors to this volume have concentrated on this aspect. At several points, training has a contribution to make, since key executives may initially be involved in policy formulation through the medium of executive seminars. Also, workshops for supervisors, prior to the implementation date, may assist them in developing those skills necessary to ensure the adoption of new behaviour by their workgroups. Commitment to and support for the new policy by both first-line supervision and top management is necessary to its success and the judicious use of training, including briefings about the policy, its necessity and what it is designed to achieve, may go some way towards obtaining such commitment. For obvious reasons, however, training of the front-line workers in a service organisation, whether they be patrolmen or policewomen, social workers, teachers or local government officials is a necessity. These are the people in any service agency who have greatest contact with the public and who are often the cause for complaints from aggrieved groups for alleged insensitivity, discrimination, ignorance or, in some instances, harassment. While briefings about the need for the policy and plan and its objectives are important, training which allows exploration of attitudes but especially the modification of role behaviour is especially necessary.

Evidence has accumulated to show that the use of discussion groups to explore previously hidden or taboo subjects helps to moderate attitudes which are inimical to system's goals of good race relations, equal opportunity and positive action. Provided such discussion is clearly seen to be working towards defined policy goals and are conducted by credible individuals, they can be made effective in relation to organisational renewal. Provided also that a balance of supportive and confronting forces within these groups can be obtained and also that the corrective experiences in the groups can be generalised and applied to relevant work situation, there is great value in them. It seems clear that experiential training used in the service of personal development within organisations should never lose sight of its ultimate systemic purpose if is to be successful.

As already mentioned, training of the front-line servants of a public agency so as to modify inappropriate and discriminatory behaviour is a key issue. Such behaviour may range from the patrolman who quite unnecessarily shoots a fleeing felon who is unarmed to that of the housing officer who regularly gives the better housing allocations to majority clients. The best ways to proceed here involve the use of role plays, simulations and the discussion of case material drawn from actual practice. The latter is particularly good in raising the level of awareness so that the new policy is seen to be required by the current shortcoming of the service in question. Role plays and simulations create a capacity for empathy and provide the opportunity for individuals to reflect upon role behaviour which may have previously been automatic, unreflective and repetitive.

Several contributors have emphasised the importance of the evaluation and assessment of training interventions in race relations. This is important for several reasons. First, to discover whether any progress is being made in combating racism at the personal level. Second, to redirect and reorganise training when it is clearly missing the mark or has successfully achieved its objective. Next, the use of a concluding evaluation will enable a final judgment on the training programme's effectiveness to be made. Again, such evaluation contributes to a diagnosis of a system's 'racial health' which can be fed into the ongoing consultancy and planning process. Finally, evaluation counteracts unwarranted and idealistic optimism, especially by trainers, about the extent of progress being made (see Chesler, 1976).

One key learning in training has been that it should, as far as possible, be job specific in the context of the implementation of the plan. By this we mean that the training requirements for each level in the organisation must be carefully considered and training carefully tailored to each group's needs for fulfilling the plan. While some majority personnel can be relied upon to make changes in their role behaviour solely because of the moral case for equality of treatment for all, many are best approached from an instrumental point of view. In a society where most individuals' overriding personal goal is personal effectiveness and professional development, discriminatory or insensitive behaviour will, if shown to be impeding the achievement of that goal, often be abandoned in favour of more instrumentally effective behaviour. For such an approach to be effective, training should, as we have stated, emphasise the specifics of behaviour in a given role. It should show where current practices fall short of desirable outcomes and how they can be modifield so as to make personal role behaviour and organisational performance more effective in reaching mutually shared goals. This principle is now widely accepted in role training, as was indicated earlier in the discussion of role plays and simulations.

Finally, the importance of monitoring the outcomes of an equal opportunity and positive action plan should be emphasised. Procedures have to be established to monitor compliance with the new policy both through the analysis of the normal statistical data available in the organisation and through the collection of data specifically for this purpose. Organisations have often found it necessary to provide counselling, and in the last resort, disciplinary procedures, to deal with individuals unable or unwilling to comply with new requirements which may run counter to the pre-existing formal and informal norms of the system. Periodic reports are needed both from the statistical side and subjectively, through involvement in the monitoring process of organisation members and consumers or clients. Clearly members of ethnic minority groups who have been on the receiving end of discrimination, whether within the system or outside it, have a key contribution to make in the monitoring process.

A thoroughgoing example of a monitoring exercise in the U.S. Army has been described in chapter four above and shows how by the use of organisational data on selection, promotions, re-enlistments and discharges the effects of the new policy are measured. For such monitoring to be possible, data on the ethnic composition of the workforce and their clients needs to be available. There is currently some objection in some quarters in Britain to the collection of such data on the grounds that it infringes privacy. However, the Commission for Racial Equality in its Code of Practice in 1983 states unequivocally the need for such data to be collected. With this point of view, one must, on practical grounds, agree.

Equally important, once a policy is established and when data shows that it is beginning to have an effect, is the need to institutionalise the changes that have been made. In this way, if, example, regular returns of relevant data are required as a matter of course, and if the subject matter is permanently incorporated into training, if permanent staff appointments are made, and if the new demands are incorporated into the job specifications of supervisors and managers, then the changes are more likely to become permanently established within the system.

Not less important, however, is the need for continuity of commitment throughout changes in command, especially the overall command of an organisation. Just as commitment and support at this level is vital to get a programme off the ground, so continued support is essential, we believe, for the survival of the policy. Again, our contributors show how these changes can impair the success of an equal opportunity and positive action policy. It is also true that such commitment cannot be demanded or engineered. Its presence or absence may well be regarded as a 'given', which is outside the change-agent's control. However, if, as we suggest, the new policy has been thoroughly institutionalised and the system has changed its rules so that the problem is less likely to arise in future, then one is less at the mercy of new chief executives with different orders of priority from their predecessors.

Schemes to improve community and race relations in local communities, as described in chapter four, through collaboration between various social agencies, should follow the criteria we have specified, as well as attending to other issues. In particular, it is important that cooperation between the different agencies who are party to the schemes should be obtained in advance. The evidence is that this may be readily obtained between statutory agencies although even here differences of perspective to be explored in prior discussions. The real difficulty often lies in the sharp differences of ideology and philosophy between criminal justice agencies, for example, and some voluntary bodies, relations between whom may be vitiated by suspicions over the others' real intentions in wanting to get involved.

If initial suspicions are not brought out into the open, misperceptions corrected and a basis for cooperation established, then the effectiveness of the scheme will be impaired. One may have either the establishment of an uneasy alliance or, in some cases, a refusal on the part of significant voluntary agencies to be involved at all.

The second factor of importance is the role of communication. We have noted how, within organisations, organs of communication, both formal and informal, exist which can be utilised in the service of a programme of systematic change. Similarly, in communities, channels of communication exist, particularly the broadcast and print media. Our evidence indicates the importance of these channels being fully utilised so that the change programme and the public for which it is intended can interact in a beneficial way. Where the media are not utilised, such schemes may die from lack of support and an opportunity for understanding across race lines or between the police and various races and communities may be partially lost.

Several of our contributors have warned against the danger of taking too rationalistic a view of systemic change. Perhaps we can underline this point in concluding the chapter. Emotion and conflict are inevitable in the implementation of any programme of change, especially in those concerned with reducing racism. Such irrationality may appear dysfunctional but is, if faced and worked through, both in training and in the resistances of key individuals, likely to prove functional and creative.

In conclusion, we commend these case studies to all those interested in making our societies and organisations more socially just by elminating racial conflict, discrimination and insensitivity. In recent years in Britain, and still earlier in the U.S.A., the problems of racial injustice and disadvantage have been catalogued and analysed, but the test of our seriousness about these matters is whether we are prepared to act on these analyses. The practical problems of translating theory into practice is the uniting thread that links our contributors. They have shared their mistakes and successes with you, the reader, in the hope that you will be encouraged to take up and contribute to the task of transforming society, step-by-step, in a rational and systematic way.

REFERENCES
- Chesler, Mark A. (1976), 'Dilemmas and Designs in Race Education/Training', paper presented at Second International Symposium on Race Relations Education and Training (NIMH/WRAMC) Washington D.C., Sept. 15–17
- Commission for Racial Equality (1983), *Race Relations Code of Practice*, London, Elliot House, 10–12 Allington St., SW1
- Jaques, E. (1952), *The Changing Culture of a Factory*, London, Tavistock Press
- Marrow, A. J., Bowers, D. G., and Seashore S. E. (1967), *Management by Participation*.

New York, Harper & Row

– Scarman, Lord (1981), *The Brixton Disorders 10–12 April 1981*. London, H.M.S.O.
– Whyte, W. F., and Hamilton, E. L., (1964), *Action Research for Management*. Homewood, Illinois, Dorsey Press

Notes on contributors

MARK CHESLER is Co-Director of the Program in Conflict Management Alternatives and is a member of the Department of Sociology, University of Michigan, Ann Arbor, Michigan, U.S.A.

JOHN F. COFFEY is President of CZA Associates, Washington D.C., U.S.A.

GUY CUMBERBATCH is in the Applied Psychology Division, Management Centre, University of Aston, England.

HECTOR DELGADO is in the Department of Sociology, University of Michigan, Ann Arbor, Michigan, U.S.A.

RICHARD O. HOPE is Director, Intercultural Studies Programme, Indiana University at Indianapolis, U.S.A.

RAYMOND G. HUNT is at the School of Management, State University of New York at Buffalo and William O. Douglas Institute for the Study of Contemporary Problems, Seattle, U.S.A.

PETER G. NORDLIE was formerly President, Human Science Research, Inc., of McLean, Virginia and is now Senior Research Scientist at Laurence Johnson and Associates, Washington, D.C., U.S.A.

BHIKHU PAREKH is Professor of Politics at Hull University and Deputy Chairman, the Commission for Racial Equality, London, England.

ANGELA M. RODRIGUEZ is Executive Director, Urban Studies Institute Inc., at Barry University, Miami Shores, Florida, U.S.A.

RICHARD M. SHAPIRO is Deputy Director of Operations, U.S. Office of Refugee Resettlement, Department of Health and Human Services, Washington D.C., and former Chief of the Rascism and Mental Health Program, National Institute of Mental Health.

JOHN SHAW is Senior Staff Tutor in Psychology, Department of Extra-Mural Studies, University of Manchester and a Director of National Seminars in Race Relations.

PETER B. SMITH is Reader in Social Psychology, School of Social Sciences, University of Sussex, England.

METASEBIA TADESSE was in the Applied Psychology Division, Management Centre, University of Aston in Birmingham, England, and is now a developmental psychologist working in London.

WENDY TAYLOR now runs the 'Race for a New Age' programme at the Meta Centre, Clent, Stourbridge, West Midlands, England.

Index

222 INDEX

$+$ $\dfrac{c}{+}$

1, 172, 173, 74, 75, 7 , 182, 83, 89, 97, 202, 36,

07, 08, 10,